Confessions
of a
Society Columnist

Confessions
of a
Society Columnist

ROSEMARY SEXTON

Macmillan Canada
Toronto

Canadian Cataloguing in Publication Data

Sexton, Rosemary
 Confessions of a society columnist

Includes index.
ISBN 0–7715–7365–0

1. Sexton, Rosemary.   2. Gossip columns—Ontario—Toronto.
3. Globe and mail.   4. Gossip columnists—Ontario—Toronto—Biography.
I. Title.

PN4913.S48A3   1995   070.92   C95–931525–X

Macmillan Canada wishes to thank the Canada Council, the Ontario Ministry of Culture and Communications and the Ontario Arts Council for supporting its publishing program.

Macmillan Canada
A Division of Canada Publishing Corporation
Toronto, Ontario, Canada

1 2 3 4 5   99 98 97 96 95

Printed in Canada

To Edgar, Stephanie and Robin

Contents

Acknowledgements

I am grateful, first of all, to Macmillan vice-president, Denise Schon, who has always had faith in me, for her invaluable guidance and advice.

I would also like to thank those at Macmillan who have had a hand in making an author out of me. A book in its final publishable form is always a collaboration between the author and many other people. This book, like my last one, would never have come to fruition without the existence of people like Ron Besse, who owns Canada Publishing Corporation; Macmillan president, Michael Richardson—who is always ready with a word of encouragement; my hardworking and talented editors, Kirsten Hanson and Karen O'Reilly; and others too numerous to mention.

I would also like to take this opportunity to thank *The Globe and Mail*, my esteemed employer during a very important five years of my life. May it continue to reign as influential daily breakfast fare for many Canadians, even if it is not the paper it used to be.

Finally, I would like to pay special tribute to my late cat, Beaumont, who met a quick and untimely end while defending his territorial rights against a pair of foxes lurking in the Rosedale ravine. It was he who kept me company for the months it took to write this book and I miss him more than I can say.

Part One

Social Columnist
At Large

Prologue

How I Got Started at The Globe and Mail

Yakkity Yak—The *Globe* Loses Its Cherry

The Globe and Mail recently replaced society columnist Zena Cherry with Rosemary Sexton, a younger version of the name-dropping journalist. A contest was held to decide the column's name. The winners were *Globe* environment editor Craig McInnes and Metro editor Paul Palango, who headed their 114 suggestions with the words "Rosemary Sexton," which, in fact, was the winning name. (The prize was a "not bad" bottle of wine.) But when we came across the 113 rejected suggestions, we couldn't believe the judges' lack of imagination. Some of our favourites were: Nabob Roundup, Mostly WASPs, Tiny Sandwiches, The Scum Also Rises, Loafing with the Upper Crust, Private Schools—Public Faces, Snobs, Rosemary's Babies, Not the Fred Victor Mission, For Whom the Belles Toil, Not Valpy, Rosemary's Landing, No Lefties Allowed, It's Not What You Know. . ., Rosedale Diary, On the Make, Money Talks. . . . The only suitable title they missed was Dames at See.

—*excerpt from* Toronto Life *magazine in early 1988*

Never in my wildest dreams did I think I would ever become the society columnist for Canada's foremost newspaper. There was little in my background, either interest-wise or talent-wise, that pointed to such a job.

I was born in 1946 in the small Northern Ontario town of Haileybury (pop. 2,600), the eldest daughter of District Court Judge John Beverley Robinson and his wife Julia.

My father's father, Robert Sheriff Robinson, whose parents had emigrated from Ireland, settled in the north after he was given a land grant by Queen Victoria for fighting in the Boer War. He made enough money on mining claims, the stock market and downtown real estate in New Liskeard, a town five miles north of Haileybury where he settled, to retire in his mid-thirties, despite having a large family to support.

My mother's father, William Reginald Pritchett Bridger, whose father was the canon of Liverpool Cathedral, came over from England after graduating from Cambridge University with an M.A. He taught at Trinity College School in Port Hope before becoming head of English and history at the Royal Military College in Kingston, a post he held till his retirement.

The oldest of five children, my handsome, dark-haired, intellectual father graduated from honours political science and economics at U. of T. at the age of 18 before going on to law school. As he told it, he fell head over heels in love when he met my headstrong, auburn-haired mother, the youngest of three children, while both were taking a staff course in Kingston, she having left Queen's University before completing her degree to do so. My father was a 34-year-old major in the army and my mother a 24-year-old captain in the Canadian Women's Army Corps when a movie camera recorded their large wedding reception, an event we four children still love to watch.

Unlike my siblings Julia Ann (better known as Judy), John Bridger and Nora Minette (who calls herself Minette), I was not christened with a middle name. Just Rosemary Robinson. The four of us were brought up in a rambling old grey stucco house with a big veranda, overlooking the shores of Lake Temiskaming. It was a boisterous household, but our parents were strict disciplinarians. My father ruled the roost, but my mother ruled him (indirectly, of course), and woe to any of us if we crossed either of them. Though rarely used (the back of my father's hand was the corporal punishment of choice), a leather strap hung on the back of the kitchen door as a reminder of what would happen if we got out of hand.

My parents may have been strict, but they were also a lot of fun and a popular couple with young and old alike. They entertained nonstop—visiting judges on the circuit, out-of-town relatives and friends, and their children's playmates, who incessantly filled the house with the sounds of their laughter and sometimes their tears. At any given time, there were usually cousins, aunts and uncles, and friends from around the world staying in our upstairs bedrooms.

My mother made everything into an occasion, from our wintertime birthday parties where about thirty of us would head out into the countryside on a one-horse open sleigh, to summer gatherings on our large front veranda. My father loved taking us and our friends out on his boats which were kept at a nearby marina, trips often ending in minor catastrophes of one sort or another—a conked-out motor or an approaching storm.

My parents were voracious readers. Our old house literally bulged with bookcases and books. Although my mother frequented the library weekly and took us with her, a habit I continue to this day, we children never had to go outside our house for background research when doing school projects. There was always a book to be found at home on any topic under the sun.

Looking back on my childhood, I would have to compare our household with that of the Gilbreth family in the 1948 best-seller *Cheaper by the Dozen*. Like Frank Gilbreth, my father believed that families should do everything together, despite the minor revolts and rebellions among his offspring that this philosophy engendered.

On a freezing morning in February, for example, you might see him heading off with his ragtag group of four on a skiing expedition across the lake, at least one of us crying, two of us fighting and the fourth straggling along reluctantly. During the summer months, he would herd the four of us out into the large garden to perform our appointed tasks. He purchased four lawn mowers so that Judy, John, Nora and I could mow the lawn at the same time, much to our chagrin when passers-by stopped to stare. Reading was not allowed until we had completed either household chores or some outdoor activity. And sleeping in was absolutely verboten.

Observing family tradition, our parents sent us off to boarding schools for the high school years—Bishop Strachan School and Havergal College in Toronto, and Trinity College School in Port Hope. I endured only one year at Havergal (Grade 11) before begging to come home. In my senior year, I was elected football queen and graduated at the top of my class from Haileybury High School, which, at its largest, had 135 students, and enrolled in modern languages and literature at the University of Toronto.

My year at U. of T. came to a quick end when, after delaying the inevitable for several months, I was taken in February by my roommate Natalie Little to see a doctor who announced that I was six months' pregnant, too late to have an abortion.

Terrified that my parents would find out, I made arrangements to have the baby in Toronto and put it up for adoption. But the father of the baby, Murray Black, my boyfriend in Grade 13 and the son of the Crown attorney in Haileybury, told my sister Judy. He and she then went to my parents with the news. Successfully hiding my increasingly protruding stomach, I stayed in residence at Margaret Addison Hall at Victoria College until I wrote my final exams the first week and a half in May. Then, according to my parents' bidding, I married Murray on May 11, 1966. I was 19; he was 20.

It was not a joyous occasion. My father refused to come to the wedding, and the first night of our honeymoon my new husband left for Kirkland Lake, about 100 kilometres away, to begin his summer job working the night shift at a mine. Stephanie was born on June 7, 1966, a beautiful blonde, blue-eyed baby.

Murray and I received our B.A. degrees two years later at Laurentian University in Sudbury, where he had spent his first year after turning down hockey and golf scholarships in the U.S.. With the assistance of my uncle Dick Taylor, MPP for Temiskaming, Murray obtained a position as stockbroker with Doherty Roadhouse. He worked in Haileybury for one year before being transferred to the Owen Sound office, where he became manager.

After attending summer school at the Ontario College of

Education (altogether I spent six summers at OCE, the first two qualifying to teach English and French, the next four obtaining my specialist certificate in guidance and counselling), I taught English, Latin and physical education, first at New Liskeard Secondary School and then at West Hill Secondary School in Owen Sound. When Murray was transferred to Toronto's Bay Street from Owen Sound in October 1972, I was 26 and our daughter was 6. Although I was in my fifth year of teaching, I couldn't obtain a teaching position in Toronto until January, so I went back to U. of T., where I took the fourth year I'd missed earlier. I received a fellowship to take my master's degree in English, but turned it down at the last minute to attend Osgoode Hall Law School. I took my master's courses at York University at night, and three years later (1976) received both my M.A. in English and my LL.B.

I then articled at a downtown corporate firm, got pregnant with my second child and, as my marriage was falling apart, started dating the litigation counsel at the firm, Edgar Sexton. It was another turbulent time. Robin was born on June 14, 1977, just after my articling year was over and two months before the bar admission course was to begin. In contrast to Steffi's cool, blonde prettiness and gentle manner, Robin was dark-haired, red-cheeked and feisty. He was born with no right hand and almost died that summer due to some internal complications. His fighting spirit and raw determination pulled him through as much as anything. I spent most of that summer down at the Hospital for Sick Children, only going home to sleep.

The day after the bar admission course ended, Edgar and I moved in together. It's hard to put into words the personal fulfillment I have experienced in our relationship. Suffice it to say that the years since I have met Edgar Sexton have been the happiest in my life. We married on May 9, 1979, immediately after our divorces came through. Edgar was 42 and I was 32. This time my father gave me away.

During my bar admission course I had been hired by the Official Guardian of Ontario to represent children's rights in court, but the first day I appeared on the job, I was fired by lawyer Lloyd Perry after I told him, in reply to a question about my marital status, that I was living with lawyer Edgar Sexton. Edgar and I considered suing the government to get my job back, but decided against it. He had an excellent career, and at that point my new relationship with him mattered more than my job. I was, however, truly devastated by the firing, which forced me to scramble around to find any job in the legal profession, since by then most were taken for that year.

At first I worked as a tax editor for CCH Canada Ltd., a law publishing company. Then, reading *The Globe and Mail* one morning, I noticed an editorial complaining about recent decisions made by the Ontario Censorship Board and saying more liberal members were needed. I applied for and got a position that I kept for two years, resigning in 1980 over cuts that board chairman Mary Brown had ordered in the movie *The Tin Drum*.

In a new marriage, with a teenaged daughter and two-year-old son, as well as three stepchildren who visited, I decided to stay at home for a while, look after my husband and family and just enjoy some free time.

In the beginning, I loved the freedom. But as my children got older and needed me less, I started to do some volunteer work. I might as well be getting paid if I'm going to work like this, I thought. Thus began my search for any job in which I could get reimbursed for my efforts and not spend too much time away from my family.

Why not go back into law? my friends urged me. But in the ten years since I had been called to the Ontario bar, I had forgotten everything I'd learned. I would have had to retrain or at least rewrite my bar exams. I was not willing to do that or to go back to working the long hours required at this stage in my life.

I was also unwilling to return to teaching. Granted, I had the certificate and the experience. The retraining required would be less onerous than for law. But I had no desire to be marking papers and spending my days with adolescents en masse. I had really enjoyed my five-year teaching career doing just that, but I wanted to move on.

So I typed an up-to-date curriculum vitae (actually, at this point, I couldn't type, so Sheila Roche, my husband's obliging secretary, did it for me) and applied for all sorts of jobs from youth counsellor to editor to truant officer. Those who deigned to answer sang praises for my qualifications but showed absolutely no inclination to take me on.

So back I went to immerse myself in volunteer work once again, which at this juncture was careering out of control. Except for the six months I took off in 1984 to work as volunteer co-ordinator for Julian Porter when he ran unsuccessfully for the Conservatives in Rosedale against Liberal Ian Scott, I turned down very few requests for help. As a result, by 1988, I was sitting on nine boards (Family Day Care Services of Metropolitan Toronto, Toronto Symphony Women's Committee, Wellesley Hospital Auxiliary, Arthritis Society, Toronto Pops Orchestra, St. George–St. David's PC Association, Canadian Psychiatric Awareness Committee, Society for Educational Visits and Exchanges in Canada and Laurentian University) and my fund-raising duties, which at first had been fairly light, became increasingly time-consuming.

In fact, my quest for a job was as much an attempt to get out from under the morass of volunteer activity as it was to start earn-ing money again.

One day in August 1987, I read in *Toronto Life* magazine that a going-away party was being held for Zena Cherry, who had been the legendary society columnist for *The Globe and Mail* for sever-al decades. "Why don't you apply for her job?" my husband asked.

I was intrigued, but first I felt I should visit Zena to find out what the state of things really was. I knew her, but not well. Over the years she had written several columns on parties I had held. I didn't want to run in and try to wrest her job away from her if she still wanted it.

In any case, I thought my best bet to be hired by the *Globe* would be as an assistant to Zena. I could help her edit her copy. I knew from reading her columns that she had been suffering from memory loss lately. She had always been so precise, and now some really glaring errors were beginning to appear.

So I went to see Zena, and she told me that Geoff Stevens, managing editor at *The Globe and Mail*, had fired her out of the blue. "Would you like me to speak to the *Globe* about getting your job back?" I asked her. "Yes, dear, thank you" was the reply.

I called Geoff Stevens, whom I didn't know but had once seen across a crowded room at a University Club reception, and made an appointment to see him. Thus began an unforgettable comedy of errors that nearly cost me the job before I even began.

As bad luck would have it, the day before the appointment I woke up with the flu (later diagnosed as mononucleosis). I cancelled, giving no reason, because I didn't want Geoff Stevens to think I was a sickly person and thus unreliable.

One month later I set up another appointment. Although I was still pretty weak from mono, I thought I could pull off an interview. But disaster struck again. My mother suddenly had to go into the hospital for an operation, and my father, who at this point was in the advanced stages of Alzheimer's, came to stay with me. I literally could not leave his side. Again I cancelled my appointment with the *Globe*. I was beginning to think that fate was against me; anyway, I really didn't have the strength right then to cope with any more than my mono, my father's sickness and looking after my family. A job seemed out of the question.

Another month went by. My strength returned, my mother was out of the hospital, and I started thinking about that job. I had not heard that anyone had been hired to replace Zena, and I knew there was a distinct possibility that the *Globe* might not replace her at all. But I thought I'd give it another try.

However, this time, surprise, surprise, Geoff Stevens refused to see me at all. Screwing up my courage, I called his secretary, Sue Garapy, whom I was beginning to know from arranging and cancelling appointments. "Do you think I could wait outside his office and maybe catch him at an off moment?" I asked her. "Sure," she said. "Come in around noon tomorrow. I'll show you where you can sit and wait for him."

I sat in the middle of the *Globe* newsroom for 20 minutes dying with embarrassment, but knowing, from Stevens's point of view at least, I deserved to be treated this way. He finally walked by, curtly showed me into his office, and we started talking.

I began by saying I was there on behalf of Zena and I wanted to assist her in the job. "If we hire you," he said, "it will be your column. We're not having Zena back."

Geoff Stevens and I immediately hit it off. He started asking me questions to test my knowledge about goings-on around town. He asked me about socialite Catherine Nugent's wedding, which had been given a whole column by Zena. I knew more about it than he did. However, when the conversation veered toward politics, I was totally outshone; Geoff was a walking encyclopedia. But I knew that didn't matter much; I wasn't trying to be hired as a political columnist.

I was so nervous that I'd forgotten to bring my CV, so just before I left I scribbled some of the boards I was a member of on the back of an envelope.

I left Geoff's office after our 30-minute talk feeling quite good. The interview had gone as well as could be expected, and despite my two cancellations he was going to consider me for the job.

Several weeks later, the phone call came through. "It's Geoff Stevens. We'd like to offer you a job."

And so began my five-year stint as society columnist for *The Globe and Mail*, five of the most interesting years of my life.

And, by the way, I learned to type in about two weeks when I was practically thrown a little word processor by the *Globe*'s computer expert Terry Christian and told to use it. My request to do the column in longhand was, not surprisingly, denied.

Chapter One

A Day in the Life of a Society Columnist

A Social Columnist's Lot is Not a Happy One

December 2, 1989

Some people may labour under the misapprehension that a social columnist's normal routine consists of the following:

9:00 a.m.   Breakfast in bed while opening morning mail.

9:30 a.m.   Dictation of correspondence to secretary while glancing over appointments for the day.

10:00 a.m.   Hair appointment.

11:00 a.m.   Manicure and massage.

12:00 (noon)   Lunch at Fenton's followed by a fashion show at the Gardiner Museum.

3:30 p.m.   Aerobics and dancercize classes.

4:30 p.m.   Gown-fitting at Holt Renfrew.

6:30 to 8:30 p.m.   Dropping into various chichi cocktail parties around town.

9:00 p.m.   Late dinner and drinks with a) the Mulroneys; b) the Petersons; c) Princess Diana when she's in town.

12:00 (midnight)   Final round of late-night parties until deposited at my door by chauffeur-driven limousine.

I'd like to set the record straight. Herewith an outline of a social columnist's typical day:

7:00 a.m.   Telephone rings. Did I or did I not receive an invitation to the fifties sock hop at the Royal Canadian Curling Club on Broadview Avenue? Will I be gracing the hop with my presence? Why not?

7:30 a.m.   Husband goes to front door to retrieve morning paper. Is greeted by three giggling witches carrying broomstick heralding upcoming Wizard of Oz gala. They leave him with broom.

9:00 a.m.   Arrive at dentist's office in North Toronto to get son's braces tightened. Work on final touches for my column due down at the *Globe* at ten-thirty. Computer crashes and wipes out three columns. I cry.

9:30 a.m.   My first "congratulatory" call of the day from a previously respectable woman I had interviewed for a piece appearing in today's paper. The dialogue goes something like this. Dumb columnist: Hi, M——. How did you like the story? Irate caller: You f——ing idiot. Wait till I get my f——ing hands on you. Protestations from columnist; more obscenities from caller. I hang up. Phone rings incessantly.

10:30 a.m.   Put in a load of laundry, including a well-worn polyester dress that has seen better days, in case I decide to cover an evening event.

12:30 p.m.   Go to kitchen and make myself a sandwich and pour a glass of milk. Hear commotion at door. Peer out. Large black perambulator sitting at doorstep. With trepidation open door and look under blankets. Breathe sigh of relief. No baby. Instead, pair of baby booties accompanied by invitation to a shower. Retrieve invitation. Furtively wheel baby carriage to corner for next day's garbage pickup.

2:30 p.m.   Busy writing, I refuse to answer doorbell. Livid courier, who has caught sight of me through the window hunched over computer, circles house banging on all windows. I crawl into hall where I can't be seen and curl into a ball on the rug. Phone rings fourteen times. I laugh hysterically.

5:00 p.m.   Drag along a protesting son to a cocktail party at the Art Gallery of Ontario. Wander around the room hoping that someone, anyone, will talk to us. Strike up several conversations with strangers who look at me oddly. Pretend to hold fascinating conversation with my son, who gets bored and pulls me over to the hors d'oeuvres on the sidelines which he devours shamelessly. We tour the gallery and look at pictures, then go home.

6:00 p.m.   Open bag of mail delivered by courier from *The Globe and Mail*, most of which consists of dull press releases or juicy tidbits too gossipy for serious upscale newspaper. Also one fan letter and five critical ones. Keep the fan letter. Deposit rest in large green garbage bag, which I take outside and put in pram.

7:00 p.m.   Pull on polyester dress and drag my daughter along to an auction. Despite said dress, organizers of gala, thinking that we're two girls out for a night on the town, try to pick us up.

8:30 p.m.   Climb into hot bath, forgetting to take phone off the hook. It rings four times. Will I be an auction item? Will I hand out free chicken legs in front of Honest Ed's? Will I serve in a soup kitchen? Will I donate money to the University of Western Ontario?

9:45 p.m.   Call from my mother, who warns me not to get a swelled head from all the attention I'm getting.

11:00 p.m.   Crawl into bed. Doorbell rings insistently. Husband groans and puts pillow over his head. Stones hit the window. I wearily open window. "Invitation for a native people's gala tomorrow night," courier yells up. Not wanting to offend one of our visible minorities, I descend stairs and answer the door. Before climbing back into bed, go over to shut window. Hear rustling in the bushes. Peering out, discover courier making off with pram and garbage bag.

What happened to the bright, ambitious women we were in our twenties? We were determined then "to be the best we could be," to compete to our utmost and "get to the top." We were disdainful of stay-at-home wives and mothers—"What on earth do they do all day?" we would ask. Now former colleagues ask us the same question. To their enormous surprise, the driven forty-something women they knew are quite content puttering at home, walking the dog, reading all those books they always wanted to read, going to movies, gardening and playing mah-jong.

> —Sheila Robb explaining why the can't-stop-'em women
> have stopped, published on the Facts and Arguments
> page of the *Globe and Mail*, June 29, 1994

I used to be a free man. Now I spend half my day answering letters. I used to go to Portofino for holidays. Now I stay [at home] because I am accosted whenever I go out. I can't even go to a newspaper kiosk and buy a copy of *Playboy* or everyone says: "Look, there's Eco, and he reads *Playboy*.

People say that success brings you women, horses and champagne. I don't drink champagne, I don't like horses, and I've never paid for a woman.

> —Umberto Eco on the success of his
> novel *The Name of the Rose* in the
> *Independent* magazine.

Although I only experienced a small fraction of the harassment doled out to best-selling author Umberto Eco, I can't say that I liked it any better than he did. To be perfectly frank, it got to me. In 1988, when I was hired by the *Globe and Mail*, I was 42 years old. Staying at home, having drinks and dinner and reading with my husband, was, and still is, my idea of a perfect evening, not going out on the town to a party every night and writing a column on it afterward. And it wasn't only my evenings and weekends that the job threatened to take over. It was all day, every day. (Having said this, I realize that most jobs take over most of your life. But at this stage, I wasn't sure that was what I wanted.) Like Sheila Robb's 40-something women, I was too contented and happy in my personal life to be willing to take the flak that goes along with a fairly high-profile job.

One of the greatest hazards of being a gossip columnist is that one's phone rings incessantly. Why not unplug? suggested a visiting friend one day, doubtless tired of all the interruptions. Or take the phone off the hook? Or get an answering machine?

I employ the first two strategies all the time, I told her. As for the third option, several weeks into my job, beseiged by the constant calls that were interfering with my getting my columns done, I went out and bought an answering machine. It was the worst thing I could have done. It was true that at last I could have a peaceful afternoon when I turned it on. But there were dire consequences.

The first day the machine was put to use, I turned it on at 2:00 p.m. and retrieved my messages four hours later. There were more than 25 of them, mostly from people I had never heard of. It took me the whole next morning just to return the calls, and in many cases it turned into a game of telephone tag. This absurd turn of events went on for a few weeks until I gave the machine to my daughter, who lived at the back of my house, and who, on call at Global Television, had far greater need of the infernal contraption than did I.

The result was that I might have occasionally had to put up with a barrage of calls, but that was only when I chose to leave the phones plugged in or on the hook. At least when I left the house to perform some errands, I was not greeted, when I returned, with dozens of messages that people were expecting me to return. The added advantage of no machine was that all but the most persistent callers eventually gave up, helping me to shorten the process, albeit not very selectively, of winnowing down potential column subjects.

I was two years into my job when I published this list of invitations, so that those on the sending end would perhaps understand why they never heard back from me. It also gives one a glimpse into a typical 14 days of choices presented to me as the *Globe's* society columnist.

Long List of Also-Rans in Columnist's Schedule

November 25, 1989

When the publicist for Maestro Guiseppe Raffa, artistic director of the International Opera Festival's *Aida*, reproached me last week for not attending his post-performance reception, I felt a twinge of guilt. Like any other well-brought-up person, I was taught to write thank-you notes and reply to invitations. Sadly, the exigencies of a social columnist's routine have caused such niceties to fall by the wayside. So here I offer a small sampling of the invitations, requests and come-ons I received in just one week to explain my lack of response.

The opening party of Paparazzi Restaurant and Nightclub in Richmond Hill (Nov. 9); a luncheon speech by Margaret Papandreou, former wife of former Greek premier Andreas Papandreou (Nov. 4); afternoon tea and a stroll through the E. R. Wood estate in North Toronto announced with the depositing of a pair of green rubber boots on my doorstep (Oct. 24); a schedule of classical guitarist Liona Boyd's forthcoming European tour (Nov. 1 to Nov. 16); the annual awards banquet of the Canadian Foundation for Ileitis and Colitis along with Rich Little and 2,300 others (Oct. 27); a buffet and fashion show at the York Mills Plaza with special guest Marilyn Lastman (Nov. 29); a dinner conference on Canadian-Soviet Cooperation in the Arctic (Oct. 23); a private preview of art and jewelry auctions by the directors of Sotheby's (Canada) (Nov. 6); a media luncheon to meet the 1990 Miss Canada contestants (Oct. 23); a public forum on sexuality at the Ontario Science Centre with June Callwood and Shere Hite (Nov. 12); the opening night of the Canadian Stage Company's production of the rock musical *Fire* (Nov. 16).

Book launchings for Allan Fotheringham and Roland Michener (both Nov. 1); *Maclean's* magazine (Nov. 6); Jack Pollock (Nov. 20); an advanced screening of Harry Rasky's film on Northrop Frye (Nov. 2); a francophone talent night to celebrate the coming into effect of the Ontario French Language Services Act (Nov. 18); Allan Gotlieb speaking at a Pollution Probe dinner (Nov. 1); a Meals on Wheels third annual recognition dinner (Oct. 4); a lecture by Dr. Liane Jakob-Rost from the Vorderasiatisches Museum in East Berlin on Mesopotamian Antiquities (Nov. 8); a climb up the CN Tower with Toronto mayor Arthur Eggleton and several firemen to raise money for the Hospital for Sick Children's Burn Unit (Nov. 12); an opening night party at Tarragon Theatre for Sally Clark's *Jehanne of the Witches* (Nov. 21); a benefit performance by an Israeli piano quartet at the Jane Mallet Theatre (Oct. 24); the November meeting of the Monarchist League of Canada; the presentation of the eighteenth annual Jacqueline Lemieux prize by Canada Council director Joyce Zemans to dancer Anuradha Naimpally at Centrepoint Stage, Nepean, Ontario (Oct. 27).

A lecture by Dr. Charles Nelson of Dublin on horticulture in Ireland at the Civic Garden Centre (Nov. 7); cocktails to celebrate the republication of the magazine the *Canadian Forum* (Nov. 6); an exhibit of Canadian art made of wood at the University of Toronto's Faculty of Forestry (Oct. 20 to 27); the sixteenth annual luncheon of the women's committee of the Dellcrest Children's Centre at the Prince Hotel (Nov. 5); the Canadian unveiling of the new Mercedes-Benz SL Coupe/Roadster by United Way campaign chairman Tony Fell (Nov. 4); a community meeting in Etobicoke to introduce the Dorothy Ley Hospice for palliative care (Oct. 26); a plea from Bishop Reynold Rouleau of the diocese of Churchill-Hudson Bay for a donation to the Esk-Omi missions (Oct. 27); a bus tour of Toronto with the wives of international IBM employees with stopovers at Ashley China, Ken Thomson's art gallery and Charles Pachter's studio (Oct. 31).

It is difficult to choose from such a variety of interesting events. I was especially keen on the climb to the top of the CN Tower, but declined after being informed by Chief Bev Gilbert that *Sun* photographer Silvia Pecota's firemen calendar pinups would not be participating.

I received an inventive response to this column from a trio who offered to organize my timetable for me:

November 24, 1989
CAP Associates were dismayed to read of the dilemma you find yourself in at the present time—to which [*sic*] too many invitations and not enough time! We feel that *The Globe and Mail* could do its readers and yourself a great service by hiring CAP Associates to "job share" with you in attending and providing coverage of these vital social events.

In case you are not familiar with CAP Associates, we are a two-women and one-man social consulting group with a broad spectrum of concerns and interests. Our talents, qualifications and social contacts are without parallel:

- We hold between us eight university degrees (including an earned doctorate from the University of Toronto) with areas of specialization ranging from ancient history to modern art and business;
- Our social circles run the gamut from the Rosedale and Forest Hill set to contacts with high-ranking government officials; CEOs and executives in the business, banking and legal communities; the equine and athletics set; the "Old Boys Network" of University of Toronto, McMaster University, Massey College and the University of Waterloo; the amateur and professional theatre crowds, and so forth;
- While at university, each of us had experience as a working journalist. Our work experience ranges from employment in a wide variety of government ministries and agencies, educational institutions ranging from elementary schools to university, as well as employment in the private sector. All three of us have extensive experience with making presentations and giving speeches.

We feel that the extended coverage CAP could provide would not only enhance your column's range of cultural and social experiences but also bring a more balanced perspective to the column by appealing to men, an often overlooked segment of your wide audience.

CAP Associates would be more than willing to discuss our proposal with you and negotiate a formal agreement to job share. We feel the following arrangement would constitute a more than equitable arrangement:

- an honorarium in the amount of $7,500 per annum to be shared by the three members of CAP Associates;
- an allowance for personal expenses such as hairstyling, manicures, facials, dry-cleaning of clothing, and so forth.

In return, we would cover two lunch-hour events, one evening event (during the week), and a minimum of one weekend event. This would allow you to expand your horizons by a minimum of 15 events a week. We are also willing to travel out of town to cover such events as theatre openings, polo exhibitions, hunt club balls, and so forth. . . .

(Dr.) Anne Lloyd–Adams
President, CAP Associates
Toronto

Being a society columnist, especially for Canada's national newspaper, was a heady experience, I don't deny it. People clamour after you, willing to do almost anything to get into your column. You get to meet lots of stars and rich and/or famous people. The public, at least those who read your column, consider you an authority on everything from what band to hire to play for a high school prom to how to start a business. It's all very flattering, and I suppose it could go to your head.

Unfortunately, there was not much chance of that. For the three years that I wrote three columns a week for the *Globe and Mail* (much less so in the two years following, during which I wrote one column a week), I had little time for myself. Maybe I'm a slow worker, too much of a perfectionist, or a combination of both, but during those three years, activities such as lunching out at a favourite restaurant, wandering through antique stores or just talking on the phone with friends became rare.

It is not that I am naive as to what a job entails. Indeed, I have never had a job that didn't involve most of the hours in the day. When I taught high school, I was usually in the school by eight-thirty in the morning and, after teaching all day, had extracurricular activities, frequently until six o'clock. After supper, marking and lesson preparation often took several hours.

Law was even harder. The complex issues that one had to deal with as well as the competitiveness of the profession usually meant I worked a 12-hour day, seven days a week. And I had two children by this time, as well.

So writing a social column was much easier in comparison. But writing a social column for Canada's national newspaper entailed an invasion of privacy I felt uncomfortable with.

At first, my close friends thought that I had abandoned them to hobnob with the jet set, and were quite cool the few times that

I caught up with them. But as the months went by it slowly dawned on them that not only was I not living the glamorous life they so envied, but that my life was a bit crazy and out of control. Quite often, party organizers themselves came to my door with invitations and requests. When I appeared, they were doubtless taken aback. Instead of the elegant, well-put-together society figure they might have expected, there stood greeting them on the doorstep, in a T-shirt and long jean skirt, hair akimbo, face bereft of makeup, a somewhat different spectacle.

(These incidents remind me of the time I, an aspiring column-subject, rang Zena Cherry's doorbell in the mid-eighties only to be confronted with an apparition in a torn raincoat over a house-coat surrounded by piles of letters and invitations on the floor. "You can't come in right now, dear, I'm not dressed," she said sweetly, but she very kindly engaged me in conversation on her doorstep. I have no doubt that the eager, well-dressed, young and not-so-young society matrons who appeared on my doorstep were as shocked by my dishevelled appearance as I was by hers. And Zena had a much better excuse. She was then, though few knew it, in the early stages of Alzheimer's. At this point in my life, as I opened numerous invitations, dropped in on never-ending parties, and stumbled over countless names and spellings and titles and corrections, I became convinced that Alzheimer's might well be an unavoidable hazard of the job.)

Unfortunately, the den in which I worked had a big window right beside the front door. When I refused to answer the door, people would come and knock on my window. It was really quite amazing the lengths to which some of them would go, either to catch a glimpse of the *Globe*'s social scribe or, if they were couriers, to obtain proof that they had dropped off their envelopes and/or parcels at the requisite destination.

I was asked to perform many offbeat and crazy tasks in my role as a society columnist. I wrote the following column after being invited to come on CBC Radio's "Morningside" to teach Peter Gzowski how to waltz. I really didn't want to do it—my awkwardness at conversational repartee is only matched by my gracelessness on the dance floor. But I'm a big fan of Peter

Gzowski's, and, consummate host that he is, he made it as easy for me as possible. Unfortunately, the *Globe* cut the column by two-thirds when it ran on Saturday, March 2, 1991. I'm reprinting it here in full.

On a cold, frosty morning one Thursday in February, having set my alarm for 7:00 a.m., I leapt out of bed, put on a twirly black pleated skirt over an olive-green crushed velvet bodysuit and headed down to the CBC Radio studios at Jarvis and Carlton streets. My mission? To teach a self-proclaimed unteachable dance student by the name of Peter Gzowski, host of CBC Radio's popular "Morningside," how to waltz.

I had been selected for this daunting task, so senior producer Willy Barth told me, because my credentials were impeccable. In countless balls over the years during my three-year stint as this national newspaper's society columnist, I had waltzed with the best of them. But, unbeknownst to Willy and crew, my enviable status was based on false pretences. Refusing unless absolutely necessary to dance with anyone but my husband, whose most complicated dance pattern was the two-step shuffle, I hadn't a clue how to perform on a dance floor. Now my lack of prowess as a ballroom dancer would be revealed from coast to coast.

Fortunately, the request came at an opportune time. I had just attended the Canadian Stage Company's Dreamland Ball where society mavens Heather Thomson, Robin Vaile and Betsey Atkinson Crang had put on superb ballroom dancing demonstrations for the ritzy crowd. I had been expertly whirled out on the floor by Mrs. Thomson's partner, a professional dancer from the William Pollock Dance School.

So I put in a quick, desperate call to Mr. Pollock, who graciously taught me the steps over the phone in a couple of minutes. There are six waltz steps for the man, he instructed. 1. FRONT LEFT 2. SIDE RIGHT 3. TOGETHER LEFT, then 4. BACK RIGHT 5. SIDE LEFT, and 6. TOGETHER RIGHT. My steps were the same, he said, but in reverse order. I jotted down his instructions, my anxieties disappearing. This was radio, not television, after all. I could take my notes into the studio and read them off. No one would discover that I was a ballroom dance fraud.

I had turned to a master for advice. Mr. Pollock has been teaching dancing for 37 years. He said that the waltz has always been in favour, especially at balls and at weddings. But its popularity waned somewhat in the sixties. "During that decade it was more of doing your own thing on the dance floor," he explained. "But partnership dancing is definitely back." Many society women and their husbands, such as Julie Medland, wife of former Wood Gundy chairman Ted; designer Norma King and her husband John, an architect; and Mrs. Vaile's husband Sigmund, who is an eye surgeon, flock to Mr. Pollock's dance classes.

One of the most famous, and unlikely, of Mr. Pollock's students is entrepreneur Ed Mirvish, who has taken dance lessons for 30 years. He comes two to three hours a week, just for the exercise. Although 77 years old, he can still lift his 147-pound dancing teacher. "I wish I could do the same," Mr. Pollock, who is 57, said with a laugh.

But back to my radio debut. It all went as planned. My genial host (the recalcitrant waltzer) and I chatted away for a few minutes and then were miked in preparation for our debut as dance partners. "This is a piece of cake," I said to myself. "I can't possibly make a fool of myself." The tape of Strauss's "Blue Danube" began, and we got up to dance. I placed my left hand on Mr. Gzowski's shoulder as, with my right hand, I picked up from the table where we'd been sitting the little card on which I had typed RIGHT FORWARD, LEFT SIDE, TOGETHER RIGHT.

"Why, Rosemary," sputtered an astonished Mr. Gzowski, loud enough for all his listeners from Newfoundland to Victoria to hear, clear as a bell, "you've brought notes!"

Usually I turned requests down with the only-too-true excuse that I hadn't the time. But if the truth be known, neither did I have the inclination. The requests ranged from testifying at a mock trial as a rape victim at the University of Toronto Law School (immediately vetoed by my husband), and sitting on numerous boards (vetoed by the *Globe and Mail*'s conflict of interest rules). I was asked to serve Big Macs on McHappy Day with then premier

David Peterson, McDonald's president George Cohon, television czar Doug Bassett and publisher Paul Godfrey (I did one year, and it gave me a good column); make television appearances (I assented to some); and speak before various public interest groups (ditto). I was asked often to be an auction item, that is, lunch with me was auctioned off to the highest bidder, and I did agree to do it for one charity, but it was a mistake. The first time, the wife of the man who bid for me came on the "date" instead.

Not knowing I had agreed to be an *annual* auction item, I failed to withdraw my name from the charity's list, and so came up for auction again the next year. When the highest bidder was contacted that he had won me as a luncheon companion, he was so terrified or embarrassed or both that he denied ever signing his name to the list of bidders, saying that his friends had forged his signature to play a joke on him. Instead of some unfortunate wife who had to step in to honour her husband's obligation, this time there was no lunch partner at all and it appeared as if the charity would end up without the money. Luckily for me, socialite Pat Appleton stepped in and took Catherine Nugent, Cathie Bratty and me out to lunch at Winston's, picking up the tab for the lunch and the charity.

It was typical of Pat to make such a generous gesture, but it's not uncommon to find wealthy socialites doing favours for members of the media. They know well that the connections they make may prove invaluable to them in the future.

The recognition factor is just one reason women fund-raisers get involved in charitable causes. There are a whole host of other reasons that vary from individual to individual. Often the reason they volunteer for a disease charity, for example, in the first place, is that they themselves or members of their family have suffered from the disease. It's a wish to help and to nurture others, which seems much stronger in women than men.

Or it may be as simple as just a need to get out of the house. These women have often spent years staying at home and raising a family. Their children are grown; their husbands work long hours; and they are unlikely to pursue careers, either because their years at home have left them ill-equipped for the professional world or just because they don't need the money. They still want to be able to pick up at a moment's notice to join their husbands on a trip or celebrate the birth of a grandchild, and a full-fledged job would not allow them that flexibility. So they immerse themselves in volunteer work.

And, because it is not paid work, it often goes completely unrewarded. During the eight years I worked as a volunteer on a number of boards and committees, there were times when I felt I had worked especially hard with no thanks or recognition. But there were also times when I had not worked as hard as I would have liked, due to lack of time or conflicting appointments, and had received accolades I thought were undeserved. Usually it all balances out in the end. And it's important for women volunteers to be mature enough to keep their cool when something unfair happens.

By the same token, the society columnist must expect some abuse if he or she occasionally takes potshots at others. You can't hold others up to ridicule, no matter how light-hearted or well-intentioned, without taking it yourself. Here are some Letters to the Editor—some published, some not—to prove my point.

January 20, 1988

Correct Social Forms

I read with interest in yesterday's *Globe* of the appointment of Rosemary Sexton as your new social columnist, and I looked forward to reading her first column. I was much dismayed, therefore, to find that she had committed a solecism that, while common enough among the ignorant, is surely inexcusable in a writer who is expected to be *au fait* with the niceties and usages in high social circles.

In the second half of her column she correctly identifies the new British High Commissioner and his wife as Sir Alan and Lady Urwick, but later refers to "Lady Marta Yolande Urwick." This is quite incorrect as the two forms of address are, generally speaking, mutually exclusive. Lady Blank refers to the wife or widow of a marquess, earl, viscount, baron, baronet or knight; Lady Mary Blank is a courtesy title given only to the daughter of a duke, marquess or earl. If Lady Mary marries a peer she adopts his title even though his precedence is lower than hers; if she marries a baronet, knight or commoner, she retains her courtesy title along with her husband's name (like Lady Margery Bellamy in "Upstairs, Downstairs"). Only if she marries a courtesy lord or the younger son of a duke or marquess does she have the option of retaining her courtesy title along with her husband's name, or adopting the usual style of wives of such persons. But these matters need not concern us here, since it seems most unlikely from the description that Lady Urwick is the daughter of a [British] duke, marquess or earl. If she were, of course, she would be known only as Lady Marta Urwick and never as Lady Urwick.

I suggest that you promptly provide Mrs. Sexton with a copy of *Debrett's Correct Form*, which is an authoritative reference for these and related matters. But in the present instance, it should have been quite sufficient to reach for one's nearby *Fowler* and look up the article on *Lady* (the second edition is somewhat more informative than the first).

Frederick W. Burd
Denman Island, B.C.

January 21, 1988
Re your new columnist Rosemary Sexton and her first column, "800 Attend Gala Dinner Welcoming Japan's PM" (January 19):

Am I correct in assuming that you have replaced one name-dropping, porch-climbing columnist only to take on another? Not only did Mrs. Sexton's first column read like the list of begats in the Bible, but among "those who did not show up," my name was, along with millions of other Canadians, conspicuously absent.

Marc Tessler
Toronto

July 10, 1989

Wait For It

The idea behind Rosemary Sexton's column is, presumably, to include as many names as possible so that everyone mentioned will buy extra copies of the *Globe and Mail* to send to friends and relatives. Ms. Sexton does well. The total of 184 names—including God and Prime Minister Brian Mulroney—on July 1 eclipsed the record of 118 names set by her predecessor on December 17, 1985.

Ms. Sexton lists not only people who were at the function, but also those who were not there. Accordingly, I look forward to seeing my name regularly in future columns.

Ernest Wotton

Toronto

Re: Beatty dinner honours retiring NATO chief—March 12, 1988.

The above-mentioned military dinner that you have written about seems almost incomplete without such military guests as Kurt Waldheim and Oliver North in attendance.

In view of the many hungry and needy children in Canada, I am sure glad you did not mention the cost to Canadian taxpayers.

A taxpayer

June 9, 1988.

Attention: Rosemary Sexton re article "Royal Guest Marks 25th Anniversary of Awards for Youth."

With regards to Catherine Nugent. I agree that she is ubiquitous. Socialite, maybe, too. But why not just say the notorious courtesan, which is really what she is (we all know that, anyway) along with her buddies Anna Maria de Souza and Mercedes (Mimi) Skinner. . . . The way they *appear* is only a front, a facade. . . . You should know better (if you claim to know the so-called jet set and society). They would *never, never* be accepted, let alone invited, in the good old establishment, and you know it (or should), mentioning these people the way that you do. Ubiquitous socialite is as ridiculous and tasteless as mentioning the Rosedale mansion owners, their past, private affairs, etc. Wake up, lady, and put a better photograph of yourself in the newspaper. It really does not flatter you. Have a good day.

[Unsigned]

Though I was often amazed at the vitriol from some letter writers (such as the untrue accusation that the above socialites were courtesans), I was relieved that people were reading my column at all. It had been my fear that I would die out in about week two of my new job. I really didn't mind the criticism, indeed almost welcomed it as a sign I was being read.

And when I got complacent and a bit boring, there was always Geoffrey Stevens around to give me a poke. "Say, Rosemary," he would remark to me, "you haven't been stirring things up around here lately." And back I would go to the drawing board, intent on throwing a dart or two.

But even I was surprised at the force of the reaction to some of my columns. The first time that it was really brought home to me was in May 1988. I had only been on the job for five months and was still trying to cope with the glare of publicity brought on by my thrice-weekly columns. In April my husband and I escaped to Longboat Key, Florida, for a ten-day holiday. In order to really relax, I had worked especially hard to write columns ahead and had sent down four columns on the Friday we flew out. But I was apprehensive about my return to Toronto. How was I ever going to get columns done for my week back when we weren't flying in until Sunday night? I was still pretty new to the column-writing game and hadn't yet discovered an easy way out.

So, instead of napping with Edgar in the afternoon as I usually did on holidays, I waited until he was asleep and quietly went into the living room of our condominium to work on a column. The only topic I could think of off the top of my head that I didn't have to attend a party for but that did involve society was Rosedale real estate, so I sat down and wrote what turned out to be two columns. I took a stroll in my head through winding Rosedale streets and described who lived where and what was for sale. I knew most of it by heart. I hope, I thought as I wrote it all down, that the *Globe* will print this, since it's not about parties. It never entered my mind that there was anything controversial about it.

When I got back to Toronto I transferred my notes to my computer. A friend of mine, Cathy Scott, who has since moved to Vancouver, dropped in, and since I had just printed the columns out, I let her take a peek. As she leaned over my shoulder to read, she erupted into an outburst of "Oh, oh, oh!" and then shrieks of laughter. "Omigod Rosemary," she exclaimed, "you're not going to print this stuff!" I was utterly taken aback by her reaction. So that night over dinner, I showed the columns to Edgar. He had exactly the same reaction I had had to them, which was the opposite to Cathy's. He was even a little bored by them. "They look fine to me," he said. "What's the problem?" I explained to him Cathy's reaction. Like me, he couldn't understand it, so the next morning I sent the first instalment down to the *Globe*.

The response was instantaneous. At around five that afternoon, as soon as the copy editors had begun to work on my piece, two fact checkers called me on and off for about half an hour to check if what I had written was all factually correct. This had never happened before. Usually after I sent down a column, one person might phone to check on a fact or two. This time it was two people checking and asking a whole lot of questions with an excited timbre to their voices. That was my second indication, after Cathy's shrieks, as to the storm on the horizon.

The next morning Edgar and I were sitting reading the paper after breakfast and discussing whether or not we should take a stroll over to the park for the annual Rosedale Mayfair. The phone rang. It was David Rose, the real estate agent who had checked some of the dollar amounts for me in the article and whom I had quoted. "Have you been to Mayfair yet?" he asked me. "If not, don't go. I was just there and everyone's talking about your column. They're very upset."

For the first time since I'd started on the column I was scared. It's one thing to create a bit of controversy; it's another to become an object of hate. I envisioned a groundswell of public opinion with pickets outside the *Globe* demanding my resignation. Needless to say, Edgar and I did not go to Mayfair.

The next week, when I went to the local grocery store, Summerhill Market, I could actually feel the tension around when I walked through the door. Disgusted stares were directed toward me, and people stood in twos and threes whispering in corners. This kind of thing went on for a few weeks. At home, phone calls and letters poured in filled with so much hatred that I finally got annoyed and threw them all out. Ever since I was a teenager, and cared too much, I have never really cared about being liked. But I did find this virulent reaction disconcerting. I found it especially bemusing since I had so misjudged the situation.

Looking back over the columns several years later, I have the same reaction to them I had when I first wrote them—that there's really nothing controversial about them. I have laid them out here exactly as the *Globe* printed them, in two instalments, with headlines intact. The reader may decide.

Charm Is Never Cheap in Rosedale Real Estate

May 12, 1988
Rosedale, that prime area of residential real estate in the heart of Toronto, is unique in both its location and its character. First of all, few cities can boast so elegant an enclave so near to the downtown business core. Second, with its winding streets, and lots and houses of every shape and size, it recalls an English village more than a modern Canadian city.

The rapid rise of the real estate market is even more evident in Rosedale than in the rest of Toronto, because the prices are so astronomical. There are few houses on the market these days, and those that are require wealthy purchasers.

Dean Muncaster, former president of Canadian Tire, and his wife Brenda recently sold their house on a private lane at the east end of Douglas Drive for $2.4 million, down from an asking price of $2.6 million. One prospective buyer was singer Gordon Lightfoot, who owns a large old house on Beaumont Road, a dead-end street lined with some of the most coveted properties in Rosedale.

Besides Mr. Lightfoot, its inhabitants include architect Eberhard Zeidler and Emmett, Cardinal Carter, Roman Catholic Archbishop of Toronto. A few years ago, several Beaumont Road residents launched a losing legal battle against plans to redevelop one of the most idyllically situated pieces of real estate in the city, at the very end of the street. Food magnate Galen Weston and several co-owners sold it a few years ago to builder Peter Kellner, who planned to erect town houses on the site. However, he in turn sold it in May 1986 for $1.6 million to Gaylord Lindal, president of Viceroy Homes, who has begun to build a single-family house on the property.

At present, Mr. Lindal rents a modern coach house on Castle Frank Road at the rear of the Seagram mansion, a marvellous old stone structure that builder Adam Smuszkowicz turned into five elegant condominiums in the early eighties. Its owners include dentist Steven Small and his wife, Sandra, and stockbroker Gordie Eberts and Mary Joyal.

The Georgian mansion of Ken Thomson, chairman of The Thomson Corporation, and his wife, Marilyn, is also on Castle Frank Road, and just down the street where Castle Frank Road turns into Elm Avenue is the Tudor-style residence of Senator John Godfrey and his wife, Mary. Their son John is the editor of the *Financial Post*. Being the editor, not the owner, of a newspaper, he rents an apartment in an old house on the same street.

Nearby on a private laneway called Hawthorn Gardens and overlooking the Don Valley Parkway is the massive brick mansion that Adrian Edwards sold two years ago for several million dollars to John Haney, one of the inventors of the game Trivial Pursuit. It was on the market a few months ago for $4 million plus, but is no longer for sale.

Also overlooking the Don Valley is the oldest house in Rosedale. Called Drumsnab, it was bought from art collector Budd Feheley in the mid-eighties by Dr. Alistair Thomson and his wife, Sheila, who chaired the International Polo for Heart event in Gormley last July. The asking price was $1.4 million; it probably is worth double that at today's prices.

Drumsnab is on a private little street that bears its name; it used to be called Castle Frank Drive.

Another house on that street has an interesting history. It was a brothel for many years; then it was sold in the seventies and rented to Conrad and Shirley Black while their house on Park Lane Circle was under construction.

There is also a Castle Frank Crescent, south of Bloor Street, on which stands the pink-stuccoed residence of Attorney General Ian Scott. Artist Harold Town lives nearby.

The confusion of street names, part of the quaint charm of Rosedale, causes untold misery to visitors in the area, who sometimes end up driving around in circles.

Walls surround many Rosedale residences, among them the beautiful Elm Avenue house that used to belong to Robert Macaulay, chairman of the Ontario Energy Board, and stockbroker Geoff Boone and his wife Elaine's house on Dale Avenue. Their wall protects their swimming pool from passersby. The old Band mansion across the street from the Boones was bought several years ago by Central Capital Corporation chairman Peter Cole. He sold part of the property to developer Brian Magee and his wife, Susan, and turned the large house into a duplex, keeping the south side for himself. The north half alone was for sale last year for around $800,000.

Just around the corner on McKenzie Avenue, a lovely walled red brick house needing some work was sold recently for $1.4 million by businessman Bruce Westwood and his wife Lyn, whose marriage had broken up. An earlier offer on the house made by stockbroker David Birkenshaw and his wife, Nancy, had fallen through because Mr. Birkenshaw's former wife, television broadcaster Bodine Williams, refused to vacate its backyard coach house that she rented.

Marital Discord a Factor in Rosedale Real Estate

May 14, 1988
In Toronto's famed Rosedale there have been a couple of house sales brought on by domestic disputes. When the marriage broke up of insurance broker Douglas Jones and his wife Margaret Ann, a director of Planned Parenthood, their house on Hawthorn Avenue, relatively small by Rosedale standards, was bought by Allentharp Construction for $670,000 and flipped over in six months for $770,000.

Mrs. Jones is now dating boating enthusiast Dan Finn, who lives in the back coach house of the huge mansion at

1 Chestnut Park Road. Its bottom floor is inhabited by Ada Slaight alone, since she and husband Allan, chairman of Standard Broadcasting, have parted. Upstairs lives interior decorator Robert Dirstein, who bought the second-floor condominium for $1.4 million in July 1984 with his partner James Robertson, who died in January of this year.

A few doors down is the square grey house belonging to venture capitalist David Scott and his wife, Cathy. They bought it for $540,000 six years ago when they came to Toronto from Montreal. They are now moving to Vancouver and it was sold in one day for more than $1 million.

One of the most beautiful streets in Rosedale is Chestnut Park Road. The house that Eaton's chairman John Craig Eaton moved out of years ago has just been bought for about $1.4 million by the Mojtahedi family, who are dealers in Iranian carpets. Former federal finance minister Walter Gordon used to live on this street, and his former neighbours, Cathy and Bill Graham (he's the federal Liberal candidate for the area in the next election) have recently moved into the Sherbourne Street North residence of former provincial minister Allan Lawrence. It has no garage and no backyard, but they have sunk a lot of money into its restoration.

A corner condominium a block to the south with an asking price of $1,295,000 was just sold by its owner, Tom Smythe, grandson of Conn Smythe, who built Maple Leaf Gardens.

Dunbar Road is also interesting, though not so scenic as Chestnut Park. A couple of big old houses owned by CTV president Murray Chercover and his wife, Barbara, and the Mackenzies, parents of socialite Catherine Nugent, coexist with smaller ones. These include the one owned by television broadcaster Valerie Elia, which she has rented out at different times to columnist Barbara Amiel and her estranged husband, David Graham, and also to publisher Adrienne Clarkson when she returned from France. A renovated house at the end of the street is up for rent for $5,000 a month.

At the end of Highland Avenue, a dead-end street, is a huge house just sold by an elderly lawyer for more than $4 million to the architectural firm of Armstrong Molesworth

Shepherd, which plans to turn it into town houses. The scenic piece of property owned by the University of Toronto to house its president is on this street, as are the massive mansions owned by Harlequin Enterprises chairman Larry Heisey and wife Ann; American Barrick Resources chairman Peter Munk and wife, Melanie; and businessman and lawyer John Finlay and wife, Janet.

On Glen Road at the eastern end of Highland stands a house in the style of a French château owned by former MPP Margaret Scrivener and her husband, Richard. Next door live lawyer Ian Angus and his wife, Daphne, who a few weeks ago sold their ravine property to Leland Verner for $1.6 million and bought the Batterwood Estate in Port Hope for more than $2 million.

A few doors down from them is the former Rosedale Golf Club clubhouse inhabited part-time by its owner Donald Davis, when he is not in New York. Across the street resides plastic surgeon Charles Kilgour and his wife, Mary.

Roxborough Drive, Binscarth Road and Whitney Avenue run perpendicular to Glen Road and parallel to one another, or as parallel as is possible with Rosedale's asymmetric streets. One of the most beautiful corners of Rosedale is the eastern end of Roxborough Drive, and the largest property there is owned by Colonel Maxwell Meighen, son of former prime minister Arthur Meighen. A few doors down is the house of Liberal senator Lorna Marsden and her husband, Edward Harvey.

Other owners in the area include Olympia & York vice-president Marshall (Mickey) Cohen and wife, Judi; Imperial Optical president Peter Hermant and wife, Katie; and retired Baton Broadcasting chairman John Bassett and wife, Isabel.

Residents on Cluny Drive and Rosedale Road include Empire Life Insurance chairman Hal Jackman and wife, Maruja; Burns Fry chairman Jack Lawrence and wife, Janice; and Onex president Gerry Schwartz and Heather Reisman.

Nearby is Park Road, where hockey negotiator Alan Eagleson has settled into his third Rosedale house imaginatively decorated by his wife, Nancy. At one point they considered buying the yellow brick mansion up the street that David Thomson, son of Ken Thomson, was trying to sell, while it was still being renovated, for around $4 million.

Author Timothy Findley and Finance Minister Michael Wilson grew up on South Drive, and lawyer Julian Porter's boyhood home was on Pine Hill.

Rosedale resident David Rose has the best of both worlds. Not only did he buy a house in Rosedale when he moved from New York 15 years ago, but he started a new career selling real estate in the area. His net income last year, he says with a twinkle in his eye, is satisfactory.

I was extremely fortunate to be working for the *Globe* at that time. Worried that the paper would want to fire me after receiving a number of threatening letters, including a rather nasty one from then Burns Fry chairman Jack Lawrence, who had written to Norman Webster complaining about me, I telephoned Norman.

"I'm just calling to apologize for causing you so much trouble at the paper," I said to him. I particularly wanted to let him know that I had not written the headline for the second instalment of the Rosedale columns—Marital Discord a Factor in Rosedale Real Estate—which several people, including Mr. Lawrence, had taken exception to. I'd put my own aunt and uncle in that column, Dr. Charles and Mary Kilgour, so I was quite upset at the letters.

"You're not to be concerned," Norman told me. "That's what a newspaper editor's job is—to field storms of controversy. I do it all the time and I expect it to happen."

"I realize that you don't think up the titles for your columns," he reassured me. "We have a staff down here that does that." I was extremely grateful to Norman for his objective approach and his refusal to allow me to become the scapegoat.

The next column that caused quite a stir, but in a rather more positive way, was a column I wrote the next September on the Spruce Meadows equestrian centre in Alberta started by Calgary businessman Ronald Southern and his wife, Margaret. When I had been contacted about writing up a black-tie dinner that had been held for the centre, I had decided that this was a must-write column because, along with the Southerns, *Globe and Mail* publisher

Roy Megarry and his wife, Barbara, had hosted the dinner. To give Roy Megarry credit where credit is due, he did not, in all the time I worked at the *Globe*, put any pressure on me to cover any particular event. Nor would I have faulted him if he did so. He was my boss, after all, and if the boss can't get a few things that concern him in his own paper, well, then, who can? But he never did. Whenever I covered events that he was involved in, it was entirely my own choice.

First of all, to get background for the column, I called Spruce Meadows and asked for Mrs. Southern. I usually found wives to be more helpful concerning the social side of things, so I thought I would start with her. Unfortunately she was not communicative at all. Maybe she didn't know who I was, or maybe she did know who I was and didn't like my column, or maybe dealing with the press scared her, as it does many people, but in any event I got nothing but monosyllabic replies to my questions.

Usually when this happened, I gave up and went on to another story. I was not an investigative reporter, and there were scores of people out there dying to have their parties written up. There was no point giving the space to someone who was not interested. But I had already called Roy Megarry's secretary to ask him if he had any objections to my writing up the dinner. It would look pretty funny if, after that, no story appeared. So I called the centre's general manager Ian Allison, who was very helpful and who, during the course of our conversation, put Mr. Southern on the line.

Mr. Southern was much more forthcoming than his wife, and we chatted away for a few minutes. He told me all about the dinner and who had come. I wrote down everything he told me. Finally I was getting some good information for a column. But then he made a request that absolutely floored me. Yes, he was happy for me to write up Spruce Meadows, but, please, would I not mention the names of any important people who had attended his dinner. Spruce Meadows wasn't really about fancy black-tie dinners and my column would give the wrong impression.

Now, the ethics of journalism are such that, technically speaking, I did not have to abide by Mr. Southern's request. He had freely and willingly given me the information and then asked me to withhold it. In cases such as this, the reporter is not obliged in any way to comply with the request. (It is different, however, if the request is made before the information is given.)

I was caught in a real bind. This man was a friend and cohost of my publisher. Obviously, he would be very upset if I printed the names of his guests. His wrath would immediately come down on my publisher, who would be embarrassed and angry himself and who also, as a result, might lose a powerful and wealthy advertiser. Yet I had told Megarry through his secretary I would be doing a column on the party he had cohosted, and now Mr. Southern expected the same.

What was I to do? I sat down at my computer and in desperation produced the following few paragraphs:

Last Saturday A. Roy Megarry, publisher of *The Globe and Mail*, and his wife, Barbara, were hosts, with the Southerns, at a dinner attended by several notable Canadians. It was a glittering affair, but at Mr. Southern's request, the guest list won't be published.

Mr. Southern obviously does not place reading social columns high on his list of priorities. "Suzanne," he said to me, "I'd appreciate it if you wouldn't single out any of my guests for publication. They're all important."

So, if you want to know whether former Alberta premier Peter Lougheed and his wife, Jeanne, Sir Ronald Trotter, head of New Zealand's Fletcher Challenge, or Bank of Montreal chairman William Mulholland mingled with such eminent riders as Canada's Ian Millar, three-time European champion Paul Schockemohle or former Olympic champion from Great Britain David Broome, you won't find it here. . . .

Unlike the Rosedale real estate column, this time I knew I was playing with fire. It's not that I thought that people in general would pay much attention to my little joke; it's that I was poking fun at an important businessman and friend of my boss. And I was printing information he had specifically asked me to withhold.

But I couldn't resist it: I had worried that I wouldn't have any story at all and here was Mr. Southern unintentionally providing me with a little comic relief. Ethically speaking, I could use the names he had given me, and he had called me Suzanne without knowing it was not my name. I liked people who didn't pay attention to social columns, and, though I was poking fun, I was also giving Mr. Southern a plug at the same time for being his down-to-earth, unpretentious self. I had enjoyed talking to him and I admired his philosophy. So down to the *Globe* went the column. I thought either it would go totally unnoticed or be cut.

But I was wrong. Again, as with the Rosedale article, I got a call, this time from sports editor David Langford. "Did that exchange with Mr. Southern really happen?" he asked. "Yes, it did," I replied. Now, it is highly unusual for another person down at the *Globe*, apart from a copy editor, to see one's column before it is printed. And, not only to see it, but to question its veracity. Although I didn't ask, I concluded from Dave's call that there had been discussion down at the *Globe* about the column, and that he had been enlisted to check on it. Certainly, after it was published, there was a lot of discussion from the readers, who mostly thought it was very funny.

There were other columns I wrote that people either loved or hated, especially the latter. Not surprisingly, some people are very thin-skinned and hate criticism of any kind, even when it's meant in fun, such as the following column comparing the Brazilian Ball to a university dance. I got the idea from the clever Lee MacLaren, wife of Liberal Trade Minister Roy MacLaren, who is profiled in *The Glitter Girls* and whose son was attending the Trinity dance.

Brazilian Ball Contrasts with Students' Formal

February 9, 1988
The swing to conservatism in the 1980s often makes it difficult to distinguish between adults trying to escape middle-aged ennui and their straight-arrow offspring. A case in point occurred last Saturday night when Trinity College students held a formal dance at the same time as their parents were whooping it up at the Brazilian Ball.

It was the 105th annual Conversazione held by the students. It began as a social evening to gather and talk and has evolved into a formal ball. In celebration of this year's

theme—Babylon Revisited: An Evening in the Jazz Age—
the students staged a week of events culminating in the ball,
including a showing of a 1920s gangster movie, waltzing
and Charleston lessons, a debate on "Heaven Knows, Anything Goes," and a prose reading titled "Martinis and
Modernism."

About 600 college students and their dates attended the
ball, some of them, such as Malcolm MacLaren, son of pub-
lisher Roy and his wife, Lee, holding dinner parties before the
main event. The conveners of the evening were Michael
Szonyi, in his third year of Chinese studies, and Francine
McKenzie, a history specialist. The guest of honour, singer
Maureen Forrester, was entertained beforehand by Robert
Palmer, provost of the college.

The ball on Saturday night, which was a black-tie affair,
took place in five or six rooms decorated to different themes.
The students could take their pick of, say, waltzing in an art
deco ballroom or dancing cheek-to-cheek in a hall fixed up to
resemble the New York Stock Exchange.

Their adult counterparts, meanwhile, had no such choices.
Packed like sardines into the barn better known as the Metro
Toronto Convention Centre, there was little opportunity for
conversazione, at least once the raucous music began. All one
could do was get up and dance or gawk at the endless parade
of young men or women either decked out in outlandish cos-
tumes or wearing almost nothing at all.

Some of the onlookers were Mayor Arthur Eggleton and
his wife, Brenda, who'd just finished her stint as model at fashion designer Marilyn Brooks's twenty-fifth anniversary; fund-
raiser Inta Kierans with Wellesley Hospital urologist Dr. John
Rankin; lawyers Robert Lindsay and David Purdy, both with
wives named Ann(e). Anne Lindsay is in the process of writing
The Lighthearted Cookbook on behalf of the Heart and Stroke
Foundation, the recipients this year of the ball's proceeds.

The Brazilian Ball, which was started by Anna Maria de
Souza in a church basement 22 years ago, and was co-
convened this year by Anne Laurier, has become one of the
main events of Toronto's social season. For that reason it attracts

a high percentage of the Toronto society crowd that you run into at every big function: Senator Jerry and Carole Grafstein, Alf and Louise Powis, David and Catherine Nugent, Hal Jackman with wife, Maruja, etc.

Several people had parties before the event, including Grafton Group chairman William Heaslip and his wife, Nona Macdonald. Among those admiring the view of the city from the Heaslips' spectacular living room were Harry Seymour, a founding director of Yes Canada, and his wife, Lillian; *Flare* magazine publisher Donna Scott with her management consultant husband Hugh Farrell; and William Weldon, a managing partner of Arthur Andersen & Company, and his wife, Audrey.

Those dancing up a storm at the ball included Ruth Grant, vice-chairman of Women's College Hospital, and her husband, Douglas, chairman of Sceptre Investment Counsel; sociology professor Merrijoy Kelner, who was columnist Doris Anderson's husband's second wife; and businessman Morris Kerzner and wife, Miriam.

There was no dearth of egos in the room. At one table sat Peter Nygard, chairman of clothing enterprise Nygard International, with his blonde-of-the-moment; and CITY-TV president Moses Znaimer accompanied by Erica Ehm, a miniskirted deejay from MuchMusic.

A brief word of advice to the organizers. The ritzy but drawn-out evening (the prize-giving took forever) was not the appropriate time for a restricted bar. Cocktails such as Manhattans and martinis were surprisingly not available. The Trinity students would have laughed.

The last paragraph was merely meant as a little joke and a device to tie back in to the Trinity students and their dance. But it was objected to strenuously by some Brazilian Ball committee members who bombarded the *Globe* editorial desk with complaints. Fortunately, Norman Webster and Geoffrey Stevens were at the helm of the *Globe*, a duo not loathe to rise to the defence of their columnists. Although I saw copies of the angry letters sent by irate readers, my bosses never brought the matter up with me.

Not surprisingly, some of the most positive reaction came from columns dealing with the plight of the sick, handicapped or disadvantaged. I first learned that that was going to be the case when I wrote about a fortieth birthday party thrown by *Toronto Star* columnist Janet Enright, who has since died of cancer, to raise funds for the mentally retarded. The late wife of CBC Radio's Michael Enright and the sister of former federal cabinet minister Barbara McDougall, Mrs. Enright had a daughter who was born mentally retarded. I had heard about the party through Geoffrey Stevens, who knew the Enrights. The day my column on the party appeared in the paper, Geoff's secretary Sue Garapy called me. "I just wanted to let you know, we've had great response to your column on the Enright party," she said. I'd been a little apprehensive about the article, because I was afraid I'd be criticized for writing about a topic that wasn't really my bailiwick.

Fortieth Birthday Bash Assists the Retarded

April 12, 1988

Toronto Star columnist Janet Enright and her husband, Michael, host of CBC Radio's "As It Happens," have three children. Their third child and only daughter was born retarded. Searching for some respite from the constant care of a handicapped child, Mrs. Enright was appalled at the lack of facilities available.

Last Thursday was Mrs. Enright's fortieth birthday, and, after enlisting corporate sponsors to donate various elements of the event, she invited several hundred friends for dinner at the University of Toronto's Massey College. In return, they were asked to send a contribution to the Metropolitan Toronto Association for Community Living, the euphemistic new name for the former Metro Toronto Association for the Mentally Retarded.

Master of ceremonies for the evening was Employment and Immigration Minister Barbara McDougall, sister of the hostess. Speakers at the event included *Toronto Star* columnist Joey Slinger (his comments were very funny but unprintable), who came with his wife Nora McCabe, a sportswriter, and publisher Paul Rush, who was accompanied by his wife, Mona. Grace was sung by the leader of The Gents, a male vocal group. Reflecting the atmosphere in the hall, he sang songs going back decades, closing with a spirited rendition of "New York, New York."

Among those attending were critic Robert Fulford and his wife, Geraldine Sherman; *Toronto Life* publisher Peter Herrndorf and his wife Eva Czigler; Dr. Murray Frum and his wife, Barbara, host of CBC-TV's "The Journal"; writers Martin O'Malley and Karen O'Reilly; and Irving Abella, professor of history at York University, with his wife, Rosalie, chairman of the Ontario Labour Relations Board.

As well, Geoffrey Stevens of the *Globe*, with Lin Shannon; lawyer Eddie Greenspan and his wife, Suzy; author Morley Torgov, who has twice won the Stephen Leacock Award for humour, and his wife, Anna-Pearl; and Bob McGavin, vice-president, public affairs, Toronto-Dominion Bank.

Also in attendance were Robert Lewis, managing editor of *Maclean's* magazine, and his wife, Sally; June Callwood and her husband, Trent Frayne, both *Globe and Mail* columnists; and artist Charles Pachter.

Three of the most generous donors who were present were Jalynn Bennett, vice-president of Manufacturers Life; composer Harry Somers with his wife, actress Barbara Chilcott; and kidney surgeon Dr. Michael Robinette and his wife, Marni.

Also attending were Mrs. Enright's high school friends Cinny Powell and Dale Butterill, and camp-mate Megan Whittingham.

It was a warm evening that almost turned into an overnight affair for the Enright family. Attempting to leave Massey College after midnight, they found themselves locked in and had to ring for a porter, much to the disappointment of son Daniel, who thought he might enjoy a sleep-over in the building.

The evening proved to be a financial as well as a social success. Approximately $9,500 was raised for the association for the retarded, twice the amount the hostess had hoped for.

There was an ironic twist to the piece. Geoff Stevens had told me about the party, which was one of the reasons I had decided to write it up in the first place. But, much to his chagrin, the first two words of the story, in capital letters, were *Toronto Star!* The copy editors, in rearranging my first paragraph, had caused the unfortunate result. We had a good laugh over that one.

As a result of the positive feedback I had received, I began to write every once in a while about different social causes.

Another person fairly close to me, the wife of my ex-husband's brother, was diagnosed with breast cancer to the shock of our whole family. Since a number of women I knew had been stricken with the disease, I tried to work her illness into a column on a breast cancer symposium.

One Woman's Fight with Breast Cancer

October 9, 1990

This is the story of a friendship. The centre of the story happens to be my sister-in-law. But it could be the story of any number of today's women.

Christine Black is 40 years old, five-foot eight and, I would guess, 135 pounds. She is the picture of health, a tall, strapping blonde who laughs a lot. If it weren't for the fact that she is a devoted wife and mother, you might easily classify her as one of those good-time girls. She is usually the life of the party, outgoing to the point of being boisterous and, even though an outrageous flirt, equally popular with women and men. I have known her since the early seventies when she married my first husband's older brother.

I remember being jealous of her. In 1972, for example, I was a full-time student at Osgoode Hall Law School, attending night courses toward a master's degree in English, and had a 6-year-old daughter. She was footloose and fancy-free and looked better than I did in a bikini. Whenever I heard the song "The Girl from Ipanema," I thought of Chris. While I was busy studying and doing housework, she and her husband were buying expensive clothes and Cartier watches and taking trips down south from where they would return looking tanned and fit.

As the years went by, our fortunes reversed somewhat, and our paths crossed less frequently. I escaped from my foundering marriage to settle down in Rosedale with my new husband and family. She and her husband, a stockbroker, faced some business reversals not made easier by their spiralling bills. Though Chris and her pretty stepdaughter Shelley appeared on the cover of the July 11, 1981, issue of the *Toronto Star's Today* magazine as the ideal stepmother and stepdaughter, their relationship went through some stormy periods during Shelley's adolescence. I saw her less and less as I became absorbed in my new husband and volunteer activities, and she in her busy life. She spent long hours at the Etobicoke Swim Club, where her daughter Courtney became a promising swimmer. As well, she worked part-time at Cactus, an upscale women's clothing store in First Canadian Place.

But though our daily phone calls ceased, Chris and I always stayed in touch. With my children, I would drop over to her pool in Mississauga in the summer months. She and her husband were always welcome guests at my parties. On my birthday every year, she would arrive armed with a giant cake. She even accompanied me a few times on the requisite social whirl.

After I started working for the *Globe and Mail*, she would often drop into my house on her way to the city. As ever, she would waltz in, nails freshly manicured, hair coiffed in the latest fashion, dressed to the nines, catching me in my son's T-shirt and a long jean skirt. She would tease me good-naturedly about my less-than-glamorous appearance, but I sensed that, underneath her deprecating humour, lay a tinge of envy for what appeared to be my life of comparative ease.

Last fall, after taking a whirlwind trip to London and Paris, getting my son ready for school and receiving extra writing assignments, I found myself flat on my back with the flu. It was Chris I turned to. "Please come over and cheer me up," I croaked. "Rose, I can't," she replied. "I have a doctor's appointment."

It wasn't until a week later that I found out that a lump she had had on her breast since the summer, initially diagnosed as benign, was discovered to be malignant. She didn't want to talk to me when, in shock, I called her. "I don't want people feeling sorry for me," she said. "I don't want my breast gone and my hair falling out. I'm not ready to become one of the walking wounded."

She's lucky. She hasn't. After several operations, her cancer is in remission, her hair and breast intact. If anything, she is more beautiful than ever.

Today the Canadian Women's Breast Cancer Foundation is holding a full-day symposium at Toronto's Sheraton Centre. Carole Grafstein and Dr. Richard Hasselback are the honorary chairs of the luncheon, and Nancy Paul is the present chairman of the CWBCF. A special award will be handed out in memory of Constable Carol Nicholson, on duty at last year's luncheon, who, less fortunate than Chris, is a recent victim of the disease.

I wrote the following column about one of my favourite people, Pat Appleton. She died ten months later, leaving a devoted husband and three children. There is a chapter on her in my book *The Glitter Girls*.

Charity Fund-raiser Battling Scleroderma

February 23, 1991
Upon first meeting Patricia Appleton, you might think she has it all. A petite brunette with a friendly smile, she glows with a tan acquired on recent vacations to Hawaii at Christmas and Mexico in November. The wife of lawyer Michael Appleton and mother of twin daughters in post-grad school and a son in medical school, she lives in a large mansion in the Bridle Path area, with a mirrored master bathroom bigger than the living room of the house in which she grew up in the Bathurst-Dundas area of Toronto. Draped in gold lamé, she herself was the subject of the *Globe and Mail's Report on Business Magazine's* March 1990 cover. Her life, it seems, is a never-ending round of parties and social gatherings.

But a serpent lurks in her paradise. In September 1988 she was diagnosed as having scleroderma, a painful and potentially fatal tissue disease that hardens the skin and internal organs. Primarily affecting women between the ages of 30 and 50, the disease strikes its victims in a variety of ways: some live for years and others die as their kidneys, esophagus and lungs slowly harden. There is no known cure and the cause is unknown, though some doctors say the overproduction of collagen (a protein in connective tissues and bones) plays a part.

So far the disease has invaded Mrs. Appleton's lungs (she is often out of breath and even has difficulty climbing stairs) and her esophagus (she must sleep practically sitting up to avoid choking). Her voice is raspy; her hands have become stiff and clawlike, making simple tasks such as doing up buttons and opening jars difficult to perform. "It's very frustrating," she said, "when your mind is going 90 miles a minute and you want to do everything and be everywhere, and not miss a party until you're a 100 years old." Another problem for her is the fact that her glamorous image is incongruous with the unseemly disease. People who see her out partying, all made up and in a designer dress, find it difficult to believe that she is sick. Not only acquaintances and good friends, she says, but even close family members have expectations of her that she cannot meet. Not surprisingly, parking her large Rolls Royce is a problem. "Although I have a handicapped sign, people look at me oddly when I park in a handicapped spot, because, especially with my weight gain, I look healthier than ever."

An intensified appetite (it already was naturally intense, she says, laughing) is just one of the side effects of the steroids she is taking to combat the disease. The others include changed hair texture, pockets of cellulite and a tendency toward osteoporosis.

But Mrs. Appleton didn't get where she is by giving up. She's a fighter, and ever since her world came crashing down, she's been fighting hard. "I have no intention of letting this get to me," she states determinedly. She continued in her role as chairman of the 1989 Opera Ball even after being diagnosed, finding that the hard work and busy schedule helped her forget about her painful symptoms. She realizes, however, that although a positive attitude and a refusal to give in to the disease are very important, they are not always enough to change the prognosis. She is being treated by a rheumatologist at the Toronto General Hospital, Dr. Carl Laskin, as well as a gastroenterologist and a respirologist.

She finds it ironic that although she has raised funds for 20 years in Toronto for a variety of causes, the disease that is affecting her has no fund-raising body in Canada. Even though scleroderma in various forms is said to affect more people than multiple sclerosis and muscular dystrophy, little has been done in this country to raise its profile.

In the United States, Sharon Monsky, a 37-year-old management consultant who was once a nationally ranked figure skater, has single-handedly initiated a scleroderma research foundation and has been involved in a public crusade to raise funds and publicity for scleroderma since her own diagnosis in 1983. Ms. Monsky has created a board with prominent business people and has enlisted celebrities to help. Actors John Candy, Robin Williams, Linda Gray and Lesley Ann Warren have donated time and money. The total raised over the past four years is $750,000.

A world-class research centre for studies in autoimmunity is presently being set up at the Wellesley Hospital, which could unlock the key to autoimmune diseases such as scleroderma, lupus, rheumatoid arthritis, muscular dystrophy and multiple sclerosis. Mrs. Appleton has already discussed with her friend Anna Maria de Souza cochairing a future Brazilian Ball to raise funds for the centre. "Once the economy picks up, we plan to have a dynamite party and raise a million dollars," she says.

Just last Friday, she was surprised to receive a telephone call from Ms. Monsky, whom she has never met, asking her to sit on the board of directors of the California foundation, with the view of possibly setting up a Canadian arm in the future. Ms. Monsky also invited Mrs. Appleton to a star-studded celebrity fund-raiser that will be hosted in March by Robin Williams in Los Angeles.

Knowing these courageous people reminded me that but for the grace of God there go I. Possibly having a child born with one hand has made me even more aware of the courage of those with handicaps.

Chapter Two

Highs and Lows of a Society Columnist—Columns

Celebrities, Homegrown and Otherwise

Readers always like to read about celebrities, but I tried not to lace my columns with big names. In the first place, one can read and hear about them every day in magazines such as *People* and *Vanity Fair* and on various television talk shows. In the second place, my job was to write for a Canadian newspaper about society and parties, not about the entertainment world.

There were exceptions to this rule, of course, especially when I was given a chance to do columns on the British Royal Family. But, after writing several of them, I turned down the *Globe's* request to follow Charles and Diana around when they came to Canada. The assignment was probably every reporter's dream; Christie Blatchford and Rosie DiManno, better reporters than I would ever be, were already doing the same job for the *Sun* and the *Star*. So I suppose I should have acquiesced. But I would have missed several weekends in the country with my husband; in addition, I couldn't imagine anything worse than becoming part of the rat pack that follows royalty around, so I declined. Not the route to getting ahead in one's job, but for me, the best recipe for personal satisfaction.

I got the following scoop, I was told, after everyone else at *The Globe and Mail* had turned it down. It was an interview with Andrew Morton, author of the best-selling *Diana: Her True Story*. *Globe* publishing reporter Val Ross sent me over the book, so I called Key Porter and the talk was set up. I wasn't even sure the *Globe* would publish the fruits of my labours, but, thanks to Michael Valpy, who was deputy managing editor at the time, and then national editor Jerry Johnson, it was run as a front-page story.

StoryBook Marriage Lacks Happily Ever After

July 18, 1992

While in Toronto recently, British author and royal watcher Andrew Morton discussed the controversy surrounding *Diana: Her True Story*, his best-seller chronicling the trials and tribulations of the Princess of Wales.

The tall and bespectacled young writer conceded that his portrayal of her marital hardships is less than balanced, but noted that "Charles's friends have already started to tell his side."

Q: You say in the book that Diana made five suicide attempts while suffering acute depression. Do you think that a woman who behaves that way, no matter how much one may sympathize with her, is suitable to step into the role of Queen of England?

A: I think that she is suitable and has demonstrated that. In many respects she has faced more traumas than the rest of us, yet she has come through. She has gone through more between the ages of 20 and 30 than most people have in a lifetime. And she is not the first woman who has married into the Royal Family to have done so. It was not an easy transition for the Queen Mother, for example, who was snubbed by society and nicknamed the Dowdy Duchess. And back then the spotlight was not on the Royal Family with the intensity it is now.

Q: The book portrays Charles as a selfish, uncaring husband and implies he drove his wife to what turned out to be pitiable attempts to kill herself. Given that your sources were entirely the family and friends of Diana, do you think that your

portrayal may be somewhat one-sided? Do you think that Prince Charles's friends will start to tell his side of the story?
A: Yes, it is a one-sided story, very much her truth and her perception, and yes, Charles's friends have already started to tell his side in the *Sunday Times*. There are always two sides.

Charles comes from a family where control, distance and formality are the modus operandi. Its very insularity makes it difficult for outsiders to come close. But Diana and Charles aren't the first royal couple to be under public scrutiny. There were endless stories about the Queen and Prince Philip in the 1950s, in fact, so many that Buckingham Palace had to issue a statement in 1957. But Philip was a prince and Diana was brought up as a commoner.

If royal marriages fail, it is usually due to this insularity on the part of the Royals.

Q: What did Diana hope to gain by telling all about her disastrous marriage?
A: The princess was not behind the book. She didn't co-operate. I've said it so many times, I'm sick of saying it. Diana lives in Kensington Palace. Her friends can't drop in. So she spends a lot of her time on the telephone. It's a release for her.

What does the book contain? Maybe fifty stories all told. And many of these things are ten years old. The phrases Diana is quoted as saying are phrases she has used over and over again to her friends. Words such as "the things I do for England" and "I don't rattle their cages and they don't rattle mine." The Diana of the early years is not the Diana of the present. She's no longer the same person she was as a teenager.

The Royal Family have known for years that the marriage was on the skids, yet they have done nothing about it. This is one of the interesting things about this sad affair. Nothing ever seems to get done. The members of the Royal Family live their lives in separate compartments and ignore one another until a crisis comes along. And then it's crisis management time. We tend to think that because these are important people, they have a sophisticated machinery for dealing with these things, but it doesn't happen that way.

Q: Diana has become, arguably, the most popular, sought-after public figure in the world. And doubtless quite wealthy into the bargain. Does she truly understand the consequences of giving all that up, as well as her claim to the throne, merely because she feels that her husband does not pay her enough attention?

A: Ivana Trump said a few days ago, if I may paraphrase her, that all the yachts and castles don't make a difference if one is not happy. That view, which is probably one shared by Diana, highlights the difference between commoners and Royals brought up as Royals. The latter are raised to choose duty over personal happiness. Princess Margaret, on the other hand, sacrificed happiness to royal duty.

Anyway, Diana hasn't given up anything yet. The status quo remains at Buckingham Palace. Everything's the same, things haven't changed one jot. Diana's having as difficult a time as ever. The only difference is that since my book there's been a tremendous up-surge of public sympathy for her.

Q: What about within Buckingham Palace?

A: Oh, there's a definite down-surge there. She gets more isolated day by day.

Q: Is it possible that Diana has played her cards right after all and that Buckingham Palace, frightened by all the negative press resulting from your book, will do anything now to keep her happy?

A: That's a good Machiavellian question and I think it makes Diana out to be more manipulative than she really is. Yes, I would agree that she is in a strong position. But she has been for a very long time and hasn't recognized it. Concerning the public, she has been a very popular figure. But her dominant perception is that her role is that of junior partner to Prince Charles and she has to defer to him. She is adulated by crowds, yet must come home to an empty palace. She has absolutely no allies within the Royal Family....

The book is told according to her perception because it is very different from our perception of her. In our world we see her as adored, loved, celebrated. In her world she exists as an outsider, a threat, a junior partner.

She felt rejected as a young child by her mother, who lost custody of the children in a divorce suit, felt rejected early on in her marriage by her husband in favour of another woman. And now she fears rejection from the public.

Charles's friends perceive Diana as a sideshow, as a fluffy blonde in a ball gown.

Q: Did the *Sunday Times* pay you 250,000 pounds' serialization rights? How much might you make from this book?
A: The *Times* paid that amount to my publisher and I get a proportion of that. If it sells as well as it seems to be doing, it will do better than my last book, titled *Inside Buckingham Palace*, which had a loss. I write books because I'm interested in the subject. If I had wanted to make money, I would have become a property speculator.

Ultimately, doing this book was a conflict between a writer trying to find out the truth and the preservation of an institution built on mythology, illusions and dreams. People don't want the fairy tale to be pricked. I feel like the little boy who discovered that the emperor wasn't wearing any clothes.

I enjoyed meeting another member of the Royal Family, Lord Patrick Litchfield, the famous photographer of beautiful women, when he was also in town to promote a book. Like most of the members of British royalty, he was down-to-earth and unpretentious.

Jet-setter Unveils List of the World's Best

October 8, 1988
It's not every day one meets an English lord, so stumbling into a reception for Lord Patrick Litchfield, the great-nephew of the Queen Mother, hair awry and an hour late, was not exactly the entrance I had planned last Monday afternoon. However, the construction barriers out on Dundas Street blocking access to the Art Gallery of Ontario and the surly glances

from Ontario premier David Peterson's bodyguards when I mistakenly crashed his party in the same building may have had something to do with my slightly dishevelled and unnerved state.

The reception was to celebrate the launching of the second edition of Courvoisier's *Book of the Best*. The idea for the book evolved when Courvoisier of France, the company that makes the cognac of the same name, approached Lord Litchfield, a frequent traveller, for his views of the best places to eat, stay at and visit in the world. He was considered the ideal candidate for the job, since he travels 400,000 kilometres a year, spends 150 nights in hotels and eats out virtually every day.

So, Lord Litchfield got out his little black book in which were recorded his likes and dislikes and contributed a list of the former to provide a witty commentary on the very best in the categories of Food and Drink, Travel, Culture, Social and Night Life, Fashion and Shopping in countries around the world.

More than 200 jet-setters and experts were also consulted, and many of their comments are also included in the book. Thus you can find out what author Barbara Cartland, actor Douglas Fairbanks, Jr., and magazine editor Helen Gurley Brown have in common (their favourite hotel is Claridge's in London); how British author Auberon Waugh's taste buds react to crocodile, snake and kangaroo; the secrets of Joan Collins's desert island survival kit; and Peter Ustinov's travel hints.

The lists appeal to those with varying tastes and from every walk of life. The Rosedale Diner appears on the same page as Winston's; Frederick's of Hollywood lingerie is alongside Calvin Klein underwear; and Sporting Life and Roots sportswear are on the same pages as designer labels from Creeds and Ira-Berg.

The commentators, like the lists themselves, are an eclectic mix. They include British author Jeffrey Archer, New York interior designer Mario Buatta, Australian columnist Dorian Wild and Japanese fashion designer Hanae Mori.

Stirling Moss recommends the best cars—his first choice is a Ferrari. Karen Kain tells where to buy a trench coat—at Clotheslines. There are opinions on who gives the best parties, where the best horse races are run, and where the best nightclubs and shopping districts are.

Whether the reader agrees with the selections or not, the book is, to quote Lord Litchfield, a jolly good read, especially if you're stuck in an airport for an hour or two.

Among those at the reception were several Canadians who are included in the book. Restaurateur Roel Bramer, who owns the Amsterdam Brasserie and Brewpub on John Street in Toronto, chatted with George Butterfield, whose luxury bicycle tours are also mentioned. Not content with trips to Italy and France, Mr. Butterfield is leading 24 people on a bicycle tour of China in three weeks.

Former World Cup skiing champion Steve Podborski, who suggests heli-skiing in the Rockies as the ideal vacation, came with his wife, Kathy, whose brothers used to race with her husband. Mr. Podborski is now host of "Pod's Perspective" on CKVR-TV and is involved in various sports promotions.

Though his advice appears freely in the *Book of the Best*, Bob Ramsay was hard-put to explain why he was chosen one of *T.O. Magazine*'s 50 sexiest people.

Patrick Litchfield began using a camera at the age of 6. He was educated at Harrow, and his first picture of his cousin, the Queen, was taken during a cricket match against Eton. It was promptly confiscated.

He travelled the world taking pictures, and in the 1960s was known as the man in the Burberry trench coat. His big break came when he was summoned by Diana Vreeland to shoot fashion pictures for *Vogue*. In July 1981 he was appointed official photographer for the marriage of his second cousin Prince Charles and Lady Diana Spencer.

Lord Litchfield has a reputation as one of the best photographers of beautiful women. He neglected to ask me to pose for him, an oversight no doubt due to my failure to create a favourable first impression.

I gave the following party a write-up because it was the sixtieth birthday celebration of a columnist who, by virtue of his wit and longevity, has become a Canadian institution. Allan Fotheringham was also a help to me, a fledgling journalist, taking time to go for lunch occasionally and offer sly and sagacious words of advice.

Columnist Gets Party with Poetry Chez Porter

August 22, 1992

It is well-known among the literary party-going community in Toronto that there is no better place to find oneself on a cool summer's evening than at the comfortable and decidedly unposh Moore Park residence of lawyer Julian Porter and his publisher wife, Anna. As their home is invariably run amok with children and dogs, celebrities everywhere you turn, loud speeches and scintillating conversation, it might be argued that no more coveted invitations to house parties exist elsewhere in the city.

Last week's reception to celebrate the birthday of sexagenarian columnist Allan Fotheringham was no exception. If anything, it was even more uproarious and more outrageous than ever, due, no doubt, to the lethal one-two punch packed by both the controversial writer and his celebrated hosts as enticement to the party-goers. Rather than ask who was at the party, a more pertinent question might be who was not.

As might be expected, members of the Toronto literary community abounded: Margaret Atwood and Graeme Gibson, Jack Batten and Marjorie Harris, Sondra and Allan Gotlieb, Alexander Ross, Richard and Sandra Gwyn, Peter Worthington and Yvonne Crittenden, Robert Fulford and Geraldine Sherman, Phyllis Bruce and Malcolm Lester.

Lawyers, diplomats and civil servants included former British high commissioner Donald Macdonald and his wife, Adrian; economist Sylvia Ostry and her husband, Bernard; former Canadian consul general in New York Bob Johnstone and his wife Popsy; and Central Capital Corporation vice-chairman Stanley Beck and his wife, Barbara. Also Pierette Lucas, chief of staff, External Affairs, and new TVOntario head Peter Herrndorf with his wife Eva Czigler.

Society types mingling included Catherine and David Nugent, Sarah Band, Valerie Jennings and Pia Southam. Not to mention family and friends, including Anna Porter's mother Maria Szigethy.

Host Porter was in enviable form, popping up every half hour or so to lend his laconic, ofttimes incomprehensible, speech-making abilities to the already noisy gathering. "I always knew that no one but a genius could coin Fotheringham's one-liners," he said at one point. "And I was right. When he said of 'Thumper' Macdonald that 'he had so much conceit that he could strut sitting down,' he was quoting from none other than H. L. Mencken, who used the same turn of phrase in 1928."

Not to be outdone, Fotheringham leapt to his feet with a slew of lawyer jokes. And so it went throughout the course of the evening: thrust and repartee, parry and response. Acerbic verbal contributions were made by the selfsame "Thumper" Macdonald and broadcaster Jack Webster, who told a joke about Timbuktu not repeatable in this column.

To cap the evening off, the ever-prolific Peggy Atwood came up with "Ode on the Birthday of A. Fotheringham" (with apologies to A. A. Milne and Edgar Allan Poe) in honour of the boisterous occasion:

When a Fother's
In a dither
Or he's (rather)
In a lather
He's a bother
To the other
Creatures living in this zoo.

But I'd rather
Have a Fother
In a highly coloured
Fluster
Than a blastid [sic]
Politician
And I'm sure that you would, too.

My mother, in 1937, as she appeared in the *Kingston Whig Standard* at 18 as one of Kingston's "lovely younger set."

When my father retired in 1983, at 74, this portrait was presented to him by the lawyers of the District of Timiskaming. It now hangs in the courthouse in Haileybury.

Guess who at 18 months, surrounded by my father's three beautiful sisters: (left to right) Barbara Brooks, Nonie Taylor and Mary Kilgour. Taken the summer of 1948 at my parents' first house in Moore's Cove, several miles north of Haileybury.

A picture of me, crowned Laurentian University home-coming queen, appeared on the front page of the *Sudbury Star* on November 4, 1967.

My sister Judy (right) and me at the ages of 3 and 4 sitting on our front steps in Haileybury in 1950. My mother is holding Judy, my father is sitting behind her. That's my uncle John Bridger in the middle and his son, Tony, holding me.

My daughter, Stephanie, my son, Robin, and I cavort for the camera in Sherwood Park on the day I resigned from the Ontario Censor Board in the fall of 1980. This photo appeared on page 2 of the *Globe*, September 3, 1980. *Photo Credit: The Globe and Mail.*

Celebrating with Bill Keenan, a fellow
English teacher at West Hill Secondary
School in Owen Sound, on the day I
was called to the Ontario bar, April 1978.

Testifying at the parliamentary
inquiry into the workings of the
Ontario Censor Board, June 1980.
Photo Credit: Steve Patriquen.

Censor Board members: (left to right) Douglas Walker, Wendi Enright, Joseph
Cunningham. *Photo Credit:* Steve Patriquen.

My sisters Judy (left) and Nora (middle) sitting with me on Judy's screened-in veranda in North Bay, Ontario, the summer of 1985.

Before I began to write up parties, I held a few of my own. This picture appeared in a Zena Cherry column on January 31, 1984 about a fundraiser I had held. *Photo Credit:* Peter Caton, Gerald Campbell Studios.

Edgar and me on our wedding day, with his two sons, Jim (left) and Chris. May, 1979.

The Robinson clan at our Rosedale house, Thanksgiving 1981.

With Edgar (right) and members of his family at Charleston Lake, Ontario, summer 1986.

Sitting on our award-winning 1941 Chris-Craft named *After Taxes* at the Muskoka Boat Show, Port Carling, Ontario, July 1987.

Stephanie's school picture, age 16.
Grenville Christian College, 1982.

Robin's school picture, age 16.
Grenville Christian College, 1993.

Stephanie on location in Florida with her
"Global Kidsbeat" cohost, Mark Foerster, 1993.

So three cheers for Father Fother
And his blither
And his blather
And his bluster
And his blister—
Making bracing verbal stew.

(Sometimes nasty, but it's tasty,
Racy, rich and super-pacey;
Just a spoonful of this brew
Is extra special good for you.)

Another house party I enjoyed writing up took place several blocks south from the Fotheringham affair in the heart of Rosedale. World-famous violinist Yehudi Menuhin visited Toronto, coincidentally just one week after I had finished reading his autobiography, which I couldn't put down. Going to meet celebrities is not my favourite pastime—much to my daughter's disgust, I had turned down a request from Gino Empry to interview Hollywood heart throb Richard Gere the week before because I didn't want to miss my Friday afternoon train to Brockville. But Yehudi Menuhin, although he is world-famous, is much more than a celebrity; he is a multifaceted human being with many talents, not the least of them an elegant writing style. I knew that from reading his book. So when philanthropist Joan Chalmers asked my husband and me to a party in his honour, I accepted with alacrity. There were two other reasons I wanted to be there: to meet another celebrated guest, actor Peter Ustinov, and to gawk at the interior of Ms. Chalmers's recently renovated $2 million condominium.

Award, Dinner Mark Visit by Menuhin

November 4, 1990

Several years ago, upon hearing that I had just met author John Irving, the inimitable Liz Tory exclaimed in her usual understated way: "I would have grovelled at his feet." I haven't felt like grovelling since—until last Monday night when I had the opportunity to meet Sir Yehudi Menuhin, the world-famous violinist who made his debut with the San Francisco Orchestra at the age of seven, and who, though he never received any formal schooling, has received 24 doctorates from universities around the world. (The story of his life is portrayed in his eloquent autobiography, *Unfinished Journey*.)

Since he was held in high regard by another great twentieth-century musician, Canadian pianist Glenn Gould, it was entirely appropriate that Sir Yehudi come to Canada to receive the 1990 Glenn Gould prize.

When Mr. Gould died, one of his closest friends, John Roberts, then head of music at the CBC, arranged a memorial service for him. It was held in October 1982 at St. Paul's Anglican Church, Bloor Street, to encompass the throng of 3,000 who attended from all over the world to pay their respects to arguably Canada's greatest twentieth-century musician. Maureen Forrester and the Elmer Iseler Singers sang, the Orford String Quartet played, and the service ended with Mr. Gould's recording of Bach's *Goldberg Variations*. Said Mr. Roberts: "I thought he should have the last word."

In the intervening years the Glenn Gould Foundation has been set up in Mr. Gould's memory. Mr. Roberts, who has since become the dean of the Faculty of Fine Arts at the University of Calgary, first approached lawyer John Lawson, chairman of Roy Thomson Hall, to prepare the legal groundwork. Others who were involved from the outset included television producer John McGreevy, former Toronto Symphony Orchestra general manager Walter Homburger, and arts patron Arthur Gelber. When the group needed a cornerstone fund to get off the ground, philanthropist Floyd Chalmers came to the rescue with a start-up donation of $150,000. At the same time, the foundation asked Mr. Chalmers's daughter Joan to become a director. Today the board includes impresario Nicholas Goldschmidt, dancer Veronica Tennant and executive director John Miller.

Every three years the foundation gives out a prestigious prize to someone who has made a distinguished contribution to music and communications. On Tuesday evening of this week, Sir Yehudi was presented with the $50,000 cheque and a work of art by Fay Rooke of Burlington, Ontario at a dinner hosted by Sunlife of Canada chairman John McNeil and his wife, Esther. Dinner guests included Governor General Ray Hnatyshyn and his wife, Gerda; 1987 prize laureate Murray Schafer and his wife, Jean; Canada Council chairman Allan Gotlieb and his wife, Sondra; and Mr. Gould's parents, Bert and Vera. Miss Forrester was the master of ceremonies.

The previous evening, Joan Chalmers hosted a small formal dinner to welcome Sir Yehudi to Canada. Ms. Chalmers's Rosedale condominium, which she purchased from Ada Slaight for $2.5 million about six months ago, is still undergoing renovations, but it will soon be converted into a showcase for the Canadian crafts of which she has been such a valued supporter. At the small, select dinner Monday night, the guests stood around the large empty rooms for some time awaiting the arrival of another special guest, Sir Peter Ustinov, who arrived with his exotic-looking daughter, Pavla, on his arm. After he and Lady Menuhin, a wonderful mimic herself, bantered back and forth beside the grand piano, Sir Peter toasted Sir Yehudi as only Sir Peter can do—in Japanese with repeated obsequious bows, in staccatolike effusive German and as a formal and stuffy Brit. . . . .

Yehudi Menuhin and Sir Peter Ustinov notwithstanding, homegrown celebrities were my favourites. I couldn't resist a chance to see and cover Canada's foremost journalists being honoured one November evening.

Giants or Gerbils? Only Journalists Know

November 13, 1990
If you thought that we Canadians didn't have any heroes, then you weren't among those attending last Saturday night's love-in titled Gathering of the Giants at Toronto's Metro Convention Centre.

Jeffrey Simpson, Robert MacNeil, Peter Mansbridge, Barbara Amiel, Allan Fotheringham, Richard Gwyn, Barbara

Frum, Peter Gzowski, Lloyd Robertson, Peter Jennings, Morley Safer et al. strutted their stuff before an august crowd of several hundred who lapped up the proceedings with glee (and paid a cool $500 a couple for the privilege of doing so).

Never mind that hyperbolic metaphors and inane questions ran rampant, or that the tempo of the event was definitely not full speed ahead (I finally had to run downstairs to Queen's University's John Orr dinner to get a bite to eat). These giants (and Amazons), Canadian-born and bred, put up with it all without a fuss. Besides which, the money raised was going for a good cause, the University of Western Ontario's School of Journalism.

Once seated in the John Bassett Theatre, gala guests were confronted with a large video screen upon which flashed scenes of huskies pulling a sleigh, vast expanses of wheat fields on the Prairies and the CN Tower looming over the horizon, to the accompaniment of a jazzed-up, rather maudlin rendition of "O Canada." (We don't need to rely on our American neighbours to stereotype ourselves; we can do it very well ourselves, thank you very much.)

Individually, the participants ascended the stage and, after more videos, were peppered with questions from fellow Canadian journalists and students of journalism whose curriculum obviously doesn't include such niceties as etiquette. Since when did "Hi, there" become an adequate substitute for "Hello" or "Good evening, Mr. So-and-So"?

Host Peter Desbarats, dean of the journalism school and mastermind behind the fund-raiser, took the podium and provoked some of the best responses of the evening from an eloquent Mrs. Frum and Mr. Gwyn, the latter playing down the value of a formal education in becoming a journalist (maybe he was fed up with the "Hi, theres," too).

The svelte and short-skirted Ms. Amiel lived up to expectations, hopping on her bandwagon of dismantling orthodox feminism—to a few chauvinist male huzzahs in the crowd. NBC broadcaster Henry Champ asserted that television journalism is not more superficial than print. Mr. Fotheringham deftly fielded the question of whether a good journalist's status depends on the number of libel suits against him. (Yes, if he wins them.)

Former *New York Times* executive Sydney Gruson, who was interviewed by the *Globe's* Stephen Brunt, revealed that his first job was as a message boy at the Royal York Hotel for $9 a week.

Mr. Gzowski was given the daunting task of defining Canadians in four minutes flat. Mr. Jennings was asked if a celebrity journalist felt like a gerbil in a cage. Mr. MacNeil, creator of the "MacNeil/Lehrer Newshour," spoke up for slower, more thoughtful and quieter news. Once the initial laughter died down at younger, long-haired versions of Messrs. Mansbridge and Robertson, those gentlemen fielded their questions with finesse.

Globe columnist Mr. Simpson made some choice remarks about his favourite subject, patronage, while veteran newscaster Mr. Safer managed to prick a few balloons with his humorous remarks on print journalists in particular and Canadians in general.

Two hours later, the journalists were led across the stage, if not exactly like gerbils in a cage, then maybe like lambs to the slaughter. They lined up facing the audience and were presented with an autographed picture of themselves and a Parker pen, then slowly led offstage to join the gala guests for a reception and dinner.

The predinner finale was a video titled *A Sign of Our Times*, an endless procession of clips of Farrah Fawcett, Che Guevara, Jimmy and Tammy Bakker, Chuck and Di and Elvis, interspersed with clips of the foregoing journalists, as a raucous rap song practically blew the audience out of the theatre.

It was close to 9:00 p.m., and drinks, dinner and, believe it or not, another video (of the journalists reading a prewritten script playing themselves, which turned out to be quite funny) awaited the guests.

If they weren't convinced that broadcast journalism was the sign of the times before the evening began, for better or for worse they were assured of it now. Peter Mansbridge and Peter Gzowski as our own homegrown Canadian heroes? We could do worse.

Cross-Canada Events

One of Roy Megarry's lasting legacies at *The Globe and Mail* is that he turned it into a truly national newspaper. I was expected to cover events from St. John's, Newfoundland, to Victoria, B.C., and I did as often as I could. Canadians get tired of hearing about Toronto all the time, so I was always pleased when I got phone calls and mail from the rest of the country asking for some coverage.

Unfortunately, I could rarely be there in person, mostly due to budget and time constraints, but I had some good spies who proved to be excellent eyes and ears.

Camels Hard to Cast for *Aida* in Montreal

January 26, 1988

At this very moment in the city of Montreal, casting calls are going out for camels. And, believe it or not, camels are hard to find. These efforts are the result of that city's staging of one of the most elaborate operas ever performed, Teatro Petruzzelli's $7-million production of Verdi's *Aida.*

The world premiere of this lavish production took place in Egypt, the opera's actual setting, at the foot of the pyramids of Giza near Cairo. Not only is Montreal the North American premiere, but it is also the only other staging of the production. . . .

Edmonton Can Party as Richly as Toronto

December 15, 1990

The city of Edmonton may not rejoice in Christmas parties and balls to the extent Toronto does, but it's certainly no slouch. "We're not a hinterland exactly," said Joan Shimizu, wife of Edmonton plastic surgeon Dr. Henry Shimizu, a bit taken aback at being questioned about the party-going habits of her fellow citizens. "I've been to galas across Canada and to closing parties at conventions all over the world, and we rank with the best. Moreover, since Edmonton is oil-based, it is not as affected by the recession as other parts of the country."

Most of this fall's large galas in Edmonton have sold out. A November black-tie auction/dinner-dance called Effort raised $150,000, which was dispensed to various charities in the city. The dinner of the Minerva Foundation, set up by Edmonton businessman Gary Campbell in memory of his wife and two children who were killed in a car accident, was very well attended, although the ticket prices were a steep $365, $1 for every day of the year. Two other popular events were the opera masked ball at $125 a ticket and the annual tree auction titled Festival of Trees, which raises money for the University Hospital Foundation.

And recently, the sixth annual Holly Ball, which is being chaired by Mrs. Shimizu for the third year in a row and which takes place tomorrow, was a table and a half away from being sold out. It is a family affair at which, in many cases, three generations come together, so ticket prices are kept relatively low at $100 each and the committee concentrates on bringing in abundant sponsorships. Last year the ball proceeds, which were about $30,000, supported one-quarter of the Edmonton Art Gallery's exhibitions.

Ball patrons are Tri-Jay Investments president John Schlosser and his wife, Patricia. Those who have bought tickets include former Alberta premier Peter Lougheed and his wife, Jeanne; philanthropist Francis Winspear and his wife, Harriet; kidney transplant surgeon Dr. William Lakey and his wife, Shirley; architect Craig Henderson and his wife, Isabel; Alberta's chief human-rights commissioner Gil Fraser and his wife, Gladys Odegaard; and Citadel theatre founder Joe Schoecter and his wife, Kayla. . . .

Sports an Important Part of Vancouver Social Scene

March 11, 1989

American fashion designer Carolyne Roehm came to Toronto last week to show off her 1989 spring collection and to attend a luncheon in her honour held by Hazelton Lanes boutique owner Sharon Batten. At that very moment I was winging my way across Canada, utterly dejected at being deprived of the opportunity to attend the grand event.

There were compensations, nonetheless. I was $600 wealthier—the price of a ticket to the luncheon. And the feature film aboard the plane, *A Fish Called Wanda*, was even better the second time around. The same could be said for my repeat visit to Vancouver, recently described by *Globe and Mail* editor-in-chief William Thorsell as the Marilyn Monroe of Canadian cities—lovely and lazy and famous and marginal.

There may have been snow on the primroses in the gardens outside the Vancouver Lawn and Tennis Club, but inside the fire was welcoming and the company vivacious as Cathy Scott, Sally Lambert, Jill Purdy and Lorraine Welsford chattered about in-fill sites in Shaughnessy, summer homes on Bowen Island and British Columbia's zany politics. Not much different from a lunch held by society matrons at, say, Toronto's Granite Club, except for the influx of young mothers, tennis rackets and children in short pants in tow, as we prepared to leave.

This is a sports lovers' paradise, and Vancouver people care much more about scheduling their next tennis game or sailing trip than about the next business deal.

Vancouver's downtown oasis for a visitor going first class is the Wedgewood Hotel. Resembling a private English club, it is the creation of Eleni Skalbania, whose ex-spouse, entrepreneur Nelson Skalbania, is often spotted having dinner there. The elegant hotel is often reserved for private gatherings, such as last month's wedding of movie producer Peter Bogdanovich to the younger sister of the late *Playboy* centrefold Dorothy Stratton.

Across the street are the Vancouver law courts, a spectacular structure taking up two city blocks, designed by hometown boy, architect Arthur Erickson.

Former Torontonian Carole Taylor, who left her hometown and high school sweetheart to marry former Vancouver mayor Art Phillips, and who last November topped the city polls for Vancouver alderman, has a high profile here.

Not so singer Juliette, who retired from show business to care for her husband of 40 years, a victim of Alzheimer's disease. She lives in relative obscurity on the ninth floor of a downtown Vancouver apartment building, emerging last December for a one-night stand at The Roof Nightclub where she was discovered in the 1940s singing pop tunes to the Dal Richards Orchestra.

Other Vancouverites I have met in past travels include lawyer Jack Giles and his wife Virginia, who held a reception in Florida for the American Trial Lawyers Association a few years ago, and former British Columbia attorney general Brian Smith.

The city's lively social column by Valerie Gibson, the former wife of Liberal leader Gordon Gibson, appears weekly in *Vancouver* magazine. The March issue describes ski parties at Whistler, a prime winter occupation for Vancouver people. Former prime minister Pierre Trudeau and his bride Margaret Sinclair spent a short honeymoon here in 1972. Members of the Vancouver establishment who own chalets at Whistler include the Ross Southams; Peter Brown, chairman of Canarim Investment Corporation; and lawyer Thomas Ladner and his wife Janet.

Vancouver real estate prices, as elsewhere, make front-page news, soaring ever higher, fueled by speculative Pacific Rim purchasers. There are many prime residential areas in Vancouver, including the massive residences along South West Marine Drive, and those in West Vancouver and the Point Grey area.

But the favourite area of old monied families is still Shaughnessy, about ten minutes from downtown. The massive old mansions behind large hedges and stone walls on The Crescent, with their spectacular view of the Selkirk Mountains looming over the city, equal any I've seen in cities across Canada.

Although Newfoundland is not known for its glitzy galas (and is likely proud of the fact), on January 16, 1990, I did write up a birthday party in that province held for businessman Geoffrey Peters, which his wife called me about. She got my phone number from Ed Roberts, former leader of the Opposition in Newfoundland.

On a quiet residential street in St. John's, a group of friends gathered on a foggy evening last week to celebrate the fiftieth birthday of Geoffrey Peters. Former commodore of the Royal Newfoundland Yacht Club (at the same time that premier Clyde Wells was learning the political ropes as chairman of its constitution committee), he is the fourth generation of his family to run Peters & Sons, a well-known dry-goods firm in Newfoundland.

Mr. Peters had been dreading the event for weeks, warning all who would listen that he would not be party to any festivities. Ignoring his dire threats and armed with funny presents and bottles of wine, his friends rang the doorbell. A forewarned Deanne Peters ushered them in to greet their surprised host.

Among those gathered were lawyer Ed Roberts, former leader of the Opposition in Newfoundland, and his wife, Eve, chairman of the Newfoundland Human Rights Commission.

Also present were internist Graham Young and his wife Eleanor; John O'Day, past president of the Board of Trade and a recent appointment to the Newfoundland Economic Council, and his wife, Janet; Dr. Linda Inkpen, president of the Cabot Institute, a post-secondary technical institution, and her husband, Nizar Ladha, a forensic psychiatrist.

As well, the guests included Curtis Legrow, who owns the largest travel agency in Newfoundland, and his wife, Kathy, a senior social worker for the Newfoundland Family Court; and Michael and Annette Staveley—he is dean of arts at Memorial University and she an associate professor. Mrs. Staveley recited a satirical sonnet she had penned, under the pseudonym of Wilhelmina Shakespeare, bidding Mr. Peters godspeed on his forthcoming sailing trip in Scotland.

One of the best-written and funniest letters I received in my five years as society columnist came from a reader in Newfoundland:

A Rift in Pouch Cove

March 12, 1988

Anthony P. Scoggins (Letter to the Editor, February 26) asks, "Who cares a royal hoot who attended that or any ball?" in reference to Rosemary Sexton's social column.

Well, I must say that out here in Pouch Cove (pronounced "Pooch" for all you mainlanders), we all care.

As a matter of fact, I'm sure Rosemary's column has caused a major rift in the Cove. When I went to T. G. Hudson's (general merchants) to pick up some partridge-berry jam, I asked, "Did any of you see in Rosemary Sexton's column that Conrad Black attended a ball in Rosedale?" And all I got were blank stares, and people stopped talking in mid-sentence and just stared at me.

I know that they're mad. It's something that I shouldn't have asked. It hurts that they weren't invited and yet Conrad Black was. So now we just don't talk about Rosemary's column.

And the local Captain Quick store won't even carry *The Globe and Mail*, and I know it's just because it is upset about Rosemary's column.

So now I have to start up the old Lada and drive to St. John's to pick up Rosemary's column—and my UIC cheque, of course.

David Laird
Pouch Cove, Newfoundland

Not surprisingly, the Maritimes' special events have a character all their own. The wedding of the son of actor George C. Scott and Colleen Dewhurst is a case in point.

Bay Fortune Wedding Community Affair

August 31, 1991

On a hot summer's day recently, in the picturesque province of Prince Edward Island, Irene Strang, the daughter of Hazel Strang of Cape Traverse, exchanged nuptial vows with

Alexander Scott, elder son of two renowned actors, the late Colleen Dewhurst and George C. Scott.

The wedding took place at the Inn at Bay Fortune, formerly the summer residence of Miss Dewhurst and built in 1910 by Elmer Harris, the New York playwright who wrote *Johnny Belinda*. Based on a local character, the play was turned into a movie starring Ronald Reagan's first wife, Jane Wyman, a portrait of whom used to hang above the fireplace.

The wedding took place in the courtyard of the inn, where the Scott boys used to put on theatricals when they were young. Best man for his brother was Campbell Scott, currently starring in *Dying Young* with Julia Roberts, who came up from Sharon, Conneticut, with his wife, Anne. Maid of honour was Lisa Cheverie, like the bride, a native of P.E.I.

Thirty-six close friends and family members attended the wedding, including Ken Marsolais, a Broadway producer and longtime friend of Miss Dewhurst; Paul Verdier, artistic director of Stages, a Hollywood theatre centre; and David Wilmer, owner of the Inn at Bay Fortune.

About 80 guests gathered for the reception, which featured buffet-style shellfish hors d'oeuvres, oysters on the half shell, lobster and brie in phyllo pastry, crabmeat-stuffed mushroom caps, vegetables on skewers, and sole served three ways. The occasion was a community affair. Neighbours lent their barbecues, extra chairs and tables came from the local community hall, the bride's mother picked local strawberries, and her grandmother baked homemade delicacies. Then there was dancing into the night.

The bride and groom spent the weekend at a cottage before heading off to various bed-and-breakfast places on the island.

Fortune became an actors' colony in the late nineteenth century. To reach it from New York, vacationers would take a train to Boston, a ship to Charlottetown, then a train to the fishing village of Souris, and finally a horse and buggy ride to Fortune.

Arden Cottage, now owned by Dr. Robert Welch of Toronto and his wife Penny, was built in the 1890s by New

York actors Charles Kent and Betty Barry. It has been rented from its present owners by former television journalist Laurier Lapierre and his family for several summers.

Across the Fortune River from Arden Cottage lived another well-known actor, Henry Warrick and his wife, Elsa, a Gibson girl. Actress Leslie Carter and literary figure David Belascoe, summertime visitors to the area in the early 1900s, put up a sundial on a point of land in memory of Charles Flockton, their stage manager.

The Inn at Bay Fortune has had a number of bookings for bicycle tours, a popular summer sport on the island. Travel entrepreneur Sam Blyth and Gordon McQuenn, the owner of a cycle shop in Charlottetown, are working on a plan called Rails to Trails, a scheme to use the old railway rights-of-way that span the island as a linear park for bicycles, cross-country skiing, hiking, etc.

The opening event, an inaugural bicycle trip along the route, will take place October 11 to 14.

Shaw's Hotel, a one-time hangout for the judiciary, and Dalvey-by-the-Sea are both long-established resorts on the North Shore near famous Cavendish Beach and Anne of Green Gables' house.

Since *Anne* has just completed a popular tour of Japan, Japanese tourists abound on the island and a restaurant in Charlottetown (the Selkirk Restaurant in the local Prince Edward Hotel) offers Japanese food on request.

I tried to write about native Canadians every once in a while, though galas were not, obviously, their preferred form of entertainment. However, a reception held to launch a book on Billy Diamond written by author Roy MacGregor gave me a chance.

Billy Diamond Present at Launch of Biography

May 2, 1989
There was nothing unusual about the crowd milling around the Art Gallery of Ontario's Walker Court for a cocktail party last week, but the guest of honour was remarkable. Short and

stocky, with thick glasses and a lock of unruly black hair falling across his forehead, Billy Diamond is immediately recognizable. He has, after all, met the Pope and appeared on the cover of *Maclean's* magazine. And now Mr. Diamond is the subject of a biography called *Chief*, by Ottawa journalist Roy MacGregor. The occasion was the launching of the book.

The sixth of nine children born to a Cree Indian trapper in Northern Quebec, young Billy was sent by plane to residential schools to learn the ways of the white man. He returned to his home village of Waskaganish (formerly Prince Rupert) only to be catapulted onto the public stage when Premier Robert Bourassa announced plans to build the largest hydroelectric plant in North America on Cree lands, a $6 billion project.

Mr. Diamond led the two-year battle against the government to save his band's traditional hunting, trapping and fishing lands. He eventually negotiated a settlement no one had thought possible: $137 million for 6,500 Crees, plus recognition of their rights to about 160,000 square kilometres of land.

Mr. Diamond went on to create a Cree-owned and operated airline with former Timmins bush pilot Stan Deluce. Initially, the Crees owned 40 percent of the enterprise, called Air Creebec. Six years later, in 1988, the Crees assumed full control. By then the airline was doing $8 million worth of business a year, much of it, ironically, ferrying workers in and out of the James Bay hydroelectric project they had so violently opposed.

Mr. Diamond's latest undertaking has been to form a joint venture with Yamaha Motor Company of Canada, the first North American joint venture in that company's history. The boat-building deal came about after Mr. Diamond approached the company to buy snowmobiles.

His success is not without cost. His marriage suffered from his long absences. His son Philip was diagnosed as suffering from a gastrointestinal disease contracted from the foul water supply in Waskaganish, and it was feared that he would never walk or talk. Mr. Diamond eventually developed a problem with alcohol.

Last week, those battles seemed won, as members of his family joined him on the podium in Walker Court. There were his mother, Hilda, and his sisters, Annie and Agnes. His brothers Albert, president of the Cree Board of Compensation, George and Stanley attended, as did his sons Sandy, Ian and Philip, now fully recovered, and his wife, Elizabeth.

Also present were Ike Saguchi, president of Yamaha; Roy and Bill McMurtry and their law associate Delia Opekokew, who is a Cree Indian; Donald Noble, vice-president, Northern Telecom Canada; Gary George, a lobbyist for the Crees in Northern Quebec; Narda Iulg, director of communications for the Canadian Council for Native Business; Raj Rawana, the national marketing director for Yamaha; Peter Cole, president of Central Capital Corporation, which financed Air Creebec when it recently bought the northern assets of Air Ontario; and Bill Deluce, one of Stan Deluce's seven sons, who is president of Air Ontario.

Among the speakers were Mr. MacGregor and Cynthia Good, editor-in-chief of Penguin Books Canada.

Ontario premier David Peterson dropped in, as did former Indian Affairs minister John Munro, who once fell asleep after a tough set of negotiations with Mr. Diamond, dropped a cigarette on the back of a dry tamarack goose decoy the Crees had given him, and set his office afire.

There are other memorable incidents described in the book, such as Hilda and Malcolm Diamond sneaking back to live in their shack with its outhouse and old wood stove because they hated the new house with modern appliances built for them; the old Cree who turned off his new television set every time he went outside to get firewood so he wouldn't miss any of the action; and the time Mr. Diamond, as the new chief of Prince Rupert, and his wife were invited to the local priest's house for dinner and ushered into a separate room and seated at TV tables while white missionaries and educators gathered in the dining room.

I received an appreciative letter from Roy MacLaren after the above column, which I framed and hung above my desk for inspiration. Years later, when I was in Ottawa on my book tour for *The Glitter Girls*, I called him up and he told me that he and I had both been at Laurentian University together, a fact I had not realized until then.

Mishaps and Misadventures

One of the best ways to deal with seemingly insurmountable obstacles is to try to laugh at them. Writing humorous columns after such events occurred was often therapeutic for me.

Occasionally, I wrote about personal and family problems, but I had been hired by the *Globe* to write about parties and social events, not about families. Every once in a while, though, I snuck in a few of my personal anecdotes. I wrote the following column after a particularly frustrating week leading up to Christmas. It appeared in the *Globe* on December 21, 1990, the day after my forty-fourth birthday.

Christmas in Splitsville

Stepson #1: Uh, Rosemary, I'm not too happy about these two-family Christmases. When I was growing up, I never expected not to be able to spend the holidays with my own relatives. It's confusing to have to deal with all these strangers and people I don't really care about.

Daughter: Mum, you're not going to get angry, are you, if I go to Dad's for Christmas dinner? He doesn't really get to see enough of his own kids, and you have your husband and his family to keep you company.

Son: Who's going to be with us for opening Christmas presents on Christmas morning? Just me, you, my stepfather, sister and stepsister, I hope. It's our Christmas, Mum. I don't want to share it with a whole lot of people we don't know.

Sister: Why don't you all drop over on Christmas Eve? We're going to have Mother here, and my husband's children from his first marriage, and your ex-husband's brother and sister-in-law and their children. Your children should really see their cousins more often, you know. Why don't you bring along your stepchildren—what are their names again? Sorry we can't make your Christmas party. We've booked a trip to Barbados then—not on purpose, of course.

Brother: We'd love to come to Toronto for your Christmas party. Is it OK if we bring the five boys? We have them all for Christmas this year. And only three are still in diapers. By the way, can we stay overnight? It would be really inconvenient to drive back home that evening and we want to get the most out of our visit, since your invitations are few and far between.

Stepson #2: Rosemary, sorry, we have to cancel for Christmas Day. My girlfriend's father is alone since the divorce, so we're joining him. You know how it is.

Sister-in-law: Is it all right if I spend Christmas Day with you and bring Aunt —— along? The kids will be at their father's this year.

Stepdaughter: I'm really sorry, but I have to cancel for Christmas Eve. My mother wants me up in Muskoka with her. Will you and Dad look after the cat while I'm gone?

Ex-husband: I'll drop in and pick up the kids on Christmas Day, just in case you change your mind about letting them come. Maybe your husband and I can have an eggnog and chat, ho ho ho.

Ex-wife: Rosemary, do you have any idea what my kids are doing for Christmas? They haven't gotten back to me, so I've arranged to spend the day with my current husband and his children. You *were* planning to have them, weren't you?

Old school friend: Yes, we'd be happy to drop in, but only if you promise not to surround us with all those glitzy jet-setters you cultivate these days. We have nothing in common with people like that, and, quite frankly, Rosemary, we're surprised that you do.

Socialite: Thank you for the invitation, dahling. Who else did you say would be there? How quaint. We'd love to be introduced to all your little school friends, but I'm afraid we have a previous commitment that we just can't bow out of.

Cousin #1: Yes, I'd love to drop into your Christmas party. And I'll bring J—— (wife #3) even though she threatened never to come again when you called her M——. That was my second wife's name. Can't you keep them straight, for heaven's sake?

Cousin #2: Yes, thank you, I'd like to drop over. But it was lonely last year without Bruce. Do you mind if I bring him along? It's about time we came out of the closet, and your party is about as good a time as any.

Aunt —— (mother of cousin #2): I'll be flying into Toronto just in time for your party. Alone, of course, since Uncle —— refuses to accompany me. He refuses to enter your house ever since your divorce. Some people still have standards, you know.

The following piece was written after a trip to France that turned out to be fraught with difficulties. It aroused quite a bit of reader comment. Accompanied with a cartoon of me angry and wet beside the broken shower, it didn't hurt that the *Globe* ran it on the front page of its travel section.

Her Gown Was Drowned

Down and Out in Paris

The City of Lights Went Dim for Visiting Society Columnist
December 14, 1991
As two important Canadians standing in the lobby of a Paris hotel discussed an embassy function, the red-faced society columnist for Canada's national newspaper, who was sitting nearby and also staying at the hotel, sank down in her seat. She had not attended any embassy function, nor even been able to see the Paris Ballet as planned, because of an unfortunate mishap.

It was an inauspicious beginning to a long-awaited holiday to France. Little did she know that things were going to get worse. But I'll begin at the beginning.

Tuesday

The first of three days holed up in a hotel room the size of a large cupboard while husband was at business meetings from morning to night. At 7:00 a.m., husband takes shower, but afterward it won't turn off. Trying to fix it, husband soaks and ruins party dress hanging in bathroom brought to wear to the ballet while husband attended embassy dinner. Call and cancel. Spend evening sprawled on bed in large cupboard watching *Bewitched* re-runs dubbed in French. Order dinner from room service plus two Manhattans specifying they be made with Canadian rye. Drinks arrive full of bourbon. Choke them down to accompaniment of leaky shower. Throw pillow at husband when he arrives after having hobnobbed with the Mulroneys et al. until midnight.

Wednesday

Go shopping in the cold and rain to escape hotel room. Walk for hours through the streets of Paris attempting to soak in atmosphere of City of Lovers. This attempt hampered by several things—I'm all alone, invariably ignored or berated by surly waiters, and have trouble crossing the street. At busy intersections, no one obeys the traffic lights but me. I nearly collide with either pedestrians or cars or both.

Thursday

Luggage boy arrives at 7:00 a.m. to check shower. Thinks he has it fixed and turns nozzle to look at it. Shower soaks him. At seven-thirty, room service waiter arrives armed with large wrench and hammer. Husband points to cupboard behind bathroom where shower pipes seem to be located, but waiter proceeds to the other side of the bathroom. With aforesaid wrench, manages to turn off water pipes leading to the toilet and sink. Shower continues to pour. At eight-thirty, concierge arrives. Husband again points out cupboard containing water pipes leading to shower. Concierge shakes head. In disgust, husband opens up cupboard, removes shelves, locates taps and turns off shower. Water flow ceases immediately. Concierge throws hands in the air and leaves.

At noon, gratefully check out of hotel and leave Paris to visit beautiful châteaux in the Loire Valley. Can't find Loire River. Discover it is muddy stream we've been driving along for several hours. Check into inn to be greeted by noxious fumes wafting into the room at regular intervals throughout the evening. Somewhat paranoid, proceed to check plumbing here. Discover odours are coming in window from the polluted Loire.

Saturday

Arrive at old converted monastery at 10:00 p.m. after meandering for several hours around unmarked country roads in dark. Fall into bed and try to sleep despite thin walls and loud-mouthed couple next door who review over the phone in minute detail their son's day with his baby-sitter.

Monday

Due to jet lag, long days in Paris and getting lost, husband gets flu. Ask to be transferred to a larger room in the old château—the night before we were the only guests to eat in a cavernous dining room seating 500. "*C'est impossible,*" says the desk clerk. "We are completely full." Try again with a new desk clerk who comes on duty at 5:00 p.m. "You have asked too late," she says. Spend night in château's smallest room as the other 29 rooms go unoccupied. Order up to room one dinner for me and con-sommé for sick husband. Charge for sumptuous meal when we check out: $75.

Tuesday

Decide to leave France four days earlier than planned. Drive to Tours train station from Loire Valley. Dropped off by husband to change day of prebooked and prepaid first-class train ticket while he returns rental car. Ticket agent shakes head. "*Payez-moi 240 francs en plus.*" Desperate to board train, I'm ready to pay anything, but wallet is in suitcase with husband. Turn away from wicket in tears. Just then, the agent, seeing me upset, changes the tickets to coach and calls "*Attendez,*" stamps ticket and hands me some change. "*Merci,*" I cry gratefully as I run from station, tightly clutching stamped ticket and un-expected windfall of cash.

Wednesday

After speedy train ride on the TGV, which takes one hour to go 200 kilometres (VIA Rail, take note), spend two hours in a Paris taxi driving 25 kilometres from the train station to air-port. Driver chain-smokes and turns car radio on full blast to rock music station. Proceeds to get lost at the airport looking for hotel despite clearly marked signs showing way. Finally at our destination, we pile out of cab, pay fare and go to bed. Nothing left to do but catch noon flight the next day—we thought.

Thursday

Wake up to fog. Call at ten-thirty to check on noon flight. Informed plane is delayed one hour and will not take off until 1:00 p.m. Ask if 1:00 p.m. departure a certainty. Reply is yes. Decide not to jump on Canadian Airlines plane that leaves, as scheduled, at 11:45. Arrive at airport at twelve-thirty to be informed Air Canada plane is delayed until five o'clock. Nearby counter advertised Air Liberté leaving for Montreal at 1:45. Check with ticket people; plane not full. Air Canada agrees to endorse tickets for Air Liberté. Air Liberté refuses to take us, since there is no meal preordered for us on the plane. "*Je suis désolée, je suis très désolée,*" repeats young woman dressed all in green to whom, it appears, all decisions at the charter air-line have been relegated. "No dinner, no passenger." Air Liberté leaves on time without us.

Hang around airport until 7:00 p.m. when flight finally begins to board passengers. Husband asks at gate for our boarding passes. "Where were you when we handed out the passes at noon today?" asks haughty young ticket-taker. Weary and fed up, normally complacent husband blows top. "What business is it of yours where I was at noon today? Where was your goddamned plane at twelve noon today?" he yells, catching the attention of flight director standing nearby. Flight director does double take. Points at bald★ husband and starts laughing. "I know who you are," he says. "You're that man in the Goodyear Tire commercial who points to charts that read 'Goodyear sells tuneups, not just tires.'"

"That's right," responds my quick-thinking husband. "I knew it," flight director says, chortling gleefully. Turning to young woman, he barks out a command: "This is a very important man. I've seen him on television. Issue him his boarding pass immediately."

We sink into seats on the plane, giddy with relief. Observe flight director proceeding down aisle toward us. We look at each other in horror. What next? Flight director looms over us, grinning broadly: "I really like your charts," he enthuses to husband. "Thank you," husband weakly responds, barely keeping a straight face. As flight director moves down aisle out of sight, we double over in our seats, tears streaming down our cheeks. Our loud snorts of laughter can be heard all over the plane. The trip from hell is finally over.

This article, much to my surprise, brought a storm of abuse down on my head. But there were just as many readers who thought it was funny. Here are a few of the varied responses:

★True to form, the *Globe* copy editors excised the word *bald*, which I'd used to describe my husband. I really couldn't believe it. First of all, my husband *is* bald, and if I, his wife, am not allowed to say so, then who is? Secondly, his baldness was a very salient fact in my story. The man in the Goodyear Tire ads, as many of my readers would know, was also bald, and that is the reason why the flight director had mistaken my husband for him. Ah, well, fortunately some of my readers appreciated the story, anyway.

December 15, 1991

I just finished reading your column "Down and Out in Paris," and I'm confused as to the message you were attempting to convey. Were you attempting to be funny? Or were you wanting the world to know what a sorry excuse you are as a female and a traveller? I would hope it was not the latter, but that is exactly what comes across loud and clear.

Why on earth would the "drowning" of your gown prevent you from attending the ballet? You had all day to have the damage repaired, or to find a new gown. And where on earth were you staying? I have never had the pleasure of visiting Paris on an expense account, but I have not had to settle for a hotel room the size of a cupboard or a leaky shower. If a hotel refuses to move you to another room, you find another hotel through the concierge. Management gets the message very quickly then. There are thousands of hotels in every arrondissement of this lovely city, and no visitor need accept less than what they were expecting.

Your description of Wednesday is particularly pathetic. How sad that you could not find a myriad of exciting things to see and do in such a rich venue. Being alone should not have been a deterrent at all. I travel on my own most of the time, and I have found the people in Paris charming for the most part—yes, even most of the waiters. You do not mention whether or not you are bilingual, or even attempted to communicate in French. I find an attempt, no matter how sad, to speak French makes the world of difference. I might get a smirk, but I get what I am wanting, too.

I would ask that you refrain from writing columns that reinforce the myths and stereotypes that portray women as helpless and dependent on men. You blew your trip to Paris, not the leaky shower, the cold and rain, the surly waiters, the traffic . . . you get the picture. If I had a husband take me to Paris on his expense account, none of the above would even slow me down from doing and seeing everything possible in the time available. I am saving for my next trip back to France in September, on my own, and nothing will stop me from enjoying the ambience and the people.

Your column on Paris and the Loire was irresponsible. Get a new travel agent and learn how to travel in a more independent manner.

Sharon A. McElroy

Defrocked Socialite

December 20, 1991
Re "Down and Out in Paris"
Gimme a break! A spoiled frock spoils Rosemary Sexton's evening out in Paris? Only for a spoiled society snoop. I guess it's a hazard of her job that being seen at the ballet was more important than seeing the ballet.

Nijole Kuzmickas
Vancouver, B.C.

Christmas, 1991
I so enjoyed your article "Down and Out in Paris"! It was marvellous and, of course, absolutely true—[as are] the best stories.

Haven't we all had a similar experience in an international city? One thing that came through constantly, along with your humour, was the feeling of helplessness and a little loneliness. Thank you for making my day.

(Mrs. L. J.) Mary Lou Batchelor
Oakville, Ontario
P.S. I have never written to anyone in the media before.

December 1991
I just wanted to comment on your article this week about Paris.

We had our first and I think last visit to this city in June 1988.

From the time we arrived from England, to the "no name/ no sign" train station, with no one to consult for directions, no signs in English telling us how to get out of the station, etc., our time in Paris was somewhat taxing. It turned out to be a battle of wits between them and us.

Our accommodation was decent with breakfast included, but when we were sent to our room, we had to stumble off the elevator and hold the walls to work our way down the hall to find it. The lights were out! However, small and compact as it was, our room had a lovely view of a game-playing area in the backyard with a beautiful little park around it.

We found the Parisians unhelpful and unfriendly if one did not speak French, and consequently, when we saw the only McDonald's restaurant, we fell into it with glee. I don't buy stuff from them in Canada, but I'll tell you and George Cohon, too, I was absolutely delighted to take advantage of their clean and free bathroom. I'm sure there have been reams of words written about Paris bathrooms and I won't say too much here except they are generally unappetizing in every way. Of course, we didn't frequent the same places you did.

The sewers and water running on the streets, cars parked at all angles, surly shopkeepers and restaurateurs, as well as the magnificent Louvre and other buildings, will stay in our memory.

Jeanette Chippindale
Cambridge, Ontario

December 16, 1991
I just don't know when I have had a real good laugh such as I had while reading about your misadventures in La Belle France.

However, when travelling, things often go wrong, even in that Swiss-run New York we call Toronto.

Last March my wife and I were returning from Barbados to Montreal. We left Barbados about five hours late, then instead of landing in Montreal we landed in Toronto. About three jumbos landed at the same time—utter chaos.

Customs people could not efficiently handle us on such short notice, and weather conditions prevented landing in Montreal. Worst of all, there are no toilet facilities in the customs area and no way to exit without permission. We finally arrived in Montreal 24 hours late.

Two weeks ago my wife and I decided to spend two days in Toronto, catch a play, visit the ROM and just generally enjoy a change of scene.

We booked into a hotel in the afternoon. That evening I phoned the theatre to confirm availability of tickets and ask about the distance from hotel to theatre. I was advised a ten-minute cab drive, so we decided we'd go to the theatre about two hours early, obtain tickets and then go for dinner.

We caught a cab at Front and York and told the driver, "Belmont Street, please." He replied, "Where is that?" I knew we were in trouble. Anyway, he drove around for an hour, stopping from time to time to ask directions. Apparently he was from Iran and knew about as much about Toronto as we know about Tehran. When we finally reached our destination we had to rush to find a restaurant to have dinner before the performance. Are we bitter about all that?

Well, no, not really. We are retired and travel a lot, rather than spend too much time at home vegetating, and when our trips are over, we often think back and have a laugh.

That is what life is all about.

Irv McGrail

J. I. McGrail

Greenfield Park, Quebec

Chapter Three

Dear Rosemary

I wouldn't have enjoyed my job to the extent I did without feedback from the readers, whether angry, sad, complimentary or downright disgusted. They kept me on my toes and they made me feel that there were actually people out there who cared about what I wrote.

By its very nature, writing is a solitary profession, its solitariness one of its attractions, at least to me. But you can't write a newspaper column in a void. It's important to get feedback to bring you in line when you're off base, to tone you down if you're too expansive, or even to cheer you up when you're down. I even got to enjoy the critical responses, which were often quite funny:

January 8, 1989
More or less by an oversight, I read your column of January 7, 1989, in the *Globe*—in which you described Mr. Mansbridge's wedding. According to this report, the bridal party, and you, certainly took no chances to offend our ever-so-vigilant feminist overseers—to put it mildly. In this respect, the following incomplete list of observations can be assembled:
1. The title of the bride was indicated as "Ms." (instead of "Miss" or "Mrs"). In my dictionary, *Ms.* is an extremely unpleasant word: it means multiple sclerosis.

2. The maid of honour was the bride's mother. By definition, the maid of honour is a not-ever-married female (check it in your dictionary); unless the bride was born out of wedlock, the title for the lady in question is matron of honour.

3. The bride's mother was mentioned only as Joan. Are all readers of the *Globe and Mail* on a first-name basis with this lady? The proper phrase would have been Mrs. So-and-So—provided of course she is now or ever have [*sic*] been the wife of a man.

4. The appellation "Miss" for the flower girl was omitted.

5. The bride's mother gave the bride away. Is this not the pleasant duty of the bride's closest *male* relative?

6. Mr. Mansbridge's parents are referred to as Stanley and Brenda Mansbridge and not as Mr. and Mrs. Stanley Mansbridge.

7. The title "Miss" or "Mrs." was omitted when Mr. Mansbridge's two daughters' names were mentioned.

8. The title "Miss" or "Mrs." was omitted when Mr. Mansbridge's niece's name was mentioned.

9. None of the named guests in your article were titled. Is it not curious that you accorded the title only to Mr. Mansbridge? Are people generally qualified to be mentioned with their respective titles? If yes, then everybody should be so mentioned; if no, nobody should be so treated, not even our venerated anchorman.

10. The new Mrs. Mansbridge will not be known as such.

11. The couple wrote their own vows. Was this a wedding where it is the priest who tells what *he* thinks should be told, or a ceremonial session with an attorney to sign a contract comprising those items—and only those—in which the contracting parties have agreed beforehand?

12. The new Mrs. Mansbridge will not only live in a separate bedroom or even house, but now—as you inform us—she will live in a different city from her husband! However—as you also reassuringly tell—the couple will "find some time to be together." (Is it possible that their honeymoon, which they reportedly spent together, falls into this category?)

I could continue the list, but I hope you will find the above sufficiently convincing.

The whole thing saddens me very much. Is this really the way our elite wants to appear or—*horribile dictu*—they actually *do* live that way?

In the meantime, don't be too upset by this criticism; it is strictly a one-time event. It will never happen again. For in the future I will be very careful not to read your column, not even by oversight!

Dr. Thomas Szirtes, P. Eng.
Willowdale, Ontario

February 3, 1990
I screamed with cynical laughter at Rosemary Sexton's column about the "venture capitalist" whose wife, upon transplantation to Toronto, had "worked hard forging new bonds" ("Art Gallery Assesses the Value of Heirlooms"—January 25).

I knew there was a shortcut to vast riches somewhere.

T.E.W. Gough
Toronto

Unhappy Lot
Re: your column entitled "Unhappy Lot."
Our advice:

Learn English;

Get husband or whomever of "means";

Change your mental disposition—your depressing looks spoil my breakfast.

Get laid, if you still can.

Your Admirer

July 14, 1988
I normally read with great interest your column on what the fine people of Toronto and area are doing. I recognize your support of the arts and at times your very clever recording of these events. However, I take exception to the paragraph and

particularly the last few lines,★ when Roy Megarry and his wife hosted a reception prior to the opening of *Don Giovanni*, a few months ago. As this was a *Globe and Mail* event, I thought the reporting should be more appropriate.

It is for this reason that I am writing to express my regret and disappointment; I don't think that you did the church, nor the paper, any credit by expressing yourself in those terms.

The Venerable Peter B. Moore
Archdeacon of Wellington
Rector, St. George's Church
Guelph, Ontario

★"A night out at the opera is a little like going to church. The music is lovely, and the accompanying ritual a reminder of days gone by. Best of all, added lawyer Julian Porter, who had dragged his reluctant wife, Anna, to his favourite performance, no one pays too much attention if you doze off a little."

August 8, 1988
I was pleased to read Rosemary Sexton's column (August 4) about the Amnesty International gala benefit held recently at the Museum of Temporary Art in Victoria Road, Ontario. As chief curator at the gallery, I am grateful to her for increasing public awareness of this independent, artist–run space.

However, due to misinformation supplied to Ms. Sexton, an injustice has been committed.

Ms. Sexton refers to the exhibition of paintings by artist Michael Poulton as "Victoria County landscapes." Doubtlessly the information was supplied by a rival of Mr. Poulton's from the Queen Street West area of Toronto, who would like to see him stigmatized as a "regional artist" before the public eye.

Of the actual paintings exhibited, half were of Bali, Indonesia. The rest were painted solely from that State of Mind known as the Active Imagination, where larger universal issues are played out.

When Mr. Poulton learned the news of this injustice, it

took three of our curatorial staff and the administration of strong inflammatories to subdue him. Even then he babbled incoherently for 45 minutes about defamation of character, litigation or at least a printed retraction.

We can only conclude that poor Rosemary was the innocent dupe of a secret band of urban art guerrillas, sworn to keeping the practice of serious art within the bounds of metropolitan areas.

We at the Museum of Temporary Art endeavour to live up to our motto: *Non redolemus pisce.* Artistic integrity must be maintained!

Michael Poulton
Chief Curator of Temporary Art
Victoria Road, Ontario

August 4, 1988

Rosemary Sexton confuses her Laidlaws. During the 1870s railway baron George Laidlaw built the Victoria, Credit Valley, Toronto, Grey and Bruce, and Toronto and Nipissing railways. Nancy Laidlaw Blair is a descendant of George Laidlaw, but not of lumber baron Robert Laidlaw. It was Robert, not George, who established the Laidlaw Foundation. George Laidlaw's homestead site, it is true, overlooks Balsam Lake. The original stone house itself, however, does not, having been destroyed by fire several decades ago. Then there are the trucking Laidlaws. But we need not go into that.

R. B. Fleming
Woodville, Ontario

April 15, 1988

In a recent column you had my position as Chairman of Counsel Corporation. I would like to draw your attention that I am in fact Chairman of the Frum Development Group. I thought you should have this fact for your records.

Dr. Murray B. Frum
Frum Development Group
Toronto

But, as well as brickbats, there were bouquets, some of them rather effusive:

April 5, 1988
I have just learned through a magazine article that you have been named as the *Globe's* new social chronicler and I am delighted.

I'm sure your intimate knowledge of Toronto's people, your skill with words and your dedication to purpose will satisfy all of the newspaper's readers.

John J. Arena
Winston's Restaurant Ltd., Toronto

December 19, 1988
I was so impressed with the depth, dissection, accuracy and tone of respect with which your review of the Winston's book was written, as published under your byline in 13 December's *Globe and Mail,* that not only did I purchase one copy to send out for framing, but I purchased a dozen more copies to send out to U.S. food and restaurant reviewers known to me, as an example of "how to".

And I thank you for your professionalism.

John J. Arena

January 10, 1989
While still retaining the pleasure your letter gave to me, I have placed it in our great Winston's history album for generations yet unborn to read as an example of proper English, exquisite taste and superb penmanship.

John J. Arena

Spring 1989
I would like to take this opportunity to commend you on your accomplishments. I am employed in the psychology department at a local hospital and I find your achievements to be a credit to your talent and endeavours to be personally proud of. What prompted you to become a newspaper writer? You display pride, determination, intelligence, stamina, dedication,

integrity, poise, grace, charm and beauty. You have my continued support, encouragement and interest in you and your endeavours. My best wishes.

James R. English
Edmonton, Alberta

December 3, 1989
I've just reread your "Social Columnist's Lot" article again for the umpteenth time for *sheer* enjoyment (at how someone refuses to let the turkeys get her down, in spite of the most *amazing* rudeness and lack of consideration you seem to experience!). It was *very* funny. *Thank* you for sharing some of the craziness that goes with your job! Hope some of the turkeys will now stop landing at your house from seven to eleven. . . . Best wishes, and thank you also for much pleasurable reading before this!

Cathy Schaffter
Toronto

O course, I was always happy to receive letters from prominent Canadians:

August 16, 1989
Your column of August 10 was a very pleasant surprise. Very few Canadians know anything about Charleston Lake. In fact, Eastern Ontario is unknown country to most Torontonians.

I grew up in Gananoque, and when I had accumulated a few dollars I bought some farm property at the western end of Charleston Lake. I moved west in 1960 and sold the property in 1964 to the Ontario government. It is now part of the Charleston Lake Provincial Park.

Occasionally we visited the village at the eastern end of the lake, but we always thought that end of the lake was rather crowded. Our end, with its thick forests and high cliffs, was virtually uninhabited. There was no road, so I kept a small boat at the outlet. In the spring and fall we would cruise all day to Donaldson Bay and adjacent areas and never see anybody.

The lake, of course, is full of shoals, since it is part of the pre-Cambrian Shield, but there are unofficial charts that show most of them. In eight years of boating on the lake I never had a problem, even though I travelled at night. Of course, in the late fall with low water, all the shoals appear and I make mental notes of them.

Thank you for such an evocative column.

Arthur Child
Calgary

August 21, 1989
WHAT A PARTY!

Thank you for your support and participation in the public birthday party that was given for me on the occasion of my seventy-fifth birthday, July 24, 1989.

This happy, memorable party will be an event that I will always cherish.

With best wishes to you for good health and happiness.

Ed Mirvish
Toronto

December 20, 1988

I've been away this past week, so I have only this morning caught up to the December 15 *Globe.* I'm thrilled at your sparkling, sensitive and helpful column about the toy luncheon. Everyone was thrilled to see you there—which contributed in a major way to the feeling everyone expressed that it was the best toy luncheon ever.

Merryiest Christmas, and our gratitude.

June for Jessie's
[June Callwood]
Toronto

May 22, 1991

My morning smile turned into a belly laugh when I read your column of today, March 21.

Bravo. keep Toronto on its toes.

Shelley Black
Editor
FLARE magazine

And then there were those readers who turned to me for help and advice on, it seemed, any topic under the sun:

May 23, 1988
I am a 17-year-old high school student. I live in a fairly remote area in central British Columbia. The closest village to my house is 20 kilometres away. The town, Burns Lake, has about 2,000 people. The closest city is Prince George, approximately 300 kilometres away. The nearest university is located in Vancouver, 1,000 kilometres from here.

Because of all this, I have a problem. I am an average boy who is trying to raise money to go to university. I have tried looking for a job in Burns Lake, but I have been unable to find one. It's just a small town, and there aren't many after-school or summer jobs available.

I'm in Grade 11, and will graduate in 1989. This gives me two summers to raise about $6,000 to finance my first year in university. I can't do that without an income, so I've got an idea that might help.

I want to ask if it is possible in your column to ask every reader to send me one cent to my home address.

It's even less than the stamp costs, and I think people wouldn't miss the extra penny. And enough of them would sure help me out.

Leif Ahrens
Francois Lake, B.C.

May 14, 1991
Some weeks ago I wrote asking if it would be reasonable to insert an ad — "Farmer, semiretired, abstainer, wishes to hear from Christian Lady interested in rural life in prosterous [*sic*] area." If you would consider an insertion, could you please drop me a line by mail?

George Hope

January 24, 1989
May I ask you for some suggestions regarding a wedding rehearsal dinner that I must give in Toronto on Friday, September 8.

The wedding itself will be in St. Stanislaw's Church in mid-afternoon on Saturday and will be followed by a reception and dinner in the Sutton Place Hotel for about 200 guests.

I would like the rehearsal dinner to be pleasant and not too formal. Although turning the dinner over to a hotel would be the easiest thing to do, such dinners seem to be held in impersonal conference rooms.

Unfortunately, I am not entirely sure of Toronto customs for an event of this kind, nor do I know the city well enough to identify a suitable place for this dinner. I anticipate fifteen guests and had in mind to spend about $750.

Any ideas you would have time to give me would be greatly appreciated.

Martha Lovering
Nepean, Ontario

Some letter writers penned humorous comments, perhaps unintentionally:

January 26, 1988
Congratulations on your column. We are having a big bash on Saturday, January 30th—a Toronto party! We expect about 60–80 people—great people too. We're even having a Toronto Trivia Contest. And a self-cook menu that includes every ethnic delight and my own personal breads.

I am Rhonda Katz, psychotherapist and speaker (and hopefully soon will have a Sunday radio spot on CFRB and a column in Verve: "Help Me Rhonda"—keep your fingers crossed).

Friends:

Kathy Kastner, CBC—husband Marv Burns

David Jackson, president, Astral Fox TV, and his wife Chrissie Rejman, producer, "Cityline", CityTV

Jane Hawkin, executive producer, CFRB, husband Chris Selerock, Music Brokers partner

Helena Aalto, Coles, and Josh Berman, producer, entertainers

Diana Bennett, president of Sweathearts, her boyfriend Mel Sadok, architect, Zeidler

Maybe Ben Gordon, actor, writer—his wife Terry is coming as Eglinton.

Fern Simpson Reich, buyer, partner, Town Shoes, husband Andy Reich, lawyer.

Evelyne Michaels, columnist, writer who's coming as Ms. Toronto!

My wonderful husband, Dr. Harvey Kaplovitch has been wanting to have a party but I was early in a pregnancy—NOW we're ready for one of our frequent Big Bashes. Music. Fun, Entertainment. Dance + Good food. Isn't that what a party is? I'm coming as Ontario Place.

Thank you kindly.

Rhonda Katz

October 7, 1988

Out of respect for Emperor Hirohito and his uncertain state of health, it has become incumbent upon us to proceed with suspending our November 1 reception at the King Edward Hotel. After enjoying the pleasure of inviting you to our reception, we are disappointed to have to change plans. However, we entreat the favour of your understanding for our position and your pardon for any inconvenience this announcement may bring you. Also, we should like to thank you earnestly for your patience under the circumstances.

Toshio Mori
Resident Senior Managing Director, The Americas
Tadashi Suzuki
President and Chief Executive Officer

Spring, 1990

There is a very important issue, currently under review, concerning the elimination of certain medical benefits necessary for women.

Facial hair, not "just a few," but *beards in women*, is a serious personal problem often associated with underlying hormone "imbalances." The consequences of extensive facial hair in a woman include psychiatric problems, unemployment, loneliness, spinsterhood, not to mention ridicule and adjustment problems.

The Ministry of Health is currently "studying" the probability of eliminating "epilation" or electrolysis of facial hair as a medical benefit for women with severe hormone imbalances. The elimination of medical treatment for this small subset of women is discriminatory and ill-conceived. The ministry must be stopped in its attempts to balance its budget on the backs of Ontario women.

Though the number of women affected is small, they should not be dismissed as inconsequential. They are frightened and angry and *will not be silenced.*

I implore you to read the enclosed material and form your own opinions, investigate, seek consultation . . . *but act quickly.*

The Ministry of Health is holding a meeting on July 11, 1990, to decide the fate of these women, and all are holding their collective breath.

Please help these women . . . is it not your mandate?

J. P. Donahue, MD, F.R.C.P.(C)
Sudbury, Ontario

June 7, 1988
Your column of May 14/88. I thought it was very well done, but you are really on the fringes of "How Toronto Society" plays games.

I happened to have grown up with most of them. I trust your discretion. I.E. David Thompson—soon to be the richest man in Canada—you talk about a 'lousy' $4 Million sale. Fact he is worth when his father dies (65–66 or so) will be worth about $12 billion $. I know because I know him personally. LIKE PERSONALLY.

Some of the $ are in Rosedale. *Not* the big $. Forest Hill and Thornhill is where the society and $ are.

I live in Edmonton by choice. I have several oil wells, etc. that pay my way. I grew up in Forest Hill before it was fashionable.

Drop me a note, I will give you the up-to-date.

Why? Because I believe you are a comer.

There is only one request; when I come back—only once a year—I would sincerely like you to invite my son and daughter to the Art Show. That would be kind.

If you keep in touch, off the record, I'll tell you who, with whom, etc.

Because I like you, I can arrange a 'PERSONAL' interview with David Thompson. You can write your article for many $.

What's in it for me? Nothing really.

But what a coup. Give me a time when you could sit down over lunch.

> Kenneth Coulthard
> 12025–103 Street
> Edmonton

But it was the informed, witty letters I enjoyed receiving the most:

October 4, 1990
Re your column of October 4, titled "Dalai Lama Spreads a Message of Peace."

Rosemary, Rosemary, Rosemary. I am most disappointed. *What* was the Dalai Lama wearing? Come *on*, you can do better than that!

> Rolf Auer
> Vancouver

March 21, 1989
As a devoted fan and constant reader I groaned and grumbled and darkly muttered "who the hell cares" as I plowed through your name-dropping column in this morning's *Globe and Mail*.

Mercifully you gave me a chuckle, had the last word and got in your traditional shaft by pointing out it was all in aid of pacifying those malcontents who live and love to see their name in print, and who have indicated their objection to the change of format in the column.

Having done so, I hope you get back to normal and continue the fight against flummery. I particularly enjoyed your piece on the antics of Rosedalites some time ago. When are you going to take on Forest Hill, the Beaches, the Thousand Islands and Muskoka? Perhaps, from what I hear, you have a few cogent comments about the life-style in Port Hope.

I look forward to meeting you one day, some day: either with or through David Purdy, whose brother-in-law I have the questionable privilege of being.

Gordon Heyd
Toronto

May 5, 1988

I have news for you: my husband, the late Richard C. S. Blue, several friends and I were going to buy the Royal Alexandra Theatre. The day before Mavor Moore and my husband planned to make the arrangements, the news came out that Ed Mirvish had beaten us to it. It would never have become a parking lot, I assure you.

Frances Blue
Aurora, Ontario

February 22, 1989

I can't believe I haven't written you before this. Friends sent us copies of your column about our going-away party and I thought dozens of times of how touched I was, and never did, apparently, a bloody thing about it. It's great to have it to read here because things get really weird being away from friends and gossip and whatever is happening in Canada. Every so often I whip it out and remember how much I like all those people.

I need encouragement like that. It's been so sensationally great here that coming home is going to be very hard to do. We are in the middle of paradise in the best winter in 50 years, and this place is green with blossoms all over. I was hoping that Toronto would have the worst winter ever, but we gather it hasn't been too bad. Rats. Not good for the garden.

We hear nothing about Canada at all. Zero. Zip. *Nada.* Except how disgusting B. Mulroney's original stand on the Salman Rushdie case was. Shameful. Apart from that no one seems to have heard of Canadians. Ah, yes. The French say, We have to be so careful because if we think a Canadian is an American, they get so insulted. "Oh, really." Of course the French don't care. I've learned the following:

All Frenchwomen have great legs and wear black stockings. No one is fat here (not allowed) even though everyone porks out, grazes and has access to the best food in the world.

No French person picks up any dog shit whatsoever. *Le merde des chiens* are everywhere. It is appalling.

All French males flirt with women of any age.

I could go on and on. Travel does not necessarily narrow as has so often been stated.

We are both beavering away on our books.

Best to Ed and loads to yourself. Maybe we will actually see you in May when we return.

Marjorie [Harris] and Jack [Batten]
St. Jean Cap Ferrat, France

December 16, 1988

If you hear a rumbling sound and feel the earth shaking, it's not another earthquake.

It's just the late Brigadier W. Preston Gilbride expressing his disdain at being listed as "William" and probably addressing his colleagues with "Who's that new person down there? I thought only Zena could do a thing like that to me."

John J. Brunke
Toronto
P.S. Love your column.

A slightly tongue-in-cheek column describing Joan Sutton Straus's ritzy luncheon at Sutton Place, and Cathie Bratty's glitzy Russian tea at the Markham Suites Hotel sparked a lively debate amongst my readers.

Writer Sondra Gotlieb also got on the bandwagon and produced this amusing column in the *Financial Post* about the two events.

Not Invited to Markham Party

May 10, 1991

Unhappily another week has passed by without my name being in Rosemary Sexton's column. She writes social notes for a national "church" paper published in Toronto, and lots of people here are dying to be mentioned by Rosemary.

Rosemary Sexton is "wife of" William, QC, partner of the legal firm Osler Hoskin & Harcourt. Actually, I don't know if Rosemary's husband's name is William. But it doesn't matter. It seems that the husband's first name is not too important to Rosemary. She has her special way of listing people, as in "Judy Ney, wife of U.S. ambassador Thomas." Actually, Ambassador Ney's first name is Ed.

Life of Obscurity

Since you are far away in Washington, I can be frank about my social life. The reason I never get mentioned in Rosemary's column is because nobody asks me to the parties she describes. Shunned by the Brazilian ball-goers, omitted from the list of all those celebrity auctions, I live a life of obscurity, sitting around, waiting for the phone to ring.

And when it does, it's never an invite to something like the "divine and decadent party" given in Markham, Ontario, by Cathy [*sic*] Bratty, "wife of developer Rudy." It's a call from the window washer to give me his estimate. Or from my mother, who lives in Winnipeg, to remind me to send a bereavement note to her bridge friend Edna, whose second husband collapsed in the notions' department in Eaton's.

Or from Sophie, my friend the director's wife from Etobicoke, whose husband is always away at board meetings. She invites me to go dutch with her to an early movie and have a heart-to-heart about whether she should sell her cottage in Muskoka now that her kids aren't interested.

So, Polly, judging from my phone calls, I get the feeling it will be a frosty Friday in July before anyone invites me to something like that party in Markham.

According to Rosemary, the lucky guests at the party in

Markham perched on an elaborate throne for photo opportunities, noshed at ice carvings "inlaid with Russian caviar and vodka," drank from gold-rimmed crystal flown in from New York and were treated to a sit-down, eight-course meal while psychics read their palms behind the medieval Markham tapestries.

Nevertheless, do I detect a barely perceptible Rosedale sniff from Rosemary, disturbed by ostentation in Markham? Or am I reading too much between her lines?

To be truthful, Polly, I'm sorry I wasn't invited by the Brattys, because I expect that very soon this sort of festivity is going to be history, banned or taxed into nonexistence by our provincial government. Rosemary will be reduced to writing about guests guzzling on apple juice in recycled cartons, spooning up lentil stew while being entertained by *Hymn Sing*, and [listening to] readings by columnist Michael Valpy.

Social columnists who write about parties and those who are "in" earn a lucrative fee in the U.S. You told me that it's rumoured that Liz Smith, the syndicated columnist who writes about the rich and famous in New York, earns in the high six figures—maybe more—for saying nice things about her well-placed friends.

Liz, as you told me, was the one who got the tip from Ivana Trump about Marla Maples and "the Donald."

Journalistic analyzers who write about the political and economic scene daren't even dream about what Liz makes. Except maybe for Frothingham, allegedly the highest-paid journalist in this country. But then he writes about people—not issues. More like Liz, Rosemary and occasionally me.

Speaking of Rosemary, I hope the publishers of the national "church" paper who print her will remember this when it is time to renew her contract. It's possible that she brings in more readers than Frotheringham, Jeffrey Simpson and Can Lit writers you've never heard of.

Your best friend,
Sondra

Chapter Four

Diary of a Social Columnist (1991 to 1993)

[Animals] are so much more straightforward and honest [than people]. They have no sort of pretension . . . they live within their sphere in nature, they don't pretend they're God, they don't pretend they're intelligent, they don't invent nerve gas, and, above all, they don't have cocktail parties.

> —naturalist and wildlife writer Gerald Durrell in response to the question put to him on BBC Radio as to whether he preferred the company of animals to the company of humans.

May 1991

Liz Tory stopped in today to drop off some Liver Foundation material, in case I want to do a column on the charity. She was dressed in a chic navy suit on her way to a liver meeting. She said that, despite scuttlebutt to the contrary, Roy Megarry is definitely still in power at the *Globe* and that there's no way, as rumoured, that Ken Thomson is bringing his oldest son David in to run things at the paper.

Apparently Ken and Marilyn Thomson were not too happy with my sentence (in a feature that I wrote for the Saturday *Globe* for the front page of the Focus section, titled "The Party's Over") that "thrifty publisher Ken Thomson actually purchased a table."

She also said that Maruja Jackman, tired of Hal's antics over the year, has left the matrimonial home and gone downtown to live with one of her English professors. Good for her, we both agreed. Nothing against Hal, but it's nice to see a woman with alternatives who can strike out on her own.

June 6, 1991

Had coffee with Sondra Gotlieb today. She came over this afternoon at my invitation, issued after she had written a column in the
Financial Post, complaining tongue-in-cheek about not being
invited to Cathie Bratty's ritzy Russian tea that I had written up
in my society column.

She and I had both been invited last week to a tea held at
Evelyn Huang's house to preview the 1992 Brazilian Ball. I had
declined, but Sondra went, making a quick entrance and exit. "I'm
not that comfortable with the socialite community," she explained.
"There's one in every city and they're all the same. It's women
married to very wealthy husbands who want to do something use-
ful. Their charity work is highly commendable. But I don't have all
that money, and, anyway, I'd rather garden."

It's clear that because she and her husband have just moved to
Toronto many of the names and faces are as yet unfamiliar to her.
Plus, she's used to Ottawa and Washington, where politics run
everything. But I have no doubt she'll learn the ropes in no time.
She's curious about everything and not shy.

She made several lapses into an almost uneducated dialect. It
may be just the result of her unfamiliarity with Toronto. She called
Forest Hill "Forest Hills," and a creek a "crick," though she quickly corrected herself.

We discussed computers. We both have an IBM PS/1, and she
also has a portable. I gave her tips on Toronto society, i.e., the different groups (nouveau-riche socialites, uptight WASP, etc.) and
she gave me tips on writing a book. She has written at least three
books on society already.

She declined wine and just had soda water, saying that she's
trying to lose ten pounds. She wore sandals and a long white skirt
over which she had pulled a snug, hip-fitting, long-sleeved, blue-
and-white-striped T-shirt. She wore no nylons and little makeup,
and looked quite youthful. There was absolutely no hint of the
notorious underside that caused her to slap her social secretary in
front of everyone in Washington.

When I complained to her that my column had lost its bite
due to the *Globe* copy editors, she had a few words of advice:
"Get some U.S. papers and read Liz Smith," she said. "She knows

how to toe the party line but still get in some interesting comments."

July 1991
Charleston Lake and Brockville

Our July at the cottage has been spectacular, as usual. Unlike the "castle" at Brockville, which is an old stone structure almost 150 years old, with turrets and winding staircases, the cottage is a relatively small and modern wood-and-glass structure perched high on a rock on a 55-acre island on Charleston Lake. No one can reach us except by boat. Until I got my column at the *Globe* we had no phone, television or radio there, but now we have a phone that we leave unplugged most of the time except when we need to call out.

Today, Edgar and I, feeling besieged by both family and friends circling the cottage in their boats, headed into Brockville to hide. We had barely ensconced ourselves on our big sofa in the family room to watch Jack Nicklaus and Lee Trevino battle it out in the U.S. Seniors Open when the telephone rang. We looked at it, then at each other. Should we answer?

"What if it's one of the kids?" I wondered aloud, and walked over to pick up the receiver. "Hi, Rosemary" came a hale and hearty voice I had no trouble recognizing. "It's Anne Delicaet. Leonard and I are just passing through Brockville and thought we would give you a call." I covered the receiver with my hand and mouthed who it was to Edgar. "No," he said. "We're not available to anyone, and especially not your socialite friends."

But I didn't have the heart to turn them away. "Come on over, Anne," I said, "but I can't offer you any food or drink. Our fridge and stove are disconnected since we're having some work done on the kitchen (this was true). And Edgar's asleep (not true), but I'd love to see you."

Edgar was irate. "How could you, Rosemary!" he exclaimed after I'd hung up the phone. "We came here to escape family and friends, and now you're asking people over." "I'm sorry, Edgar," I answered, "but I promise you won't have to see them. I'll deal with them and you stay here and watch golf."

I don't know what Len and Anne Delicaet thought of their host's bad manners, but that's exactly what happened. I showed them around the place except for the family room, explaining that Edgar was falling asleep while watching golf, and then Len, Anne and I sat out on the large verandah overlooking the St. Lawrence River and watched the big ships go by. I don't think that Len Delicaet was very impressed with my house tour. As we entered each room, just as I was launching into a description of the work we'd done or the furnishings we'd bought, he would erupt into a loud operatic hum complete with falsetto and quaver. The first time he did it, I almost jumped out of my skin, thinking that there was a drunken bumblebee nearby. But by the fifth or sixth time, I had gotten quite used to it and looked upon the loud eruptions as appropriate accompaniments to the ornate architecture of the old house.

August 1991
Charleston Lake
Former Ontario Human Rights Commission chairman Canon Borden Purcell and his wife, Carter, had us over for Sunday brunch at their cottage on Charleston Lake along with lobbyist Susan Murray and her father Alec, and *Saturday Night* magazine Ottawa columnist Charlotte Grey and her husband, George Armstrong, a deputy minister of revenue in the Mulroney government. The Purcells have just built a log cabin that they've decorated with early Canadiana antiques. They served lunch out on the large deck. There were roast chicken breasts and legs with a delectable prune sauce, tabouleh and green salad. I brought a peach-raspberry upside-down cake I had made for dessert.

I had never met Charlotte before, though she and I had collaborated on a couple of my Ottawa columns. She and her husband brought along two of their three little boys, Nicholas and Alexander (Oliver was at camp), one of whom walked into Borden's new screen door, which he'd just installed, knocking it down. The guests commiserated with the Purcells over their screen and helped replace it, while Charlotte and George administered to their crying son. Five minutes later his father did exactly the same thing, only this time he put a hole through the screen.

When Borden and Carter came by the next day on their floating barge, Edgar and I were in swimming. "No wonder our government has such a large deficit," Edgar called out over the water to the Purcells, "with people like George in charge." We could hear Borden tee-heeing all the way down the lake.

September, 1991

Truth or rumour? Had lunch in an empty Bemelman's restaurant during the TTC strike with a friend who said that he had heard that former Ontario attorney general Ian Scott and Toronto Maple Leafs captain Wendel Clark were an item.

During a weekend at Charleston Lake, got a call from Hugh Segal and his wife Donna to invite us for dinner. Really it was our turn, so I invited them to our place in Brockville, instead. The weather wasn't great and we had some construction to oversee there, so we came in from the lake to meet them. Donna brought the dessert, a scrumptious apple cheesecake from The Big Apple near Belleville, and I cooked a roast lamb. Hughie spent some of the evening on the portable phone taking calls from the PMO.

October 1991

Rumours are swirling around town with the impending visit of Charles and Diana. A week before the royal couple were due in Toronto, I got a call from a government official who asked not to be identified to tell me that the NDP government, which was initially disdainful of the Royals' visit, is now going all out to make sure the couple get the red carpet treatment. "Last week the *Sun* reported that the Sudbury welcome reception at Science North for Charles and Diana would be tacky," he said. "But I've seen the bills and there'll be nothing tacky about it. There will be numerous dignitaries, gobs of flowers, etc."

Government staff have had a number of phone calls, he added, from Arlene Perly Rae wanting to bring a friend along, sort of her own lady-in-waiting, and wanting to be placed beside Princess Di at every photo opportunity and insisting that she ride with her in her limousine. The latter request was directed from the secretary of state to Buckingham Palace, which refused. Arlene also put ten members of her family on the guest list of a private reception held by Lieutenant Governor Lincoln Alexander in his Queen's Park suite to welcome Charles and Diana upon their arrival. But Mr. Alexander, according to my source, had demurred, saying he had a limited number of spaces, not enough for ten members of one family.

The NDP government is between a rock and a hard place—they are damned for spending too much in the recession, yet they will be criticized if the affairs they put on are considered shoddy, said my source. Adding to Rae's problems is the fact that bureaucrats who worked under Davis and Peterson and who remain in their jobs under this government are out to get the NDP since their loyalties lie with the Liberals or Conservatives. "This is the first time I've worked for government for such an extended period," said my friend. "I didn't know that civil servants acted like this." "Haven't you watched the television program 'Yes Minister'?" I asked him. He laughed and admitted that he had.

Just as the call concluded, I said, "Well, I'll do what I can about Queen Arlene, but I don't know if the *Globe* will print it." "Actually, Rosemary," he replied, "at lunch today a couple of us government staffers were discussing all her demands and we dubbed her Arlene 'Pearly Queen' Rae." I quickly scribbled down the nickname. This was great stuff.

But the next day, Friday, when I was getting ready to catch the train to Brockville for the weekend , I started to get worried about the column. My leak had promised to call me on Thursday evening in case I had any questions, but no call came. I hadn't been able to check the facts with him and I had no corroborator. But the story he told had sounded very truthful, so I decided to send it down. Besides the stuff on Queen Arlene, he had given me a real royal scoop—the previously unpublished itinerary of the two princes. Most of the press weren't yet aware that Prince William and Prince Harry were coming.

The *Globe* printed the whole column as is, and, as was to be expected—though in this business, you can never tell—there were repercussions. After I got home Monday afternoon, Tim Pritchard, the *Globe*'s then managing editor, called. "We've had a call from Lincoln Alexander's office," he said, "objecting to what you said in your column." "Was it the number of guests they were objecting to?" I asked. Pritchard replied, "I'm not sure of all the details. Do you want to pursue this yourself?" "Thanks," I answered, grateful he was leaving it in my hands.

"By the way," said Tim, "how would you feel about the *Globe* sending you out to follow the Royals around for their trip?" "I'd just as soon not, if you don't mind," I answered, thinking how upset Edgar would be if I wasn't able to spend the weekend in Brockville with him. Although I felt badly about not acceding to the request, I was happy that Tim had made it. Obviously the *Globe* wasn't too troubled by the Lincoln Alexander complaint or they wouldn't have asked me for more coverage of the Royals.

Next, fortunately, Deep Throat finally called. "Rosemary, the shit has hit the fan," he said. "It's absolutely wild down here. They're really searching for the person who made the leak to your column. I've got a wife and children to support and I'm terrified." "Don't worry." I said. "No one's asked me for my source and I'm not about to tell. But is that statement about Lincoln Alexander's refusing to invite Arlene Perly Rae's ten family members true?" I told him the problem. "Rosemary, I stand by everything I said. It all happened just as you set out in the column. But I guess I understand where Lincoln Alexander is coming from," he replied. "I never even thought of that complication."

I asked Deep Throat what he thought of my making a retraction, since, according to Tim Pritchard, who had spoken to the lieutenant governor's office, the ten guests were indeed now invited. My source seemed a bit surprised that I was suggesting such a thing, but went along with it. "I certainly didn't intend to get Lincoln Alexander into trouble," he concurred.

I called Bren MacPherson, Lincoln Alexander's assistant, who told me that Mr. Alexander had allowed the ten members of Ms. Rae's family to attend (it wasn't made clear whether that decision was made before the column or as a result of the column) and that the lieutenant governor was very worried about offending the Raes. She had called me first on Saturday and had only called the *Globe* when they couldn't reach me. "Would it help if the *Globe* made a retraction?" I asked. (Although a retraction would look to some as if I had made a mistake, I felt others would probably realize the truth. I didn't really care, anyway, as long as the *Globe* wasn't angry with me.) "Yes," she said. "It would. But Mr. Alexander wants it made clear that it's up to you, Rosemary, to word it the way you want." "Something like, Mr. Alexander has allowed Ms. Perly Rae's ten guests to attend?" I asked. "That would be fine," she replied. I called Tim back and said I was willing to retract. The retraction appeared in the *Globe* the next day (Tuesday, October 22) as:

Corrections and Clarifications

Lieutenant Governor Lincoln Alexander has invited ten members of Ms. Perly Rae's family for a small reception in his suite on Wednesday for the Prince and Princess of Wales, contrary to a report in Rosemary Sexton's column on Saturday.

October 21, 1991
Attended a book launch for a new book out by Sherill MacLaren titled *Invisible Power*, about powerful women in Canada. It was the same night as a big party for *Saturday Night* magazine, which I skipped because I anticipated a mob scene. The mid-size gathering took place at the Woodlawn Avenue West residence of real estate agent Sis Bunting Weld (since rented to Doug Bassett and his wife, Susan, after they sold their Forest Hill mansion to Ira Gluskin). Her daughter, Leanne, and Liz Tory acted as the two hosts as Sis was in Europe.

Mostly everyone at the party was in the book. It was sort of a woman's who's who list of female Torontonians. Stockbroker Mary Susanne Lamont, who had lent her telephone system to the book's author, came. Anna Porter, in a green corduroy ankle-length suit, was leaning on a cane she had been using since a recent tennis injury. Also there was Nancy Southam, a Montreal woman-about-town who lives in a converted firehall next door to Trudeau, whom she used to date. Socialite Marlene DelZotto was there. Honor de Pencier urged me to go upstairs and look at the view. It's the same one she can see out her back window, since she and her husband, Michael, bought a house on the street. I hadn't seen the elegant Joan Randall since she and I sat on the Arthritis Society board together. Feminist Nancy Jackman enveloped author Doris Anderson in a big bear hug. AIDS activist Bluma Appel discussed the Hill-Thomas proceedings—she's the first woman I've talked to who is for Clarence Thomas. There were just a few spouses, such as lawyer Julian Porter and Michael Meighen with wife Kelly. She and I haven't spoken since she sent me a fax complaining about the way I had written about her friend Joanna Black.

October 22, 1991
5:00 a.m. Got up early to shower and dress before being picked up by a CFTO limo to be interviewed by J. D. Roberts on "Canada AM" about the royal visit. They had me on with Ashley Walton, a Fleet Street reporter from the *London Daily Express*, who had just flown in. Before we went on the air, Ashley asked me if I knew anything about the princes' timetable. I handed him a copy of my column on the princes' itinerary and he went crazy. "May I borrow this?" he asked excitedly, and went immediately to the phones where he read it verbatim to his newspaper. As a result, the English press had a field day with the NDP and Arlene Perly Rae, generally making fun of the spectacle of a socialist government trying to suck up to the Royals.

12:12 p.m. Had lunch with Allan Fotheringham at Il Posto. We were surprised to see Geills Turner and Gordon Capital boss Jimmy Connacher at the table beside us chatting away. Fotheringham and I speculated as to what had brought them together. Perhaps Geills could be asking for some job assistance to reenter the market, since she's an economist. Apparently John Turner had been one of those short-listed as Lincoln Alexander's successor, but, when the word got out, Mulroney received so many phone calls protesting Geills Turner's being the wife of the lieutenant governor that he dropped the idea.

Fotheringham's full of all sorts of information and is really quite funny in person. He's also very insightful about people's motives and personalities, and he really listens when you talk, which a lot of people don't do. He's much more clued-in than I am about what's going on, because he keeps in touch with everyone, whereas, when I'm not working, I tend to hide away. He thinks that Sarah Band was handed a raw deal by Herb Solway. Four days after Herb walked out, according to Allan, Sarah discovered she was pregnant and he refused to come back. Okay, Herb, said Sarah. You can come to Zoe's graduation in 21 years, but as for visiting her before that time, you can forget it. However,

I know Ann Shortell, Herb's new live-in, and I heard a different story from her.

Fotheringham drank one martini and a glass of wine and I had a beer. He had the minestrone and then osso buco; I had a salad and then calf's liver.

I asked Allan how one of his current flames, Mary Kelly, was doing. Mary and I worked together on the Julian Porter campaign team when Julian ran against Ian Scott in the 1984 provincial election. At that time Mary was dating Sam Hughes, the son of a retired Ontario Supreme Court justice, who has since married London newspaper heiress Martha Blackburn. He and I then speculated as to why Martha, with all her enormous fortune, had married Sam.

October 24, 1991
Interviewed this afternoon by Donna Tranquata on CFRB about the Royals' visit. I asked her to interview me as quickly as possible since I was throwing a dinner party that evening. "Are you having any surprise guests from Buckingham Palace?" I was asked. Ah, such is the stuff that legends are made of.

Even my own kids are amazed when I tell them Edgar and I are skipping town this weekend instead of attending the Toronto gala honouring Charles and Di. A lot of people are clamouring for tickets. Cartier president John Lauer asked Edgar and me to be his guests at the Cartier table. As Cartier is sponsoring the event, its table is right next to Diana and Charles, so I would get a chance to talk to them or even to dance with Prince Charles. If it were on a weeknight, I would, of course, go. But I'm not giving up a quiet weekend in Brockville for a ritzy gala on a Saturday night, Charles or no Charles. "Unlike Arlene Perly Rae, I don't relish being one of 800 standing in line to meet the Princess," I said somewhat snarkily during the CFRB interview.

December 12, 1991
Yesterday I attended the swearing-in of Hal Jackman as the new Ontario lieutenant governor. It was short and sweet and both Bob Rae and Hal gave to-the-point, funny speeches. I brought a friend, Jeannie Ritchie, but they wouldn't let her in—security was really

tight—so she had to wait downstairs in the hall for 45 minutes until the ceremony was over. However, I snuck her back up for the reception afterward. She was a bit worried about having to sign her name in the book and being announced when she wasn't even invited, but it all went off without a hitch. I myself was worried about having to say hello to Bob Rae in the receiving line (only he and Jackman were greeting the guests) since my column about his wife, but it wasn't too bad. After Hal gave me a kiss hello, I turned to Rae and said, "Nice to see you. I'm Rosemary Sexton." "I know who you are, Rosemary," he said, and that was that.

Tonight I'm throwing a Christmas party for the litigation department at Osler Hoskin, my husband's law firm. I don't really mind since the law firm has hired caterers for the event. But I had to spend the morning at my computer typing up the swearing-in ceremony of Hal Jackman since it would give me a story without having to go to a Christmas party.

Christmas, as usual, was a bit of a disaster. As an antidote, I sat down and wrote it up:

Christmas 1991

December 4. Promise husband before he goes to work not to hold annual Christmas party of neighbours, family and friends as we are in the midst of a recession. Suspect he just wants a year off from seeing them all (as well as paying through the nose to do so), but refrain from imputing any underhanded motives to him.

Call from husband's law firm, asking will I hold the firm party at my house this year. Conclude I was right, after all, to suspect husband's motives in cancelling party. Decide to forgive him, since firm promises no work for me; they'll look after everything right down to the smallest detail, they assure me.

December 5. Spend day writing Christmas cards to all the friends and family I won't see now that my party's been cancelled. Put on each of the 150 cards a personal note; make sure names and addresses are up-to-date and correct. Drive to post office to buy stamps and mail them. Encounter long lineup. Decide to send cards with husband to office to mail the next day.

December 6. Offer to drive my husband to work to make sure bundle of cards gets there. Park on King Street in front of his office. Though cards have been sitting on his lap throughout drive and he knows that this is the reason he has been chauffeured downtown, in haste he leaps out of car scattering them out on the pavement. I get out of car, pick them up and hand them to him. "Don't forget to give them to Sheila (his secretary) as soon as you get into the office," I call to a retreating back.

December 6, evening. Husband arrives home from work. Assuming that nothing could have happened to the cards in the 100-yard interval between the car and the office, I fail to question him.

December 7. Over breakfast bring up the subject as casually as possible. "Sheila got them off all right?" I question brightly. "Got what off all right?" he replies blankly. I can't believe my ears. "The Christmas cards," I say between clenched teeth. A look of horror crosses his face. "I can't remember what I did with them," he whispers, almost to himself. Runs upstairs to check the contents of his briefcase. No cards. We turn his coat inside out. No cards. Calls are made to his secretary, the receptionist on the floor of the building where he works, the cleaning staff in conference room E where he attended a morning meeting that day. A memo is sent around the firm. No cards.

December 9. With Christmas cards out of the way (!), decide to tackle Christmas baking. Promise my son to spend the afternoon with him in the kitchen. Somehow get busy with other chores until son, in disgust, comes to me for instructions. Hearing the loud clamouring of pots and pans from the kitchen and stricken with guilt that I am not participating (never mind my worry over the results!), I join him in the kitchen. We mix dough and cut out and decorate cookies with green and red sugar, chocolate pieces, and silver and multicoloured balls. We make dinosaurs, angels, reindeer, Santa Clauses, rocking horses, stars and Christmas trees. Afterward the kitchen looks like a disaster area and we have baked barely enough cookies to fill a single tin. We hide it away in a top cupboard to save for Christmas Day.

December 10. Tired of paying upward of $30 for a Christmas tree that drops its needles all over the house, is a nuisance to get rid of and a fire hazard besides, decide, despite protests from family, to pick up an artificial tree at Canadian Tire. Purchase the last one available in size I want. No box for it. Salesclerk and I drag it out of store to car in minus-30-degree weather. Won't fit in car. Spend half an hour in bitter cold pulling it apart to fit in trunk. Once home, spend another half hour carrying it piecemeal in the front door and another two hours trying to put it up. The top of the tree is at least two feet from the ceiling. My family is right. The worst tree we have ever had has cost me $250, is practically impossible to assemble, and it doesn't even smell like a tree. Already I miss my real trees with the dropping needles, but figure I have to go through this rigamarole for at least eight years before the tree begins to look like a bargain. Husband and son, seeing my distress, pretend to like tree and lavish it with praise.

December 11. Tackle my favourite annual Christmas chore, putting up the outdoor lights. Spend two hours in basement untangling them, twenty minutes bringing them up the stairs and out the door, and another two hours untangling them all over again to put on the hedge. By the time the lights are finally up and actually working it has taken me a good part of the day. But, that evening, as I look at them out the window, twinkling brightly against the snow, some of my Christmas spirit is restored. And they're up just in time for the party.

December 12, 7:00 a.m. Day of party dawns. This will be a piece of cake, I gloat as I return to bed after getting husband off to work. Not like my usual parties where I run around madly the day of like a chicken with its head cut off. Today the caterers will take care of everything.

7:30 a.m. Aroused from beauty sleep by knock on door. Rental company arrives with tables, chairs, trays and glasses. Cat escapes out door. Chase cat in cold in my pajamas.

8:30 a.m. Morning bath interrupted by another knock on door. Rental company again, this time with linen they had forgotten.

10:00 a.m. Girl at door with flowers for decorating the house.

1:00 p.m. Team of men at door to check out layout of house in preparation for party. Cat escapes out into the cold again. This time let *them* chase cat.

3:00 p.m. Eight waiters arrive three hours ahead of party to "set up." In despair, shut cat in basement and go upstairs to hide. Decide I might as well get ready for party now. Turn on shower. Hear a loud knock on bathroom door inquiring about oven mitts. Step out of shower and wrap myself in towel. Go downstairs to find them. Return to bedroom, lock door and turn hair dryer on full blast, ignoring any further interruptions.

4:00 p.m. Look out bedroom window and notice that outdoor Christmas lights, controlled by a timer, have not turned on. Put on expensive sheer panty hose bought especially for party and little black dress and go downstairs with wet hair still in rollers to ask what's going on. Caterers disclaim any knowledge of problems with lights. Run outside in high heels, little dress and rollers to check lights. Snag nylons in nearby rosebush. Lose rollers in snow. Discover lights unplugged and lying over sidewalk where they have been trampled on all day. Too late to get new ones in time for party. Go back upstairs, shivering and crying with frustration and cold.

6:00 p.m. Compose myself just in time to greet guests at door in runny nylons, damp hair and a red nose. Quickly down two stiff Manhattans. Spend rest of evening, under husband's disapproving eye, wobbling precariously on high heels, laughing and talking too loudly, and flirting with his male partners. Frightened guests depart hurriedly as soon as they are able to detach themselves from their garrulous hostess, tossing sympathetic glances in my husband's direction as they head off into the night.

2:00 a.m. Suffering a painful hangover, steal from bed quietly and go downstairs to forage for some food. Open fridge and gasp. Caterers have taken all food with them. Reach up to cupboard to retrieve a Christmas cookie. Cookie tin empty except for a few crumbs. Crawl back into bed and lie awake for hours with empty stomach and splitting headache.

December 14. Attend Christmas party with husband and children given by friends in their beautifully decorated house. Over cocktail party murmur, hear loud voice of my ever-tactful son, as his mother searches frantically for a sofa to crawl under. "You know, Sarah, it's a good thing your mother had the neighbours over for a Christmas party this year. We've got a fake tree over at my house and it's the tackiest thing you ever saw."

December 17, 1991
Called my old boss and mentor, former managing editor of the *Globe and Mail*, Geoff Stevens, after reading the headlines in the *Globe* about the sudden departure of Roy Megarry to go to work in the Third World. Geoff feels that the Thomson organization is keeping Megarry on for another year to act as hatchet man when they make more cuts. Geoff says that the recent financial performance of the *Globe* has been quite bad, that there was no profit in 1990, and that it looks as if 1991 will be worse.

It's interesting, Geoff commented, that Megarry is keeping the dual responsibilities of editorial and public resources. Those are run by Megarry-loyalists Bill Thorsell and Diane Barsoski. He's also staying in charge of InfoGlobe, Globe Media International and the *Financial Times*. My hunch, said Geoff, is that the *Financial Times* is a goner. Megarry paid $9 million for that and it's been losing money ever since. So Barbara Hyland will be looking for work.

What's happened to your court case? I asked him. (Stevens launched a wrongful dismissal suit against the *Globe* after he and editor-in-chief Norman Webster were summarily fired a year ago.) The judge's decision is due out January 6, Geoff said. It's been delayed because the judge had a prostate operation, then a hip replacement. An Ontario labour department hearing has already awarded Geoff $50,000 for wrongful dismissal damages.

Also called Paul Godfrey to ask about Pat Appleton's funeral and to commiserate with him over Pat, since they had been good friends. It will take me a long time to get over Pat's death. I liked her best of all the socialites. She could play the game as well as any of them, but, unlike some of them, she never forgot it was a game.

December 18, 1991

Catherine Nugent took me to lunch at Lakes today. We ran into Fotheringham with model Donna DeMarco, a current squeeze. I doubt she'll last; he treats all his girlfriends so badly. Real estate agent Janice Rennie was at a table, as was Ken Scott, a neighbour and friend, who puts out the Sponsorship Report. After Catherine sent drinks to Allan's table, he came over to talk and told us he's leaving for Whistler for Xmas until early January. Fotheringham complimented me on my piece on a trip to Paris ("Down and Out in Paris") that ran in the travel section of the *Globe* last Saturday. I thanked him and told him how delighted I was that Eric Kierans had called me from Halifax about it. I've probably had as much response from that travel article as I have from any of my columns.

Catherine told me that Hal Jackman had had quite a collection of his female friends to his swearing in—besides ex-wife Maruja and Barbara McDougall, whom I had mentioned in my column, there was Doone Massie, Sis Weld and somebody else. Apparently Hal took them all out to lunch the week before to celebrate.

January 7, 1992

What an interesting start to the New Year. Roy Megarry is leaving the *Globe* ostensibly to pursue a career in the Third World. Geoff Stevens won his court case against the *Globe* and will receive damages of $155,000. The judge declined to award punitive damages for deceit, but said that he believed the Webster-Stevens version of events surrounding the firing over the Megarry-Thorsell version.

Liz was back from Florida where she attended Trevor Eyton's annual party on his rented 150-foot yacht *Popeye*. She said that she and John were definitely not going to Mickey Cohen's March golf tournament in Boca.

Also got a call from *Globe* business columnist Bud Jorgenson asking if I had heard the latest rumour about Conrad Black. I told him what I had heard, that Conrad and Joanna had separated upon Joanna's initiative, and that he had wanted to get back together but she said no. The couple attended Trevor Eyton's boat party down in Florida together, but went their separate ways afterward. Liz

Tory told me, and her sources are impeccable, that Barbara Amiel is going after him, no holds barred.

This turned out to be a busy day—busier than I expected. I had scheduled three interviews, quite crucial ones, for my upcoming book tentatively titled *The Glitter Girls*, so when Catherine Pigott, a researcher on Peter Gzowski's "Morningside," asked me to comment on the social etiquette of kissing on "Morningside," I had to beg off. I also had to get a column started for this Saturday because Edgar and I are taking a long weekend in Brockville.

January 8, 1992

Well, it's in all the newspapers except the *Globe*. Conrad and Joanna Black have officially separated and Barabara Amiel is cited as the woman waiting in the wings. That certainly scoops my column this Saturday (where in a description of the Eyton-Bitove boat party in Florida, I described Conrad and Joanna as attending the party together but going their separate ways afterward), but I guess I'll go ahead with it, anyway.

January 16, 1992

Invited to a party this weekend at the Binscarth Avenue home of Ray Heard and Gillian Cosgrove to celebrate Geoff Stevens's judgement against Roy Megarry. I would have liked to have gone, but it was a weekend night and I'll be away. But I did want to pay my respects to Geoff. If it weren't for him, I would never have even gotten started in this writing business. He also was an excellent editor to work for. So I went down to the Bombay Company at the Eaton's Centre to buy him a gift.

At first my eye fastened on a wooden butler called James, which I thought would be a nice addition to his and Lin Shannon's Beaches house. But then I spotted hanging on the wall a beautiful mahogany case that opened to reveal a giant dart board complete with darts. "Perfect!" I thought, paid the $140 and brought it home.

Then I spent about an hour slicing carefully through the box and wrapping until I got through to the bull's eye, where I carefully stuck on a picture of Roy Megarry that I'd glued to some cardboard backing. I was worried when I first got home that I wouldn't be able to find a picture of Megarry anywhere, but then

I remembered that about three years ago Ed Roberts, a lawyer and Leader of the Official Opposition in Newfoundland, had sent me a copy of Michael Harris's two-part series outlining Megarry's firing of Stevens and Webster.

I personally have nothing against Megarry, although I have never quite gotten over the ruthlessness with which he fired from the *Globe* two of Canada's best journalists, and the resulting exodus from the paper of much fine journalistic talent. And I did worry that maybe the dart board present would be construed as a vindictive gesture. When I voiced my concerns to Edgar and the host of the party, Ray Heard, they both made light of them and encouraged me to go ahead.

I also knew I was possibly setting myself up for some flak from Megarry myself, maybe even a firing, but I don't really care. I'd like to concentrate on writing a book now; my column, though everyone says it provides me with a forum, has become more of a stumbling block than anything else. Besides, I'm bored to death with the social scene. I'm all partied out.

January 22, 1992

Geoff Stevens called to warn me that *Maclean's* might be writing up the party celebrating his judgement against Megarry. He was worried that Megarry might fire me as a result of the dart board incident being published. I thanked him for his concern, but assured him that, quite frankly, I wouldn't care too much if I were fired. "Maybe you can sue," he said, and we both laughed. We also both knew, I think, that Megarry is too smart to fire me over the dart board. He would quietly release me later with a good reason.

January 29, 1992

Angry telephone call from *Globe* managing editor John Cruikshank.

"Rosemary, I'm calling about the dart board incident. Did you give Geoff Stevens a dart board?"

"Yes, I did," I answered.

"Did it have a picture of Roy Megarry in the centre?"

"Yes, it did."

"Can you please tell me what you were thinking about?"

"I gave it to Geoff as a joke. I was unable to attend his party and felt badly—I was away for the weekend—and I wanted to send a special gift, and that's what I came up with."

"Well," said John, "Roy is my boss, Bill's boss, and when you write for the paper, he's your boss. It's embarrassing for the paper. Bill's very embarrassed because you report through me to him."

"I'm sorry, John," I said. "When I sent that dart board I had no idea that the incident would be published in *Maclean's*. I actually asked both Ray Heard and my husband if it was an appropriate gift or if it might be regarded as mean-spirited, and they said they thought it was fine."

"I think it would be appropriate," suggested John, "that you write a note to Megarry apologizing." He then proceeded to rant on for several minutes about *Frank* magazine, which also reported the incident along with an incident at the *Globe's* Christmas party where a newly acquired male editor tried to hustle the son of Cruikshank's secretary, Sue Garapy, who used to be Geoff Stevens's secretary.

"*Frank* is a disgusting magazine," he said. "I don't care about me, but Bill is very upset by the criticism. It's racist, sexist and very homophobic. But we think we know where *Frank* gets its information."

"Where?" I asked.

"From Paul," Cruikshank answered.

"Who's Paul?" I asked, genuinely in the dark.

"Paul Palango★," he replied.

"Was he at your Christmas party?" I asked.

"No, but he still keeps in touch with people here."

January 30, 1992

Today I sat down to write a letter of apology to Megarry. Not especially because John Cruikshank had asked me to—I didn't really appreciate his inquisitorial tone. I wrote it because Megarry,

---

★Paul Palango, a former city editor at the *Globe,* was let go in the purge that followed the Webster-Stevens firing. He has since written a book titled *Above the Law* about RCMP informants that was on the *Globe and Mail* best-seller list for several weeks.

despite being a henchman for Ken Thomson, had always treated me well. And though I didn't think he was a good manager of people, it was the Thomson Corporation I blamed for giving him such a free rein and letting him interfere so blatantly with the editorial side of the paper. I don't mean to suggest that Thomson gave the actual orders or even knew what was going on. He hired people such as Michael Brown and Michael Johnston to milk the paper for all it was worth so that his bottom line would improve. It's a shortsighted view. Ultimately, if you turn out an inferior product you will end up losing advertisers and revenue. I thought it was a lousy way to run a paper and I still think so.

My letter read as follows:

Dear Mr. Megarry,
I am writing to apologize for any embarrassment my gift to Geoffrey Stevens has caused you. As I was unable to attend the party, I tried to come up with a funny gift in my absence. It was not meant to be critical of you personally in any way. It was a joke. I had no idea, when I sent the gift, that the party or the gift would be written up in a national magazine. John Cruikshank called me and suggested that a note to you might be appropriate. I hope this note will assist in clarifying things.

Sincerely,
Rosemary Sexton

As I wrote the letter I realized that this was probably the beginning of the end for me at the *Globe,* but I'd had a good run and I had nothing to complain about. I had sent the dart board with my eyes wide open to the possible repercussions. If I were supporting myself or my family, or indeed if I were still keen about my job, I would not have risked my job over a joke, but I wasn't any of those things.

January 30, 1992
Handed out hot dogs at Shopsy's on Front Street today at noon to raise money for Variety Village and to give me a story for a column.

I picked up Stephanie at Global Television where she works and we parked in the O'Keefe Centre driveway so she could hobble across the street on her crutches (she'd hurt her knee in a skiing accident) to help me. Although it was cold and breezy outside, the barbecue coals were hot and the customers were friendly.

Les Miz star Michael Burgess worked a shift, as did comedian Dave Broadfoot, as funny in person as he is onstage. Lieutenant Governor Hal Jackman came without his red carpet. CFRB's Dick Smyth may have a second career as short-order cook. Shirley Solomon exchanged her bright red coat for a yellow apron. Diane Dupuy's mother Mary Thornton dished out hot dogs, as did Mayor June Rowlands. June said that she and David Greenspan have not dated for two years, ever since he decided, at his mother's urging, it was time to have a child. "Has he become a father, then?" I asked. "No, not yet," was the reply. Sixties pop star Bobby Curtola also helped out.

February 1992

Got a call from Michael Bate at *Frank* magazine asking if I'd heard anything about Peter Mansbridge and Wendy Mesley splitting up. Apparently Wendy had a fling with a soundman who was living with Jennifer Westaway, who kicked him out when she found out, and in retaliation Peter asked out Cynthia Dale, who plays Olivia on "Street Legal." *Frank* wants to run a cover story but can't corroborate it. The magazine ended up running a cover story asking the question: Is there a split-up between Mesley and Mansbridge?

Michael Bate has called me about three times in the past two weeks. I have a feeling that he's heard about the requested apology from John Cruikshank, and he's trying to get me to talk about it. Edgar inadvertently let the cat out of the bag to Geoff Stevens, when he told Geoff about my conversation with Cruikshank at a recent Canadian Club luncheon where Yves Fortier spoke and Edgar was at the head table.

Overhearing Edgar's conversation with Geoff, I chided him afterward that I didn't want anyone to know about the requested letter of apology, because I was afraid that it might end up in *Frank* and then I would be blamed. Then you better call up Geoff and tell him that, said Edgar, so I did. I'd be fired for sure if that was written up, because only John Cruikshank and I were privy to the conversation demanding a letter of apology. Not that I'm not going to end up being fired, anyway, but I might as well make it later than sooner.

February 26, 1992

Chatted with television personality Micki Moore today. She doesn't have her show anymore, but she's writing profiles for the *Sun*. She's a workaholic, she says. Even when she and her husband Leonard Simpson, chairman of Town Shoes, go to their vacation place on Williamsburg Island off the coast of Florida, she looks for work. She owns two houses on Woodlawn Avenue West, which I'm doing a column on. She first moved onto the street because, as a divorced working mother of two, she got tired of driving into the city every time an audition or television stint came up. When she and Leonard got together, she bought a bigger house on the street from Edmund Meredith of Martin and Meredith. So now they own both 28 and 58.

I first met Micki when we danced and lip-synched at a Variety Village fund-raiser. I had missed all the rehearsals, so she quickly taught me the steps a few minutes before we had to go on stage.

April 1992

I'm neglecting my diary, because my book is taking all my time. I barely have time to do my column. I have set the month of June as a deadline for finishing the book, because I want it out of the way before we go to the cottage. And I have to try to keep up my columns, at least until the book's out, so that potential book-buyers don't forget who I am.

June 1992

In mid-June, Conrad Black served divorce papers on his wife Joanna. The oldest son, Jonathan, who is a 14-year-old student at Lakefield College, was so upset that he went out and got drunk. Up till now Joanna had maintained a devil-may-care facade about all of this. But the serving of the divorce papers apparently upset her very much. She has a relationship with a priest, and she has rented a house in Nova Scotia for the summer to be with him.

Several days after serving the papers Conrad held Hollinger's sixty-first annual dinner at the Toronto Club with Richard Nixon as the guest of honour. He had invited Nixon in 1990, but he had declined due to ill health and had been replaced by Lord Carrington.

A bit bored with the Black-Amiel shenanigans, I had decided not to try to find out about the Hollinger dinner. I had reported it last year. Also, I'd heard through the grapevine that Conrad was very upset with the news piece I wrote recently for the *Globe* talking about the separation (even though he had cooperated at the time) and that he had called Bill Thorsell to complain about it. I halfheartedly put in a call to the office of Joan Avirovic, Black's secretary. She was out and I left my name, though I really didn't expect a return call. I then called John Fraser, the editor of *Saturday Night*, and asked him if I might give him a call about the dinner the next morning if I decided to do a column on it. "Sure," he said, "but you'll have to catch me before noon because I'm flying out to Vancouver."

An hour later that day, our phone lines and those of our neighbours went out. It was a cable problem and was not fixed until noon the next day. To me it was a solution to my indecision about the Black dinner. I wasn't able to catch John Fraser before his flight and Joan Avirovic wasn't able to call me, even if she had wanted to. I breathed a sigh of relief and wrote up another column for Saturday on a fireworks display and sail past in Toronto Harbour for Canada Day.

At that point I got a call from Bud Jorgenson, who writes a thrice-weekly business column for the Report on Business section. "Rosemary, have you heard any scuttlebutt about the Hollinger dinner?" he asked. "No, Bud, I've decided not to do it," I said. "Are you going to do something?" "I might," he answered. Bud had helped me in the past and I felt I owed him one. In fact, he and I had worked together on the news piece on the Black separation, but he hadn't gotten any credit for it. Only my name had appeared as the byline; unbeknownst to me, Bud had removed his, saying I had done all the digging. "Would you like me to give Conrad's secretary a call and see what I can find out for you?" I asked him. "Yes, please," he said.

I called Joan Avirovic. As soon as she heard my name her tone became quite rude. "Rosemary Sexton?" she said. "I didn't return your call because I've been instructed not to." "May I ask why?" I inquired. "Mr. Black was very angry at your write-up in the paper several months ago." "I'm sorry he feels that way," I said. She answered, "He still hasn't gotten over what you wrote, and I have been told not to speak with you in particular, nor to send you any information." This was certainly a far different response than the one I had gotten last year re the Hollinger dinner. Then I had been sent, unsolicited, the complete list of the tables and who was sitting with whom. I quickly said goodbye and left a message on Bud's answering machine as to what had transpired. I wasn't too surprised by the rudeness of Black's secretary, because I knew how sensitive Conrad Black was about any write-ups in the press that didn't go his way.

But later on that day, thinking over the call, I got annoyed. Conrad Black was a press baron—he knew perfectly well that I was just doing my job. He had dished out enough insults to others that he should be able to take them himself without having to take petty revenge on me. In my opinion he was acting like a spoiled child who kicks and screams when he doesn't get his own way.

September 1992
In late September a gala was held in Toronto to raise funds for the United Nations Association in Canada hosted by Rogers Communications head Ted Rogers and his wife, Loretta, and Burns Fry chairman Jack Lawrence and his wife, Janice. With guests of honour including the Mulroneys and Boutras Boutras-Ghali, the secretary general of the United Nations, and with a star-studded list of committee members including Liz Tory, Marlene DelZotto, ex-premier David Peterson and restaurant entrepreneur John Bitove, and with tickets costing $1,000 a couple, it was expected that it would turn out to be one of the most successful fund-raisers of the fall social season. Instead, the evening turned out to be a comedy of errors.

Invitations were printed saying the evening was going to be held "in the presence of Brian Mulroney and his wife Mila." But the only assurance the hosts had gotten that Mulroney was coming was that Jack Lawrence had called Hugh Segal, who had promised to do his best to get Mulroney to the gala. As those experienced in the party-going circuit well know, that meant little or nothing. After the Mulroneys, the next absentee turned out to be Boutras Boutras-Ghali, who, upon receiving the invitation with Brian Mulroney on the letterhead, made it clear he had no intention of coming. It was speculated that he still hadn't forgotten that it was Mulroney who had made a big play for his job the previous year. So the main guests of honour, both of whom were printed on the ticket, were already no-shows weeks before the gala was to take place.

The next problem that occurred was that, about a month before the party, Ted Rogers underwent an emergency heart bypass that greatly incapacitated him. But he didn't want to renege on a commitment, so he reserved a room at the Four Seasons Hotel, where the gala was taking place, that he could retire to if he got overtired. However, as the date approached, it became clear that Ted Rogers was not going to be able to attend at all. Complications from the bypass settled in and he ended up back at the Mayo Clinic. His son valiantly filled in, standing up to make a brave speech in front of the assembled guests despite a slight stammer. To add insult to injury, Ken Taylor, the former Canadian ambassador to Iran who hid U.S. Embassy employees from the Iranians, was a last-minute cancellation, though he and his wife, Pat, had also been featured as celebrity guests.

The speeches took forever. It was close to ten o'clock before dinner was served. Just another black-tie night out in high society Toronto. Gerald Durrell was right (see start of chapter).

October 1992
Missed the launch party for Charlie Pachter's new coffee table book. I had to pick up my mother at the train station as she was arriving for Thanksgiving weekend. I sent down a column instead on John Lauer's getting fired as president of Cartier Canada, which the *Globe* ran as a front-page story. So I was glad I hadn't done the Pachter party. Stephen Godfrey attended on behalf of the *Globe* and reported it for "Noises Off." Apparently, 2,000 crowded into the RPM nightclub down on Queen's Quay, which owner Neil

Vosburgh donated for the event. The party was officially opened by Hal Jackman, who had to go onstage with drag queens and Queen Elizabeth and Diana lookalikes. Also a man in a moose suit who curtseyed to the Queen.

October 13, 1992

Paul Godfrey and John Turner held a party at Sutton Place Hotel's Stop 33 in honour of Alan Eagleson. The purpose of the party was to show Eagleson that his friends were still onside despite the FBI investigation proceeding against him in Boston. The invitation came from the office of John Turner and read as follows:

> No one has done more for hockey in Canada or represented our country better in the hockey world than Alan Eagleson. We are hosting a small dinner for Alan to thank him and to show our friendship for him.
>
> Your hosts, John N. Turner and Paul V. Godfrey

The evening commenced with cocktails at 6:30 p.m., followed by dinner at Stop 33 on top of the Sutton Place. Dress was black-tie. Speeches were limited to fifteen minutes.

Doug Creighton was a no-show, not unexpected since he and Godfrey are engaged in a power struggle over who is running the *Sun*; those who came included hockey coach Mike Keenan, foundation head Don Rickerd and hotelier Hans Gerhardt.

November 1992

Talked to Bud Jorgenson today. He was at home with a cold, but he was also hiding out from *Globe and Mail* editor-in-chief William Thorsell and ROB editor Peggy Wente. In the past few weeks Bud had been writing critical columns on Royal Trustco, suggesting the company was paying out too many dividends and implying that it might be in trouble. As a result, Royal Trustco chairman Hart MacDougall and president Bill Inwood, who had just succeeded ousted president Michael Cornelissen, had popped into the *Globe* to see Thorsell and complain. After the meeting Thorsell spoke to Peggy Wente, who approached Bud.

The conversation went something like this. "Cool it, Bud," Wente said. "We don't want to see any more columns on Royal

Trustco in the *Globe*." "But Peggy," protested Bud, "I've already got more in the works." "No, Bud," answered Peggy, "no more columns on Royal Trustco." Bud, disobeying her, went ahead and filed another one, anyway, on a day when Peggy was out of town. It's probably the beginning of the end for him, too, at the *Globe*, and I think he senses it.

November 7, 1992
The *Globe* pulled out all the stops for a farewell party for Roy Megarry held tonight at a large recording studio. Several weeks before the party, notices were put up on the *Globe and Mail* bulletin board that the theme would be country and western, and appropriate clothing and gear could be rented at a certain place with a phone number accompanying the notice. But obviously not everyone was comfortable with this suggestion, because one week later another notice went up on the wall that employees could come as they wished.

Over 1,000 people turned up at the cavernous space. The party started at six and went till midnight. An enormous Movenpick buffet was on hand. Entertainment was provided by Michelle Wright and Prairie Oyster. As guests entered the party, they were given a bandanna to don; as they left, they were handed a cactus.

At one point in the centre of the room a group of dancing girls in pink spandex kicked up their legs, much to the dismay of the feminist female reporters on the scene.

The lighting on the dance floor was quite spectacular. At one point the letters G-L-O-B-E A-N-D M-A-I-L were brightly spelled out.

David Clark, Megarry's successor, did not go, but Mike Soliman did. Thorsell was the master of ceremonies and former Ontario premier Bill Davis, a curious choice, made the presentation of a mountain bike, chosen because Megarry had told Jorgenson that he wanted to take up biking again in his retirement. Roy Megarry said he was a very happy man, and then he said, I know how you get everyone to love you—you leave.

Such a lavish display of spending on the part of the Thomson organization was so uncommon that most of the talk the next day down at the paper centred on the cost of the extravaganza, which some estimated to be upward of $150,000. Cost-cutting doesn't seem to be a factor for the Thomson organization when a good-bye party is given for a loyal henchman.

November 1992
Liz Tory commissioned paintings of Trevor Eyton's and John Bitove's cottages to be presented at their annual joint party in Florida this January. The two hosts should get something back from their guests, she said, because it's a wonderful luncheon buffet.

She asked artist Bruce Steinhoff to do the paintings, because his work has a nice Group of Seven look and he often paints scenes of Georgian Bay. The Torys and TD Bank chairman Dick Thomson and his wife Heather both have Steinhoffs hanging in their houses. Liz went over the Christmas party's guest list and asked for contributions only from those couples who had gone to at least three annual parties. There were 27 of them. Most said yes right away, but she had to chase down the Grafsteins. Liz finally said to Carole: "I don't care if you give, but I don't want you to feel badly at the party when the presents are presented and yours and Jerry's names are left off." Carole handed over the cheque.

But Monty Black said no and so did Steve Stavro—he and Bitove are first cousins and there's supposed to be some competition there.

Unfortunately, the artist didn't exactly take to John Bitove's house, which is about 13,000 square feet and ultramodern with fake turrets. When Liz drove down to Roberts Gallery on Yonge Street to pick up the commissioned paintings, she couldn't believe her eyes. The painting of the Bitove's place was a wonderful depiction of Georgian Bay with a tiny rendition of the monstrous house—"sitting like bird poop," observed Liz in her usual salty vernacular—right in the middle of the picture. If the Bitoves noticed anything amiss when the presentation was made, they politely refrained from commenting.

December 1992
The floor of my son's bedroom (where I hide out to work because it's upstairs, and couriers and other drop-in guests can't

see me through the downstairs windows) is littered with Christmas party invitations—to Dan Aykroyd's father's book launch, to Macmillan Canada's Xmas party, to a benefit carol singing for Anglican Houses featuring singer Sylvia Tyson, to Gino Empry's annual bash complete with ethnic Greek dancers and girls from the Klondike Follies doing the can-can, to Dr. Ken Walker (alias Dr. Gifford-Jones) and his wife Sue's posh affair at the University Club, to the Canadian Women's Club Christmas luncheon with Mike Duffy as guest speaker—the list goes on and on.

Since I have to hold three parties of my own (one this week for the litigation department of Osler Hoskin for about 55 people, one next week for relatives and friends for about 150 people, and one the next week for Edgar's family), I really don't have time to go to anyone else's, but there are two that I will say yes to—one at Robert Dirstein's opulently decorated condo at 1 Chestnut Park, which is featured on this month's cover of *Architectural Digest*, and a luncheon given by Catherine Nugent at SkyDome's Founders Club. Since I started my column, Catherine has always been help-ful to me, and I felt I should attend.

I was glad I did, if only to be reminded for a few short hours of the immense time, money and effort that the glitter girls put into their parties. I drove my Jeep up to Gate 9 of SkyDome, where a valet whisked it away. Catherine's mother, Peggy Mackenzie, was in the lobby, though I failed to recognize her at first, as she was leaning on a cane due to a bout of arthritis. Together we took the elevator up to the Founders Club.

At the top we were serenaded by an accórdionist playing Christmas carols and offered drinks. Already seated on the leather couches and chairs in the area outside the private room were Marlene DelZotto in a tailored grey suit; Odette Ambar in elegant black; Trudy Bundy in one of her fabulous broad-brimmed hats; Yvonne Alexander in demure grey plaid; Saundra Mann in a black wool suit topped with a wide-brimmed black hat; Susan Cohon in apricot; and Carole Grafstein, also in a black suit.

Arriving after Peggy and me were Daniela Bruns in blue plaid with a royal blue pillbox; Adrian MacDonald in black and gold; Nancy Paul in a brown fur hat and black suit; and Cathie Bratty in shimmering black and silver décolletage and an enormous black fur hat.

Anna Maria de Souza whispered to Catherine's mother that she had been terrified that Catherine was going to invite Jacquie Latimer, Anna Maria's co-chair at this year's Brazilian Ball, to whom she was no longer speaking. She needn't have worried; Jacquie was not invited.

Most of the guests had champagne and nibbled on hot stuffed shrimps before we made our way to the dining room. "Pick your seats carefully," Catherine warned us. "There's a wrapped present from Tiffany's at each place setting, and they're all different." Catherine told me later that she had called up Tiffany's and asked the store to find sixteen different presents, at $65 each, and send them over. The gifts were exquisite, ranging from ice buckets to glasses to sterling silver key rings.

The lunch consisted of succulent rare duck and vinaigrette leaf greens, followed by roast chicken and scalloped potatoes and finally a delicious crème brulée with fresh fruit and a treacle sculpture in the shape of a dome overtop. Evian and Perrier water and white and red wine were served as well, and cappuccino later.

As the chatter wound down, Carole Grafstein, who was seated next to Catherine (Anna Maria was on the other side and Cathie Bratty and Nancy Paul were next to them; Catherine's mother and I sat at the foot of the oblong table), got up to speak. "I want everyone to say a few words about Catherine, and I'll go around the room and single you out." "I'm going to kill Carole for doing this," mumbled Saundra Mann, but despite her nervousness, she did very well. Adrian Macdonald reminisced about the time she and Donald held a party for Catherine and David in London to launch Alfred Sung perfume there. Anna Maria described a hair-raising ride she and Catherine had in a little stick-shift sports car when Catherine was nine months' pregnant with Johnathon.

I got up last to say that I was saving my favourite stories of Catherine for my upcoming book. They all laughed politely, but I'm sure they're wondering what's in store for them. They shouldn't be too worried. I'm doing my best to be fair, and, by and large, I think the portraits that emerge are flattering ones, though I have inserted a few barbs here and there.

December 16, 1992

K. C. Irving died on Sunday morning at 2:00 a.m. We were telephoned in Brockville, and Edgar flew out yesterday for the funeral. The church where the funeral was held was packed to the
rafters. People filled the basement and lined up out in the streets
for blocks. I would like to have attended the memorial service to
pay my respects, but my family Christmas party is tomorrow night.
We are expecting 150, and, to cut costs, I haven't hired caterers this
year, so I have too much to do. Last week we held the Osler
Hoskin litigation party at our house. But tomorrow night's will be
harder without caterers.

January 1993

It's the New Year and a lot of things have been happening. First of
all, as of Wednesday, January 6, I am no longer writing my column
for the *Globe and Mail*. John Cruikshank called last Wednesday and
said they would be discontinuing the column, but that they are
going to run a political gossip piece several times a week. If you
would contribute some items to it, Rosemary, he said, we will pay
you your full salary. I thanked him very much for the offer, said I
would consider it and get back to him, put down the phone and
jumped for joy. I had promised both my husband and my book
publisher not to quit my column, but now that decision had been
taken out of my hands.

A few hours later, Paul Godfrey called. He was just boarding a
plane in Calgary and had a few minutes to spare at the airport, and
he was calling to thank me for the letter I'd sent him congratulating
him on his elevation to CEO of the *Toronto Sun*. I told him about
my conversation with John Cruikshank, and he said, "Rosemary,
you can write a column for the *Sun* anytime." "Thanks, Paul," I said,
grateful for the offer, "but I don't want to do a column anymore."

Nora McCabe also called that day and said that the *Sunday Star*
might be interested. Mildred Istona, the editor of *Chatelaine,* took
me to lunch, and Stevie Cameron said that *Toronto Life* would be
interested in me. I was happy to have people make these offers, but
I really just want to finish my book and, if that is successful, get
going on another book as soon as possible. That way my time is my
own and I don't have to dance to anyone's schedule.

January 11, 1993

Took Anna Maria de Souza, Father Charles Farnsworth and Dan Ortolani from Grenville Christian College for lunch at Il Posto, trying to nail down a deal between Anna Maria and Grenville Christian College, from which the college would get future Brazilian Ball proceeds. At the next table sat Hugh Segal, waiting for Barbara McDougall and Major General Lewis Mackenzie. We kibitzed back and forth, and I introduced my tablemates to Hughie as he sat alone because he had arrived early. Part way through the lunch I went over to the table to talk to Barbara and be introduced to Lewis Mackenzie, whom I'd never met. At the luncheon we firmed up the deal with Anna and Grenville. As long as I was writing for the *Globe*, I couldn't do any fund-raising because of the potential conflict of interest. It's refreshing to be back in the real world, putting together fund-raising deals instead of just writing about them.

January 12, 1993

Suanne Kelman, who is writing the new political gossip column for the *Globe*, called today. "Rosemary, do you have any tidbits you can feed me?" she asked. "I have a phone set up here but no one is calling." "I'll see what I can do," I promised. "Don't worry, Suanne, in about a month you'll have more than you can handle."

January 13, 1993

I called Suanne with an item she could use in the morning. Also talked to Stevie Cameron about my column being discontinued. I hope they're not doing the same to me, she said.

Also talked to Bud Jorgenson, who said that the name of the new gossip column is to be "On Dit." As of mid-January, one week before it was to come to press, focus groups investigating it decided that the name was no good and they were scrambling to change the name before Monday. (The name finally decided on was "Tattler.")

Even though I feel like a black cloud has been lifted from my head with my column gone, I still wonder if I will miss its advantages. I know for sure I won't miss the going to parties and the writing of the column, but I might miss the perqs that went with it, i.e., the clout and the profile that it gave me. One thing that cheered me up immeasurably was the kindness of the people I talked to after the news got around. Catherine Nugent and Allan Fotheringham invited me out to lunch on the spot, both of them probably insightful enough to know that I might be feeling a bit insecure.

One of the reasons I feel so good these days, besides the demise of my column, is that I now have time to do things for me—such as exercise, which I really missed sitting at a computer all day. I've taken up roller-blading, which I love, though I'm a complete klutz at it.

Once I finish *The Glitter Girls*, I feel I'll be ready to start a new phase of my life. I can hardly believe I have reached this stage. The years seem to have flown by. Stephanie and Robin are mostly grown up now, and they're really good kids, so I don't have them to worry about. I'm looking forward to a life where I read, look after my houses, golf and roller-blade in the summer, cross-country ski and ice skate in the winter, travel with my husband, and spend time with my children and stepchildren. I want these years to be really good ones, perhaps my best ones, and I'm going to work hard to make them so.

Part Two

The Globe and Mail Years

Chapter Five

Fear and Loathing at The Globe and Mail

The paper Marcia writes for is housed in a bland, square, glass-walled, windowless building, put up sometime in the seventies, when airlessness was all the rage. Despite its uninformative exterior, Marcia finds this building sinister, but that may be because she knows what goes on inside it.

The paper is called, somewhat grandiosely, the *World*. It is a national institution of sorts, and, like many other national institutions these days, it is falling apart. . . . The *World* stood for something once, or so she likes to believe. It had integrity, or at least more integrity than it does now. You could trust it to have principles, to attempt fairness. Now the best you can say of it is that it has a fine tradition behind it, and has seen better days.

Better in some ways, worse in others. For instance, by cutting its staff and tailoring itself for the business community, it is now making more money. It has recently been placed under new management, which includes the editor, a man called Ian Emmiry. Ian Emmiry was promoted suddenly over the heads of his elders and seniors, while the unsuspecting former editor was on vacation. The event was staged like a military coup in one of the hotter, seedier nations. It was almost like having a chauffeur promoted to general as the result of some hidden affiliation or payoff, and has been resented as such.

The journalists who have been there a long time refer to Ian Emmiry as Ian the Terrible, but not in front of the incoming bunch: Ian the Terrible has his spies. There are fewer and fewer of the older journalists and more and more of the newer ones, handpicked by Ian for their ability to nod. A slow transformation is going on, a slow purge. . . .

—from Margaret Atwood's "Hack Wednesday,"
Wilderness Tips, McClelland & Stewart, 1991

Changing of the Guard

To have the chance to work for the *Globe and Mail* was a privilege in itself. But to work there during the years from 1988 to 1993 was a real learning experience. Not only did I work under two of Canada's premier newsmen, but I ended up, by virtue of the timing of my employment, to be around during some of the *Globe's* most interesting and turbulent years.

On Boxing Day of 1988, Norman Webster was in his office tidying up things before he and his managing editor Geoffrey Stevens were to leave on a month's visit of the paper's foreign bureaus. At publisher Roy Megarry's request, Webster dropped by Megarry's office for what he thought would be a pleasant chat. Never one to beat around the bush, Megarry got straight to the point. He had called Webster in to fire him. Several weeks later, he would give the boot to Geoff Stevens as well. Their jobs would be taken over by William Thorsell, an editorial writer, and Tim Pritchard, a Report on Business reporter. Over the next year there was a mass exodus of most of the best and brightest at the paper, some voluntarily, others not.

A few weeks after it was reported in the *Globe and Mail* that Roy Megarry had asked editor Norman Webster to step down, many *Globe* employees received invitations in the mail for a going-away party to be held for Norman Webster at the Rosedale home of Famous Players head Nat Taylor and his wife, Claire. Claire Drainie Taylor was the mother of Bronwyn Drainie, a freelance

writer who was married at the time to Patrick Martin, then editor of the Focus section, which appeared in Saturday's *Globe*.
Patrick Martin had created quite a stir around the *Globe*'s offices
when, upon hearing that William Thorsell was Megarry's choice of
replacement as editor, he sent a bouquet of balloons to his office.

What might have been described as a turncoat act by some
would become a presage of the actions of the majority of *Globe*
employees. Seeing the writing on the wall, seemingly without
much compunction or any attempt at loyalty, they quickly
switched their allegiance to the incoming group. (Two notable
exceptions were columnists Michael Valpy, who wrote a column
decrying the firings, and Jeffrey Simpson, who said openly he was
troubled by the ruthlessness of the sackings.)

No doubt there were a number of justifications for the *Globe*
employees' behaviour. First and foremost was their own survival at
the paper, which had to be their main concern. In addition, they
had experienced similar abrupt changes of the guard before this.
Newspapers' managements are notoriously unstable. As a result,
journalists are invariably subject to numerous staff turnovers.
When Webster and Stevens had ascended to their positions of
power in 1983, then editor-in-chief Richard Doyle and managing
editor Cameron Smith had been unceremoniously turfed out to
make room for them.

As with many regimes in power for a while, Webster and
Stevens were not universally popular; they had their detractors as
well as their supporters. Both had excellent reputations as newsmen and journalists; their public relations abilities were less well-
honed. Concentrating on getting out a good paper, they often
ignored administrative or personnel problems that needed to be
dealt with, their own eroding relationship with the publisher
being a case in point. Norman Webster was considered by his staff
to be aloof; Geoff Stevens was said to play favourites. (Actually it
was true, Geoff Stevens did play favourites. His favourites were
not those who kowtowed to him; they were those on his staff
whom he considered the best reporters and columnists.)

Norman Webster was a slim, bespectacled academic who had
been a Rhodes scholar. He did not suffer fools gladly. He was the
nephew of Montreal businessman and multimillionaire Howard

Webster, who had owned the *Globe* for several decades before selling it to Ken Thomson★. As one of the beneficiaries of the Webster
family fortune, Norman, born and bred in Montreal, was well-
heeled. He and his wife Pat (short for Paterson), a native Virginian,
had five children. Both Pat and Norman were fluently bilingual,
and she was active in promoting the French language in Ontario.

Since coming home from England, where he was attending
Oxford as a Rhodes scholar, Norman Webster had risen rapidly
through the ranks of the *Globe and Mail* on his own merit until he
was appointed editor in 1983. In the process, he won two newspaper awards. But although he lived and breathed newspapers, he
didn't pay too much attention to personnel problems when they
occurred. He spent most of the day closeted in his large office
thinking about the newspaper itself. He had another characteristic
that was to prove even more injurious to him. That was his will-
ingness as an editor to stand up to the newspaper's publisher when
it came to important decisions concerning the paper.

Editors and publishers of newspapers are traditionally at odds
with each other. It is the publisher's job to see that the paper is
making money, whereas it is the editor's job to make sure he or
she is printing the best and most up-to-date news. When a newspaper is operating at its full potential, those two aims should ideally
coincide. The better the paper is, the more money it should make.
But there are often factors that cut into this merging of aims. For
example, to have the best paper, the editor may need to spend
some money to pay good people or to open foreign bureaus. But
from a publisher's point of view, the costs involved in sprucing up
the editorial content may not be worth it. A publisher may feel,
for example, that it's more important to hire an extra ad salesman
or two instead of a foreign correspondent.

★Webster bought the *Globe* in 1955 with money from a family foundation started by his father, Senator Lorne Webster who, according to former *Globe* editor-
in-chief Richard Doyle, had made a fortune in coal, steamships, railways, insurance, sugar, furs and steel. In 1965 the *Globe* and FP Publications merged,
through an exchange of shares between Webster and FP. FP was a group of
newspapers, the *Victoria Times*, the *Colonist*, the *Vancouver Sun*, the *Lethbridge
Herald*, the *Winnipeg Free Press* and the *Ottawa Journal*, owned by Richard
Malone, Max Bell and John Sifton.

Webster and Megarry represented the two extremes of editor and publisher, so sparks were bound to fly. To Webster, the editorial content was sacrosanct and the publisher should not be able to interfere. To Megarry, if the paper couldn't turn a good profit, there wasn't much point in its existing. Compounding their problem was the fact that Megarry's ultimate boss was none other than Kenneth, Lord Thomson of Fleet, well-known in the business world for his cost-cutting techniques and thrifty ways. Many people believed that all Thomson cared about was the bottom line, and if he had to milk the *Globe* dry to produce better profits, he would do so. As one of the richest men in Canada and the owner of a conglomerate that included all sorts of businesses, Ken Thomson was not going to change his thrifty practices just for *The Globe and Mail*. A real chip off the old block, he had learned his lessons well from his father, Roy Thomson.

It was unlikely that Ken Thomson even read what many regarded as Canada's finest newspaper, even though he owned it. People who know him say that when he reads it at all, it is the sports pages that he turns to. Ironically, even those pages would become victim to the cost-cutting and extreme bloodletting that would characterize the new regime at the *Globe*.

Farewell Party for Norman Webster

But back to the party. Although it was billed as a going-away party for Norman Webster, the whole evening felt more like a wake. About a hundred people gathered, most from the *Globe*. Many clustered together in groups and whispered in corners. So far, Norman Webster had been the only casualty. Who would be next? It was generally assumed that it would be Geoffrey Stevens, as he and Norman Webster had worked so closely together. In fact, it had been a dispute between Stevens and Megarry over the hiring of writer Barbara Yaffe that had precipitated Megarry's final falling out with Webster and Stevens, though many said that, because of the philosophical differences between publisher Megarry and editors Webster and Stevens, and because of the Thomson Corporation's heavy hand in the cost-cutting department, the writing had been on the wall for some time.

Stephen Lewis and his wife Michele Landsberg dropped in to pay their respects to Norman. Michele had written a column for the *Globe* a year earlier, cabling back her impressions of New York, when Stephen became ambassador to the United Nations. Michele told me that she would not be writing for the *Globe* anymore, but didn't mention her new column soon to be starting at the *Star.*

John Sewell and his companion Charlotte Sykes also came to say goodbye to Norman. John mentioned that he missed writing his city column at the *Globe.*

John Fraser, editor of *Saturday Night*, and his wife, Elizabeth McCallum, who wrote a children's book column for the *Globe,* wandered separately through the various rooms of the large house. The dapper, bow-tied Fraser, always up on the latest gossip, wrote different columns over the years for the *Globe*, including its theatre and dance column. In some ways he was getting a kick out of all these goings-on. In the turbulent weeks to come, he would visit the *Globe* offices, sniffing out any and all possibilities that might be available in the spaces that would increasingly be left by departing *Globe* employees.

Outsiders who attended included then *Toronto Life* publisher Peter Herrndorf, who would later comment that he thought these things only happened at the CBC, and lawyer and civil rights activist Clayton Ruby, an occasional columnist for the paper, who was no doubt wondering how right wing the new administration was going to be.

Deputy managing editor Shirley Sharzer, who also ran the features side of the paper and who would be the next head to roll after Stevens, was busy reassuring all the nervous and jumpy *Globe* employees she had mothered over the years. Sports editor Dave Langford, with his black curly hair and perennial tan, as much out of place in the midst of his intellectual-looking cohorts as anyone, chatted up fashion reporter Beverley Bowen, who would soon move over to the *Star* as assistant city editor.

Stevie Cameron worked the room, catching what whispers she could and saving them up. A political columnist for the *Globe*, she would depart to work for a short time for CBC's "Fifth Estate" before coming back in the fall of 1991 as a weekly freelance columnist, publishing her enormous political best-seller, *On the Take*, in the fall of 1994.

For those unaware that the decision to leave was not his (and there were few of those still around), Norman Webster's words to the assembled crowd made it very clear that he had been pushed out.

Just before Norman began to speak, my husband, sensing that this was the time to escape, ran to get our coats. Fortunately, Ottawa columnist Jeffrey Simpson caught sight of us trying to sneak out. "I hope you're not leaving before Norman makes his speech," he admonished. "There will be some startling revelations coming out and you should be present to hear them." I was embarrassed that Jeff had caught me in mid-exit so early on in the evening, and I told my husband that I thought we should stay longer.

I wasn't sure what Jeff meant about the startling revelations, but I assumed he had concluded, as I had, that Geoff Stevens's head would be the next to roll. During his speech, Norman seemed close to tears and his voice broke several times. He described some of his past good times at the paper and mentioned some of the budding talent at the *Globe*, such as writer Jan Wong, who had flourished under him. He made it clear that he had not left the paper on his own initiative. "Like George Brown, I was shot from an unexpected quarter," he said, referring to *Globe and Mail* founder George Brown, who was shot by a disgruntled employee. No mention was made of Geoff Stevens.

As it turned out, Megarry, who several days previously had personally assured Stevens that his job was intact, had curtly fired Stevens several hours before the party. Even as Webster spoke to the crowd, Geoff Stevens was huddled in a corner with his assistant, Gwen Smith, whispering to her the devastating news.

The Rise and Fall of Geoffrey Stevens

When I saw Geoff Stevens in May 1991, for only the second time since his firing two years before, I was taken aback. A boyish-looking man with sandy brown hair and a youthful, impish demeanour, he had always kept himself in good shape by playing tennis or squash early every morning before going into the *Globe*. He had also been a dapper dresser, in contrast to some of the ink-stained wretches around the paper. But, instead of the fastidious managing editor I had worked for, on my doorstep stood a different man.

There were deep bags under his eyes, and his complexion was pasty white. He had also put on some weight. His hair was soaking wet and plastered flat down on his head from a just-completed game of tennis at Rosedale Park, which contributed to his changed appearance. During his visit I heard nary a complaint about the shoddy treatment he had received, but his spirits were low and he lacked his usual witty repartee.

I suppose I shouldn't have been surprised at the changes I saw in him. For almost 30 years *The Globe and Mail* had been his whole life, until with a resounding crash his world had caved in on him.

After graduating with an honours English and history degree from the University of Western Ontario, where he was editor of the school newspaper and president of the debating club, Stevens was hired by the *Globe* in 1962, where he steadily rose through the ranks. In 1981, at publisher Megarry's request, he entered into management, becoming national editor, sports editor and finally managing editor in October 1983.

Since his firing, he had been hired by the *Toronto Star* to write a weekly political column in the Sunday paper. He also taught a course in journalism at the University of Toronto. On his now-meagre salary, about half of the $110,000 he earned at the *Globe*, he was still supporting two children from his first marriage, who were both attending university. He and his companion, Lin Shannon, had just had a baby girl called Casey. Lin had also recently lost her job in the advertising department at *Toronto Life* due to cutbacks and was at home, baby-sitting Casey and a young cousin.

Soon after this episode, it was clear that Geoff had picked up the shattered pieces of his life and started anew. A year later, he had a new job, a new house and a new life. With the financial backing of Norman Webster, he started a newspaper in Florida, the *Sun Times*, for Canadians living down there. He also cowrote a book on backroom politics with John Laschinger, which became the subject of a cover story in *Maclean's* magazine.

Back in 1983, when Megarry had asked him to become managing editor, Stevens took the job on one condition, that he be responsible for the Report on Business section of the paper. He had been present on one occasion in 1981 when managing editor Ted Moser and ROB editor Ian Carman wrangled as to whether a story would go on the front page of the paper or whether ROB would get it for its front page, and Carman had won. Since ROB was the most successful part of the paper, its editor could override the managing editor, and Stevens wanted to make sure that that couldn't happen while he was managing editor.

Megarry acceded to Stevens's request. At this point, the publisher and his new editors were still in the trial stage of their relationship. But it was becoming clear that Megarry wanted more control over the editorial side of the paper. He was often heard to say that he felt that Oakley Dalglish, who had been editor-in-chief back in the late fifties, had had more control of the paper than he did. He resented what he thought to be his minimal effect on the editorial department.

Megarry was a bright guy, but for every bright idea he had, said Stevens after the firing, there were three that weren't so bright. "You know those trucks with governors? He's like a truck without a governor, and he will often charge into things that he shouldn't. He also lacks a background in journalism. That was OK as long as he stayed away from the editorial side. The publisher's job is making business decisions, not putting the newspaper together."

As the years went by, Megarry's intrusion into the editorial side of the newspaper increased. As his demands became more and more insistent, Webster and Stevens found it harder and harder to acquiesce to them. By way of an ultimatum to his two obstreperous editors, Megarry wrote a memo in August 1988, outlining his plans for the paper. These included elevating the editor of the ROB to a position at least the equal of the managing editor and downsizing the news side of the paper, as well as massive staff cuts.

But foreshadowing or even precipitating the dreaded memo, the Barbara Yaffe debacle blew up in everyone's face several months earlier that year.

The Barbara Yaffe Incident

Barbara Yaffe was a former full-time employee of the *Globe* who moved to Newfoundland, where Stevens, with Webster's OK, hired her as a freelancer. Stevens thought she was a good reporter; Megarry didn't like her, considering her antibusiness. She also had an abrasive manner. Megarry tried to reduce her payments after John Hustler of the business office had written a memo asking what a stringer in Newfoundland was doing making $40,000 a year. But good coverage in Newfoundland helps sell papers everywhere and Stevens balked at Megarry's request. Finally Megarry ordered Stevens to cut Yaffe as a freelancer. She went to Newfoundland's *Sunday Express* run by Michael Harris.

Stevens began quiet negotiations to get Yaffe back and ultimately hired her to go to Vancouver to work for the *Globe*. Megarry found out and ordered Stevens to get rid of her. Stevens tried to reason with him. "We can't fire Yaffe at this point," he said. "She has quit her job, sold her home and is in the process of buying a house in Vancouver." "That," answered Megarry, "is not my problem." When Stevens told Yaffe she no longer had the Vancouver job, she launched a lawsuit against the *Globe* and wrote to Thomson complaining about Megarry. (The lawsuit eventually settled with Yaffe accepting damages worth $67,500.)

There was a flurry of reaction about the whole affair from the public when it came to light. Stevens got calls and letters. Pierre Berton phoned him. "Aren't you going to resign over this?" he asked Stevens. But behind the scenes Stevens was still hoping that if things died down he could get Yaffe a job with *West* magazine in Vancouver, which had recently been started up by the *Globe*. However, after Ken Thomson had passed Yaffe's letter on to Megarry, Megarry refused to have Yaffe anywhere on the *Globe*'s payroll again.

Roy Megarry

The fifth of six children growing up in a neighbourhood of grinding poverty in West Belfast, Roy Megarry left school at 15, emigrating to Canada a few years later, where he took his C.A. at night school. He worked as a comptroller at several companies, then as a senior consultant at the predecessor company to Coopers & Lybrand. He was a vice-president of the Torstar Group when, in 1978, the *Globe*, then owned by FP Publications, hired him as publisher.

Under the Thomson administration, which took over in 1981, Megarry fast became an invaluable employee. When he was hired in 1978, the *Globe* was in trouble, and Megarry, in effect, revivified it. Some of his schemes were failures, but others were unqualified successes.

He developed his concept of the *Globe* as a truly national paper and convinced the Thomson board to construct five satellite printing plants to build a cross-country circulation base. He also expanded the *Globe's* correspondents both nationally and internationally.

His most significant contribution to the paper was in remodelling the business side, transforming it from a dinosaur into a model of efficiency. In ten years, from 1978 to 1988, the *Globe's* profits went up from $5 million to $20 million.

However, with the recession approaching and competition from the electronic media, revenues had started to drop. In order to please his superiors, Megarry had to find other means to continue to reap a respectable profit.

He started to reduce employees. He contracted out security, trucking and cleaning, the cafeteria, anything, so he could pay minimum instead of union wages. He eliminated the first national edition in order to shorten the hours of the press crew and get by with fewer pressmen.

And then he turned to editorial.

In his *Saturday Night* article on the *Globe's* restructuring, Michael Harris mentioned that a prominent businessperson complained to Ken Thomson about the *Globe's* persistent antibusiness bias. That person was Trevor Eyton. After that, Thomson exerted pressure to make the paper more conservative and business-oriented, which coincided with Megarry's own views.

Then came Megarry's memo to Webster and Stevens. Appalled at some of these proposed changes, and perhaps naively thinking that they could safely ignore or forestall such suggestions, Webster and Stevens began halfheartedly to do what was asked.

Their slowness to react to his mandate just reinforced Megarry's opinion that they had gotten out of hand and that the editorial side of the paper was too independent.

After the Yaffe incident, the battlelines were clearly drawn and it was only a matter of time before Webster and Stevens themselves would become casualties.

But there was some fallout for Megarry, too. Previously respected by the staff, he became feared and even disliked by some. Perhaps aware of this change of attitude toward him, he ceased his practice of coming across the hall into the newsroom to talk casually with reporters.

Rumours swirled around the *Globe's* offices about Megarry and Cecilia Modenesi, one of his advertising staff. Megarry had put her on the management committee at the *Globe* and then in charge of all of the *Globe's* advertising branch offices. Though up to then she was virtually an unknown advertising salesperson based in Vancouver, the offices in Montreal, Calgary, New York, London and Hong Kong reported to her and she reported to Megarry, often bypassing Mike Soliman, the *Globe's* head of advertising. She and Megarry travelled together on business jaunts.

Megarry was revealing other less-than-attractive qualities in a boss. He was excellent with his superiors, writing flattering memos, for example, to Thomson Corporation deputy chairman John Tory, at the same time treating those beneath him cavalierly. Staff turnover was incredible, especially on the management committee, the newspaper's executive body. Its meetings, held every couple of weeks, mainly consisted of Megarry telling everyone how right he was. He would hire employees, praise them to the skies for a time, and then just as quickly demote or fire them, making critical comments about them as they went out the revolving door. Megarry always had to have a fall guy when things went wrong.

Megarry was also determined to downgrade the managing editor's responsibilities. Stevens's successor, Tim Pritchard, neither sat on the management committee nor had any control over the Report on Business. It was Megarry's wish that the ROB have the same status as the rest of the paper and that the ROB editor have the same status as the managing editor, and, with Stevens out of the way, he made sure that that was done.

A few weeks after the firings, when I went down to the *Globe* for one of my infrequent visits, reporter Terry Christian beckoned to me. "Come here and look at this," he said, leading me to the large mahoghany-panelled office where I had first been interviewed by Geoff Stevens. I couldn't believe my eyes. It was as if a bulldozer had come in and razed the whole room. There was nothing left of the office but an enormous crater. I stood there thunderstruck. "So that's what happens when you disagree with Megarry," I said.

The symbolism was not lost on me. Anything to do with either Webster or Stevens was to be cut out from the *Globe* like an enormous cancer. It must have been a constant reminder to the staff remaining when they walked by that gaping hole every day that they, too, had better toe the line or they would quickly share the same fate. Even Stevens's washroom was gone; the new managing editor was to share the public washroom with everyone else. Megarry's order in the famous memo that the editor of the ROB have an office as least as large as the managing editor had been effected within weeks.

Rest in Peace

Within a year or two of the Webster-Stevens firing, scores of employees, many the best that the *Globe* had to offer, would be gone, either quitting in despair or just being let go because of disagreements with William Thorsell and his henchman John Cruikshank. For months copy editor Joan Danard kept an RIP list in her computer of all the people that had gone from the *Globe* since the Webster-Stevens firings. At one point there were 60 names on the list. That meant 60 people leaving from a base of 280 employees in editorial. And this was during a recession when other papers had put a freeze on hiring. In many cases, there was no place for these people to go.

Tim Pritchard had been immediately chosen by Bill Thorsell to step into Geoff Stevens's shoes to become managing editor. A low-key guy with a pleasant manner, who had worked as reporter for ROB, Pritchard was unfortunately not cut out for administration. He had a hard time making decisions. But he had one important characteristic for the job as it now existed—he was a yes man and did whatever he was told, essential in the new Megarry-Thorsell newsroom.

That same essential characteristic applied to John Cruikshank. He was first promoted to national editor under Thorsell and then given Pritchard's job when the latter resigned to go back to reporting; there were many comments made behind his back about how his head was about to fall off from his incessant nodding at everything Thorsell said.

Under the new administration, the labour beat was eliminated and Lorne Slotnick, the labour reporter, left to work for the newspaper guild. The page two columns were also abolished. When Geoffrey Stevens had become the *Globe's* managing editor, he livened up page two with a different column at the top of the page each day. June Callwood on various causes, Michele Landsberg on life in New York, a nostalgia column titled "Didn't You Used to Be?", Hugh Winsor and Stevie Cameron on politics, and Dr. Gifford-Jones on medical advice. When Michele Landsberg stopped because she was working on two books, Megarry said she was not to be replaced. Hugh's column was taken away from him; Dr. Gifford-Jones was also let go, the latter receiving a terse letter of dismissal in the mail after twelve years of working for the *Globe*. He now writes for the *Sun* and the *Financial Post*.

June Callwood quit before Roy Megarry could have the satisfaction of firing her. Megarry hated her column. "Why does June keep writing about the homeless," he once said, "when *Globe and Mail* readers all have homes?"

Respected left-wing columnists such as Tom Walkom and Judy Steed immediately saw the writing on the wall after the Webster-Stevens firings and went over to the *Toronto Star*, where they seem to be flourishing, but Michael Valpy stayed. He did so even though the day after the Webster sacking he wrote a column questioning the dismissal. Megarry, who happened to be in New York that day, heard from his secretary about the Valpy column and the calls supporting it that had come into the office as a result. Megarry cut short his trip, rushed home and made Thorsell the editor on the spot. (Ironically, Valpy, one of the best writers ever produced by the *Globe*, has outlasted Megarry, who in his 1988 memo had said, "We will eliminate the Valpy column.")

Deputy manager Shirley Sharzer, who had been at the paper for over a decade, was let go. She's now at Southam in Ottawa in charge of professional development. Gwen Smith, the senior woman in the *Globe's* editorial department, was given Shirley's position, except for features. Chris Waddell was made associate editor, a prestigious post that made him second-in-command to Thorsell and put him on the masthead of the paper.

But under the new regime Gwen would become demanding (Geoff Stevens had always managed to keep her under control, but Tim Pritchard gave in easily), and Chris Waddell locked himself in his office one day in a sulk, refusing to carry out Thorsell's commands. Eventually, Smith would leave to work at Geoffrey Stevens's *Sun Times*, and Waddell would emerge from his state of resigned inefficacy only when he was hired by the CBC.

City desk editor Paul Palango was given a rough ride by his new bosses and left to work for *Eye* magazine. A bit of a loose cannon, when sent to Montreal to look at certain aspects of the *Globe's* operations, he had written a report implying that the Thomson organization was guilty of restraint of trade. In his opinion, there was an unwritten agreement between the *Globe* and Southam not to compete. Megarry, not surprisingly, tore up the memo. But Palango knew a news story and how to go about getting it without owing any favours in the process. He was the driving force behind an investigation into York Region developers for which investigative reporters Jock Ferguson and Dawn King won a Michener award.

The *Globe's* news investigative team, which had won a lot of kudos for the paper*, was disbanded. Peter Moon was reallocated as a general assignment reporter; Victor Malarek and Stevie Cameron went to the "Fifth Estate"; Linda McQuaig was refused a leave of absence to write a book, so she quit to have a baby and write her own political best-seller, *The Quick and the Dead*, which came out in the fall of 1991. Except for an occasional freelance piece, Jock Ferguson no longer writes for the *Globe*.

The paper's Metro section was cut. Norman and Geoff had

---

*When Webster and Stevens ran the *Globe*, it won four Michener awards in five years.

hired John Sewell as a Metro columnist and added extra staff at city hall for more coverage of Toronto. Megarry decided that the section wasn't selling advertising and ordered it killed. Later, he ordered a downsizing of the previous city hall staff. So the *Globe* ended up covering municipal government with two people, down even from the sixties when four people covered the city beat.

Even before the departure of Webster and Stevens, Megarry had been pouring money into developing magazines for the *Globe*. Now, with no one around to oppose him, he proceeded to do so even more. His belief that magazines were a potential gold mine to be exploited grew out of the success of *Report on Business Magazine*, and he added several new ones to the *Globe*'s publications. But after a few years and a large outpouring of funds, it was clear that they had been an expensive failure. Four of the magazines were killed, effective Thursday, May 23, 1991. *Toronto* was launched in 1986, *Domino* was launched in 1987, *Montreal* was acquired in 1988, and *West* was launched in 1989.

It was at this point that people began to see the writing on the wall for Megarry himself. In December 1991, it was announced in the *Globe* that he had decided to leave the paper to pursue his interest in the Third World. (Although he had been an interim director for the Aga Khan Foundation and had worked on a project sending used machinery to Peru, observers were surprised that he would choose to make it his life's work.) He was, however, brought back to the *Globe* as an interim publisher for a year after his successor, David Clark, who had come from Campbell Soup, did not work out.

In January 1991 Peggy Wente became editor of Report on Business and subsequently was given a page two column once a week. Her column is well-written and controversial, but she seems to have real problems communicating with staff. When a survey was sent around to *Globe* employees in 1994 asking them to rate the managers, she came in very poorly. Roger Parkinson, who had by this time succeeded Dave Clark as publisher, told her to shape up or ship out.

By 1994, Bud Jorgenson had quit in disgust and Stevie Cameron, who had returned to the paper after a year at CBC's

"Fifth Estate," was shown the door, finally fulfilling Megarry's mandate in his 1988 memo that their columns be axed. Tim Pritchard moved over to the *Financial Post* to become managing editor in January 1995, at about the same time as Bud became the *Post's* daily bond columnist.

Sports

Perhaps the most unpopular move made by the Thorsell team was to reduce the *Globe's* sports pages. It happened this way.

The budget process for the *Globe* usually occurs in September, but, for 1990, Ken Thomson wanted budgets completed early, so at his request they were begun in July 1989, and by September 1989 were approved. The sports department with its staff of 24 came in at $2 million.

Everything seemed to be rolling along nicely until one Wednesday in December when managing editor Tim Pritchard approached sports editor Dave Langford. "Come along with me," he ordered. "Where to?" asked the mystified Langford. "Down to Thorsell's office" was the curt reply. "What's going on?" Langford asked repeatedly as the duo made their way to the editor's office. "Bad news," said the tight-lipped Pritchard, refusing to reveal anything more. "I'd rather that Thorsell told you." By this time Langford was pretty worked up.

"I felt like the world was coming to an end," he would later say. "Thorsell was delayed, holed up in a meeting with Megarry, and I had to stand there like a dummy, hanging in suspense, while Tim just looked at me mournfully and shook his head. I was sure I was going to be axed."

As it turned out, unlike many of those working for him, Langford would keep his job. When Thorsell came back from his meeting with Megarry, he told Langford that, after the budgets had initially been approved, discussions about further budget cuts had ensued. Because of the deepening recession, Megarry decided that another $1.5 million had to be cut from the editorial department's budget of $25 million. Thorsell said that he went home one weekend and spent the whole time ruminating about where the cuts should come from. He considered closing the Halifax or Tokyo bureaus, but decided against that because it would detract from the national and foreign coverage of the *Globe*, which were major strengths of the paper. Anyway, closing those two bureaus would only result in a $600,000 saving, instead of $1.5 million. The only feasible solution, as he saw it, was to cut the entire $1.5 million from Sports.

Langford was aghast. "This is a huge mistake," he said. "Why don't you spread the cuts around? Take some from Sports, if you must, but also take some from Arts. Or take smaller amounts from several areas." When he saw that his arguments were falling on deaf ears, he tried to make Thorsell see what an impact cutting Sports so drastically would have on the *Globe* readership. He also attempted to appeal to Thorsell's sentiment.

"When I was a young kid in Owen Sound, delivering the *Globe*," Langford told Thorsell, "I would sit down at the train station where I picked up my papers to read Scott Young and Trent Frayne in the sports section before I set out on my route." But Thorsell refused to budge. He and Pritchard told Langford not to discuss the matter with anyone. They would tell the sports department the next day.

Dave Langford went home early that day, around 6:00 p.m., and went for a long run. When he got back to his apartment, his phone started ringing. Marty York, the most highly paid sports columnist at the *Globe*, called from New York. The *Sun* called. And a number of radio stations. But he had turned his answering machine on and, obeying the order from Thorsell and Pritchard, didn't return any calls.

The upshot of Thorsell's decision was that the sports staff was cut down from 24 people to 10. Langford was given the task of deciding who to keep on. He chose three columnists: York, Stephen Brunt and Al Strachan. (There was some squabbling over Strachan because Thorsell wanted to use him as a Report on Business writer in western Canada, but Langford and Strachan fought him on that issue and won.) Langford also needed two general assignment people, and he chose Neil Campbell and James Christie. Gary Loewen and David Shoalts, two hockey writers, and baseball writer Larry Millson were let go, among others. They didn't get fired, but were sent to the national desk as reporters or copy editors, or to Report on Business as copy editors.

So the sports department was left with editor Langford, three columnists, two reporters and three copy editors. Veteran Jack McHale was also kept on for special sports supplements.

Thorsell didn't like to see the Truth and Rumours section, written by William Houston, go. We can keep Truth and Rumours, negotiated Langford, if you let us have one more person on staff. So Houston was kept on, bringing the total in the sports department to 11.

Before the cuts were made, Sports had occupied two pages four days a week and three pages two days a week in the national edition, and three pages four days a week and four pages twice a week in the Metro Toronto edition. The result of the cuts was that Sports was reduced to two pages six days a week.

Four months after the December cuts, in April 1990, Langford was still getting calls and letters every day complaining about the reduction in sports coverage. With the baseball season on, the calls increased again. The Blue Jays were playing 81 home games and 81 road games, but he only had the manpower to cover the home games.

Another problem then looming at the sports department, an additional indicator of poor decision-making in the higher echelons of *Globe* management, was what to do with columnist Marty York. As the highest-paid sports columnist at the *Globe and Mail*, York made more than $1,700 for four columns a week and an extra $325 if he wrote a fifth column. (Within the sports department, Dave Langford ranked second in salary; columnist Stephen Brunt, third.)

York's salary, whopping by *Globe* standards, had come about in this way. When the mass exodus had occurred at the *Globe*, *Toronto Star* managing editor Ian Urquhart had offered York a big deal, including a signing bonus of $25,000, if he would desert to the *Star*. Marty hired agent Gil Scott, a well-known football agent, to negotiate for him. It was Thorsell's first big test as editor. He matched the offer made by the *Star* and sweetened it by giving York the title of associate sports editor. At that time the salary wasn't outrageous compared to some other top people at the *Globe*. But with the new mean and lean cost-cutting regime it became quickly out of line. Only political commentator Jeffrey Simpson and the late movie critic Jay Scott ended up rivalling York in salary.

The "castle": Our weekend retreat overlooking the St. Lawrence River in Brockville, Ontario. It has 30 rooms and eight fireplaces, and, when the Hardy family lived here from 1904 to 1962, it had a staff of 20. It now has a staff of two: me (the maid), and Edgar (the handyman)! Built in 1855, Thornton Cliff, as it is properly called, was given as a wedding present by Brockville tycoon George Fulford to his daughter when she married Arthur Charles Hardy, son of an Ontario premier, in 1904. *Photo Credit:* Doreen Dickie.

Our cottage on Fisher Island in Charleston Lake, Ontario. Edgar's family has owned the 55-acre island since his grandfather, principal of the local high school in nearby Athens, paid a $100 tax bill for a friend in 1900.

Charlie Pachter draws me in a serious pose for *City and Country Home* magazine, March 1989.

Edgar doffs his top hat at the Osler Hoskin hop, 1989.

Kicking up my heels at an Osler Hoskin "Gay Twenties" party, April 1991.

Attending a fund-raising dinner that then
Tory Defence Minister Perrin Beatty
held in honour of Lord Carrington,
March 1988. *Photo Credit*: Gary Beechey.

Pouting like a spoilt child during the
photo shoot for *Chatelaine* magazine,
June 1993. *Photo Credit:* Jim Allen.

Singing with developer Rudy Bratty (hatless, back left), hamburger king George
Cohon (to my right), broadcaster Micki Moore (beside Cohon), and socialite Valerie
Fine (far right), at a Variety Village fund-raiser, spring 1992. *Photo Credit:* Ed Regan.

Stephanie, with former boyfriend Ritchie Bedder, Robin and me at my mother's wedding, August 1993.

A bevy of blondes: Stephanie (left), me and Christine Black, Stephanie's aunt and my sister-in-law from my first marriage. Taken at the launch party for *The Glitter Girls*, September 1993. *Photo Credit:* Michael Fitzgerald.

My mother's wedding to Archibald N. (Jerry) Smith, August 1993, five years after my father died of Alzheimer's disease. Smith (seated centre, to my mother's right) is a Bermudian and a Rhodes Scholar. Far left, my brother, Professor John Robinson, standing behind his seated wife, Deborah, surrounded by their five boys (two from his first marriage): Jonathan, David, Michael, Geoffrey and Stephen. Next, I'm holding my niece, Paget Ross, with Edgar, Stephanie and Robin standing behind. To my mother's left, Nora stands between her stepson Kent and her husband, Alexander (Sandy) Ross, who died of a stroke six months later. Nora's eldest daughter, Théa, kneels in front, next to Judy, whose husband, lawyer Paul Rivard, and son, Alex, are behind her. Missing is Judy's daughter, Julia, who was at summer camp. *Photo Credit:* Amora Portrait Studios.

September 1994, posing as one of "Fotheringham's women." He wrote below the picture: "To Rosemary, girl of my dreams." Wonder what he wrote to the other girls! *Photo Credit:* Beverley Rockett.

Governor General Jeanne Sauvé presents the Michener Award, Canada's highest award for journalism, to *The Globe and Mail's* managing editor, Geoffrey Stevens. *Photo Credit:* G. Stevens, files.

At the Great Wall of China, January 1989 (left to right): Geoffrey Stevens, Jan Wong (China correspondent) and Norman Webster (editor-in-chief). Back at the *Globe*, it was the beginning of the end for the Webster-Stevens duo. *Photo Credit:* G. Stevens, files.

The *Globe* investigative reporting team accepting the 1988 Michener award, November 21, 1989: (left to right) Paul Palango, national editor; Victor Malarek, Lang Michener series; deputy managing editor Gwen Smith; Jock Ferguson and Dawn King, York Region series; and Stephen Brunt, Ontario Boxing Commissioner story. All, except Brunt, have left the paper. *Photo Credit:* P. Palango, files.

In happier days, senior staff at *The Globe and Mail* take in a Blue Jays baseball game at old Exhibition Stadium. Second row (left to right): Colin MacKenzie, Geoffrey Stevens, Norman Webster, Brian Johnson, Paul Palango. Front row (left to right): Duncan McMonagle, Dave Langford, Linda McQuaig. Only Colin MacKenzie, now deputy managing editor, and Dave Langford, now sports editor, remain. *Photo Credit:* G. Stevens, files.

We were delighted when my stepson, Chris, a tax accountant at KPMG Peat Marwick Thorne, married Wendy Daniels at the Elmwood Club in May 1994. On the left is my stepdaughter, Jennifer.

Compounding the problem, York was accused of plagiarizing. Probably the worst accusation that can be levelled against any writer is that of copying. *Frank* magazine, for three issues in a row, printed what appeared to be to its editors several examples of York's supposed plagiarism, mostly from American sources.

But the wiffly-waffly *Globe* administration (wiffly-waffly on everything but cost-cutting, that is) seemed paralyzed. As the rumours swirled around the newsroom, York's writing cohorts complained to Langford that nothing was being done about York. Three examples of the plagiarism were taken to Pritchard, one from *USA Today*, one from the San Francisco Giants' program and one from the *Miami Herald*. The result was a tap on the wrist from Pritchard in the form of a disciplinary letter to York.

It was generally felt that York, whose strength lay in his relentless reporting and digging skills, was becoming a bit lazy in the Thorsell-Pritchard regime. In his sixth year at the *Globe*, he rarely attended any games, preferring to sit at his house in Thornhill, where a satellite dish had been installed as part of the deal Thorsell had made to keep him from going to the *Star*.

York denied all the instances of plagiarizing. He remains a highly paid and invaluable employee at the *Globe*, though he doesn't cover baseball anymore. Stephen Brunt has caught up to him salarywise. But Al Strachan, another respected sports reporter (who in 1994 was included in the *Globe's* rather pompous and self-serving list of one of the 25 most influential people in Canadian sports), jumped ship in April 1994 to write for the *Sun* when he was denied a salary raise by Cruikshank. Gare Joyce has been hired as his replacement.

So the *Globe* ended up reducing its sports pages at a time when other newspapers were planning the opposite move. (About a year later both the *New York Times* and the *Times of London* increased their coverage of sports.) It didn't make sense, and the *Star* and *Sun* had a heyday. In the beginning of March 1990, the *Star* ran a radio advertising campaign making fun of the *Globe's* sports cuts and, in effect, making hay over the less-than-intelligent decision to make those cuts. The ads, which ran on a number of stations, including CJCL Radio, concluded with the following line: "*Star* sports are all over Toronto and all over the *Globe*."

On Wednesday, April 17, CBLT sports anchor Bruce Dowbiggin interviewed Dave Langford about the *Toronto Star*'s radio advertising campaign. Langford described the massive reaction to the cuts, saying he got letters and phone calls every day for four to five months. And that the calls had picked up again in April with the start of baseball season.

Jim O'Leary, who had replaced Wayne Parrish as sports editor of the *Toronto Sun* when the latter was kicked upstairs to become Doug Creighton's executive assistant, reminisced on the program about how, when he was a kid, the *Globe* was the newspaper of record, but that was no longer true. He poked fun at the *Star* ads, saying they were shooting at a mouse with a bazooka, the implication being that since the *Globe* was already dead in the water, why bother making it a target?

A *Financial Post* reporter on the same program discussed how the circulation of his paper went up by 2,000 as soon as the *Globe*'s sports cuts were announced.

According to Geoff Stevens, Megarry had tried for years to reduce sports. Megarry looked at the balance sheet in an arbitrary way, said Stevens. To discover which parts of the paper make money, he took all the costs of a department, such as salary, overtime and travel, then added in the cost of the portion of ink used and the attributable costs of the building. Then he deducted from that the money brought in by the advertising. He used that method to show Webster and Stevens that the sports pages lost $4.5 million a year.

Stevens contends that that's too rigid a reading of revenue and costs. One of the main reasons that people buy the paper in the first place is to read the sports pages. Also, advertisers buy all over the paper because there is a sports section. To carry Megarry's fallacious logic through, the editorial page should be dropped because it loses money. By that method of accounting only the ROB and fashion make money (fashion, surprisingly, because of its low cost and pricey ads).

New Regime

Under Megarry and Thorsell, there was little or no respect accorded to the employees at the paper. A prime example was the way that the workings of the editorial board changed. Previously fiercely independent, the board became a mere mouthpiece for Thorsell's views.

After Webster and Stevens left, the number of editorials in the *Globe* was reduced from four to two daily. To add insult to injury, members of the editorial board were told by Thorsell what topics to cover and what to say about those topics.

Former editors Doyle and Webster never stooped to telling the editorial board what to write, and under these two previous regimes the editorial writers sometimes refused their editor's suggestions. But under the new administration, there was no beating around the bush as to what went into editorials. First it was Megarry and Thorsell who decided; after Megarry left, it was Thorsell.

Previously Webster would give suggestions and ask for ideas. But under Thorsell, the editorial writers would come in with notepads and sit like secretaries to take their instructions. The editorial board at one point consisted of Thorsell, Warren Clements, Alistair Lawrie, Stevie Cameron and Ellen Roseman. Thorsell would turn to, for example, Stevie Cameron, and say: "Stevie, I'd like to see an editorial on Shirley Carr and what a disaster she has been as head of the Canadian Labour Congress and how we should get rid of her," and that would be that.

Alistair Lawrie was very upset one day when he was ordered to write an editorial criticizing June Callwood for swearing at a black woman. He obeyed the instructions by writing a hesitant piece tiptoeing around the subject. (Alistair may have been upset, but June was devastated when the piece came out.)

Thorsell doesn't like affirmative action programs, and when Stevie Cameron once wrote an editorial supporting the Ontario College of Art's controversial affirmative action program hiring women, he killed it. Then the women were removed from the board, and it was Thorsell, Warren Clements and Patrick Martin who wrote the editorials for a while. Presently, Thorsell has three young men to write for him: Marcus Gee, Tony Keller and Andrew Cohen. These days, Keller is on study leave and writer Andrew Coyne occasionally fills in.

Under Megarry, and thus under Thorsell, who followed his every edict to the letter, journalists are employees to be chewed up and spit out, in much the same way that Megarry used his advertising staff and salespeople.

Thorsell seems to have no idea that the purpose of a paper is sometimes to give readers what they don't want. Instead, he does what's trendy or fashionable or, above all, whatever suits the publisher.

And that was so, even when Megarry, to save his own skin, was prepared to lay Thorsell's neck on the line, which is what happened during Geoff Stevens's lawsuit against Megarry and the *Globe and Mail*.

The Wrongful Dismissal Lawsuit

In June 1990, a lawsuit was launched in the Ontario Supreme Court by Geoffrey Stevens against the *Globe and Mail* and publisher Roy Megarry personally. The action sought damages for wrongful dismissal based on allegations that Stevens was fired from a job that paid $106,000 plus a management bonus and benefits that included a company car. It also claimed damages for the tort of deceit.

In his testimony before Mr. Justice Keith Gibson, Geoff Stevens said that he was fired only three weeks after Roy Megarry had promised him in a private conversation on January 2, 1989, after Stevens had learned of Webster's firing, that his position as managing editor was secure.

The *Globe*'s position, as stated by its lawyer in his opening argument, was that the decision to fire Mr. Stevens had been made by the new editor-in-chief William Thorsell alone, not with Megarry.

The trial was held in a small motions room in the Ontario trial court building on University Avenue. The only people present, besides the parties, court staff and lawyers, were Lin Shannon accompanying Geoff Stevens; Diane Barsoski, a Megarry loyalist who was in charge of human resources at the *Globe* and who has since been kicked upstairs to the Thomson Corporation; and several members of the press—Tom Claridge, the court reporter from the *Globe*; a reporter from the *Star*; and David Bentley from *Frank* magazine.

Norman Webster flew in from Montreal, where he was then the editor of the *Montreal Gazette,* to give testimony on his former managing editor's behalf. William Thorsell testified that firing Geoff Stevens had been entirely his idea and that Megarry had had nothing to do with the decision. Roy Megarry reiterated Thorsell's testimony.

In January 1991, the judgement on Stevens's case finally came down. He was awarded $155,000 for a year's loss in wages, plus interest. The judge disbelieved Megarry that it had been Thorsell's idea to fire Stevens. This judgement was in addition to the $50,000 Stevens had been awarded by the Ontario Labour Relations Board in a separate hearing, raised from $30,000 after the *Globe* had appealed it.

Finale

So what's going on at the *Globe* these days under present publisher Roger Parkinson, a former marine, who was brought up from the United States by the Thomson Corporation to run the paper?

Well, William Thorsell remains firmly in place as editor, having tried unsuccessfully to ascend to the publisher's position himself. Employees at the *Globe* have some kind words to say about him, that he is very intelligent and has lots of good ideas and that it's too bad that he doesn't have a strong managing editor to defuse those ideas. Someone like, say, Geoff Stevens.

But, in general, the dissatisfaction level among *Globe* staffers is high, their view being that there is not a clear sense of what the paper is and where it is going. Whatever Thorsell's vision, if indeed there is one, it is not communicated to the troops. That, combined with the budget squeezes, means a lot of people are just hanging in there every day to pick up their paycheque and go home.

To many, Thorsell is seen as having a Tory agenda. *Frank* magazine, for instance, calls him Bill Torysell. He remains in close contact with former prime minister Brian Mulroney whom he greatly admires. As well, the "Men's" columns he introduced, many of which have been embarrassingly antiwomen, tend to represent the right or far right of a centre point of view. Many reporters want to distance themselves from that, and rightly so. If you put out a widely circulated national paper, you should provide a forum that gives a broad range of opinions so that readers can select for themselves. If you narrow that, you are seen as ideological, so a lot gets dismissed as representing a particular bias.

A *Globe* reporter told me that at a party he attended in January 1995, people were jokingly referring to the *Globe* as the fag rag. There is a disproportionate amount of coverage being given to gay rights in the *Globe* these days, perhaps squeezing out other concerns. Fairly recently, the *Globe* ran a piece on gay rights in Russia. Given all the different minority groups suffering in Russia, it was strange to see gay rights focussed on.

Thorsell gets away with his agenda because the Thomson people couldn't care less what goes in the paper, as long as they're making the profits they want. Unlike Webster and Stevens, who fought, it turned out, foolishly and openly for what they believed in, Thorsell fulfills the publisher's cost-cutting agenda, knowing he can then turn around and do whatever he wants with editorial.

The talk around town in publishing and literary circles concerning the problems at the newspaper have become so prevalent that they have caught the attention of at least one of Canada's most notable fiction writers. The short story quoted at the beginning of this chapter in Margaret Atwood's recent best-seller, *Wilderness Tips*, titled "Hack Wednesday," features a day in the life of Marcia and Eric. The models for the couple, people say, are June Callwood and Trent Frayne. Marcia works at a metropolitan newspaper and is unhappy with her job. At one point, Marcia remarks that you don't read the paper anymore to find out about the world; instead, you read it for what is in the editor-in-chief's head.

Thorsell runs the paper like a magazine reflecting the personality of the editor. He is intelligent, quirky and charming, but he doesn't gather strong people around him, just yes men and women who nod in agreement at everything he says.

The old *Globe and Mail* had influence and power because it was a forum for the national agenda. Webster and Stevens viewed the paper as a vehicle that interpreted or mirrored the national agenda, which is what a good newspaper should do.

Thorsell is very interested in being regarded as someone influencing and leading the national agenda. The *Globe* under Thorsell is losing its power because it is seen as trying to be a power broker. It is less trusted because it is seen as having a point of view pursued for its own sake and not because people think that it is right.

And, under Ken Thomson's ownership, the cost-cutting continues, sometimes disguised as a redesign here or an innovation there. And when there are no more costs to cut, what then?

When the far-right, antifemale, pro-gay Thorsell agenda has talked itself into oblivion, and when all the cost-cutting techniques are exhausted and there's nothing left to squeeze out from the limp rag that was once the proud *Globe and Mail*, bets are on that Thomson will sell. Takers, anyone?

Chapter Six

Copy Editors, or He Who Edits Least Edits Best

My Journalistic Career (with apologies to Stephen Leacock)

The rather feeble attempt at humour that follows was a double column I wrote one day after weeks of frustration with *The Globe and Mail*'s copy editors. I sent it down to the *Globe* to run, but needless to say, it was never printed.

> Last night I had a dream. As I searched desperately through my drawers for panty hose without runs and a pair of earrings that matched, on my way to yet another party, I looked out my window and espied the owner of the newspaper that employs me out for a leisurely stroll with his dog through the streets of Rosedale. I stumbled out of the house and waylaid him. "Please, sir," I blubbered. "I can't take it anymore. Tonight I will have to see Catherine Nugent for the third night in a row. I'll be ill if I have to eat another shrimp-stuffed snow pea or quaff yet another champagne cocktail. And my neighbours have refused to speak to me ever since Pat Appleton drove me home in her gold Rolls-Royce. I'll wash all the cars in your driveway and clean your swimming pool. I'll even agree to my

paycheque coming yet another month late. Only don't make me go to another party again."

The shy, gentlemanly owner was taken aback. "Zena Cherry?" he asked. "Didn't you used to look respectable and wear your hair in a bun?" He fumbled in his coat pocket for his glasses, took one look at the apparition before him in one high-heeled shoe, unsightly hose and mismatched earrings, and literally ran down the street, dragging his unfortunate dog after him. "See the publisher. He's the one in charge," he called in a quavery voice over his shoulder.

So I screwed up my courage and went down to the newspaper's offices. The interview began propitiously. As I sat in the outer sanctum of the cavernous office, I was greeted by the publisher's secretary. "An advertiser?" she murmured in dulcet tones, smiling sweetly. "N-n-n-no, a writer," I stuttered nervously. "Don't be impertinent," she replied. "I cover social events," I explained. "Sit down over there and be quiet," she ordered crossly, pointing to a small stool. I crouched in the corner for two days awaiting my turn as advertisers came and went. On the third day I was ushered into the mahogany-panelled inner sanctum, as large as the entire newsroom, that was the publisher's office. He was a good-looking man with a no-nonsense manner. "Please, sir," I began again. "I would like to switch my newspaper beat. I will go birding with Peter Whelan, if necessary. I will do real estate searches of Alberta premier Donald Getty's family homestead. I will write editorials praising VIA Rail cuts and Brian Mulroney. Only don't make me go to another party again."

My plea fell upon deaf ears. "My dear child," he admonished. "You mustn't give up so easily. I realize that party-going is a thankless task reserved for fools and ninnies, but of all the people I know, you are the best fitted for the job." I blushed at the compliment. "I have a suggestion for you, however," he added thoughtfully. "If every once in a while you could insert a sales pitch for the latest model Toyota Corolla or slip in a mention of the Meech Lake Accord, it might spice up your columns."

I skipped gaily out of the publisher's office, buoyed by his wise advice and encouragement. But my mood of despair soon returned, so I headed off to the editor's office. "I'm on the verge of a nervous breakdown," I whined. "I greet my husband with inane party chatter when he comes home from work. I mistake my children for champagne waiters and rebuff them rudely when they approach me. What am I to do?" He listened intently. "I think I have just the remedy," he answered. He walked over to his cupboard and opened the door, revealing a moth-eaten tuxedo amid piles of invitations which fluttered to the floor. "You're just not going to the right parties," he said. He picked up a card at random. "Here's a dinner at the Frums' house in my honour. Everyone will be there. Why don't you cover it?"

I wasn't certain that this was the solution I was looking for, but I decided to give it a try. I rushed home to get changed for my command performance at the Frums. By the time I arrived the party was in full swing. Joe Clark and Brian Mulroney were engaged in a shoving match over who could take Ivana Trump home. Garth Drabinsky swooped overhead from the living room chandelier and nearly knocked the turban off an East Indian Mountie standing on guard at the door. Artist Charlie Pachter attempted unsuccessfully to sell replicas of Barnett Newman's *Voice of Fire* he had painted the previous evening for $25 each. Provincial premiers David Peterson and Clyde Wells had even less success fobbing off tickets for their upcoming Meech Lake dinner at cut-rate prices of $999 per ticket.

I dashed home and wrote up the party. Perhaps the editor was right. Maybe this would establish my reputation as a writer of note. I went to bed with a smile on my face and dreams of smoked salmon canapés dancing in my head.

The morning after the Frum party, I went to the front door to retrieve my morning paper, opened it up to find my column and recoiled in horror. It had been hacked to bits. According to the newspaper, hostess Barbara Frum had slapped Sondra Gotlieb when Mikhail Gorbachev failed to materialize; Margaret Thatcher had abandoned her date, Conrad Black, to run off with Stephen Lewis; John Crosbie had proposed to

Sheila Copps without calling her "baby" once; B.C. premier William Vander Zalm had accepted $100,000 in cash in a brown envelope to turn Fantasy Gardens into an abortion clinic; and columnist Allan Fotheringham had left the party with Minnie, Barbara Bush's dog. The damage was irreparable. I was finished as a social columnist. More important, I would become a social outcast: I would never be invited to the Frums' for dinner again.

Back down to *The Globe and Mail* offices I went, full of righteous indignation, to find out who could have done such a dastardly deed. The first person I ran into was the deputy managing editor, who had refused to speak to me ever since I had spelled John Sawatsky's name wrong a year ago. "You did it again!" she screamed, descending upon me in vulturelike fury. "You've misspelled Bharati Mukerjee. Can't you get anything right?" Embarrassed at my unforgivable error, I burst into tears and stumbled into the office of the paper's national editor. It took me a while to catch his attention, as he was busy writing lengthy memos to the editor, but finally I managed to pry him away from his work. "Don't worry," he consoled me. "No one ever reads your column, anyway. And with all the stunningly average writers like yourself at the paper, our readers are used to a few mistakes here and there."

I thanked the national editor profusely for his encouraging words and set off to find the associate editor. He was an experienced newsman who had proved helpful in the past. Maybe he had some idea as to who had made mincemeat of my column.

But before I had a chance to explain anything to him, he greeted me with a barrage of questions. Had I taken any trips lately and charged them to *The Globe and Mail*? Had I made any long distance phone calls that couldn't be accounted for? Had I drunk from the water fountain without permission? I denied everything. "Well done!" he cried. "Keep up the good work." He patted me absentmindedly on the back and ushered me summarily out of his office.

I was just about to give up and go home when I passed by the doors at the far end of the newsroom. I peered inside.

Before my eyes was row after row of industrious employees with giant shears poised in readiness over pieces of copy, hyenalike grins on their faces. "Who are you?" I asked in astonishment. "We're copy editors," they replied proudly. "We are the most important people at the paper next to the advertising department. It's up to us to whittle writers' columns down to fit the paper and make room for advertisements." "How do you decide what to cut?" I asked as the truth began to dawn on me. "It's perfectly simple," they said in unison. "We just lop off the end if it takes up too much space. Or we cut a word here, a phrase there, a sentence here, a paragraph there, making sure that the grammatical structure remains correct." A fit of trembling came upon me. "What about the story's meaning?" I whispered hoarsely. But with all the cutting and pasting going on, they were unable to hear me.

I knew what I had to do. Without a moment's hesitation, I threw away my pen and took up a pair of scissors. I am now happily ensconced in *The Globe and Mail* newsroom as a copy editor. I don't go to parties anymore. My status at the paper has risen dramatically; my pay has quadrupled; and the publisher's secretary never fails to bestow a sunny smile in my direction when I pass by her office.

Unbeknownst to the majority of the newspaper-reading public, everything they read has been gone over with a fine-tooth comb by a team of men and women who descend upon the newspaper's offices at around 3:00 p.m. each day and peruse everything written until eleven that night. To add insult to injury, these copy editors get paid as much or more than the reporters and columnists themselves. I have a word of advice for the thrifty Ken Thomson. If he wants to save money, he should fire all the copy editors.

"Why do newspapers have copy editors?" I wailed one day to my former boss Geoff Stevens after a particularly nasty round with one. "They're there to ensure that the writer writes according to the newspaper's style and to correct his mistakes," he replied. All that means to me is that they make the paper uniform and boring, and it has been my experience that they increase the possibility of mistakes.

Peter Ustinov had it right. In a Canadian Press interview printed in the *Brockville Recorder and Times* on October 27, 1989, he deplored the practice of using copy editors. Editors, he said, are unknown in Europe and are "a purely transatlantic device to create employment, which is like most of the overstaffing that is American."

I would not want to leave the mistaken impression that I was the only hapless victim of the copy-editor syndrome. One of the first things that Adrienne Clarkson said to me when she found out that I had been hired by *The Globe and Mail* was: "Be careful, Rosemary, the copy editors down there will drive you crazy." Having never heard of such a species, I didn't take much heed of her prophetic words at the time. But they came back to haunt me.

Not that there's anything one can do about them. Writer John Lownsbrough once told me about taking a book review he had written for the *Globe* to then book editor Jack Kapica, who perused it quickly and, without any hesitation, immediately erased the word *baldly*. "Sorry, John," he explained, "this won't do. The copy editors are sure to think that you mean *badly* and mess it up."

Incredibly, this is not an uncommon occurrence. Former *Globe* political columnist Stevie Cameron, who sent her copy editors a large double fudge chocolate cake as a goodbye present when she left the *Globe*, has an even better story to relate. It concerned a profile she once wrote of Michael Zaritsky, the civil servant who blew the whistle on Nova Scotia premier John Buchanan's trust funds. For the first interview she took him to singer Rita MacNeil's teahouse in the Maritime hamlet of Big Pond. In her opening column she re-created that scene, describing the music of a Rita MacNeil tape in the background. She was setting up the contrast of the romantic, cozy, cliché-ridden Nova Scotia that tourists expect against the reality of the harsh, vengeful society that destroyed Zaritsky. After she sent in the column, she got a call from copy editor Paul MacRae. (This is the same Paul MacRae who is married to Thomson newspaper heiress Sherry Brydson, Ken Thomson's niece, who caused *Frank* magazine so much puzzlement. I got a call one day from David Bentley who was writing an article for *Frank* on Rosedale homes. "Rosemary," he asked, "who is this Paul MacRae at *The Globe and Mail* who owns a mansion worth several million dollars on Cluny Drive?")

"Stevie," Paul inquired, "who is this Rita MacNeil, anyway?" Stevie explained that she is one of the most popular country singers in Canada. "Well, I've never heard of her," he said, and promptly excised the lead paragraph. "And you sent those guys a cake?" I asked her incredulously. "Yup," she answered. "There were many times when they saved my skin." I suppose that may be true for Stevie, who, though an excellent journalist, was often, due to the nature of her column, engaged in speculation and innuendo. But I was merely a social columnist writing about parties and get-togethers, hardly world-shaking affairs that warranted further scrutiny. Besides, everything I sent down to the *Globe* I checked and verified thoroughly. And I resented copy editors, most of whom were sadly unfamiliar with the social scene, revamping my copy, often adding mistakes where there were none before, almost invariably detracting from the column's style and content.

I don't mean to imply that all, or even a majority of, the mistakes in my columns were not attributable to their author. Fortunately, there were many readers around to catch me up on those.

February 25, 1990
Just a note to correct a couple of things in your piece on the Eaton gift to Trent University.

Lady Eaton's father, John McCrea, was *not* a carpenter. He was a cabinetmaker. I have a charming sofa and chair, signed, which came to me from my maternal grandmother. John McCrea was my paternal great-grandfather.

Ardwold was not in Forest Hill. It was where Ardwold Gate is now. Forest Hill Village ended at the north side of Lonsdale Road, I think, several blocks north of Ardwold. It was quite a house!

Flora Agnew
Toronto

February 9, 1990
In hopes of?
What will be next, *real* good—*real* nice—anyways?

J. Holton
Port Hope

April 25, 1989
High tea is the meal that miners and factory workers in the north of England have when they go home in the evening.

It consists of such things as tripe, fish and chips, sausages, etc., washed down with beer or very strong tea.

Surely you must mean afternoon tea?

Caroline Clarke
Unionville, Ontario

October 25, 1988
For your information, I have been divorced from Marina Taylor for some considerable time.

My present wife is amused by your mistake, but I trust it won't be repeated.

Charles Taylor
Willowdale, Ontario

Sometimes it might even be a fellow reporter who would try to get me into trouble:

SLUG: OOPS
DESK: NDESK
DATE: 19-01
TEXT: rhoward, Ottawa to NDESK.
Rosemary Sexton's column today: First item seventh para listing "Tory supporters . . ." may be wrong: "Metro ridings coordinator Susanne Warren (Michael's ex)" quit the party job two years ago and is a federal citizenship judge, I believe.

-endit-30-

From the Desk of Geoffrey Stevens
  Rosemary,
  Is the Ottawa Bureau correct on this point?
  Please let me know.

                                                    GS

MEMO
To: Geoff Stevens
From: Rosemary Sexton
What I said: "Susanne Warren is currently the senior Metro
organizer for the PC Party of Canada, Toronto region. She
used to be a citizenship court judge, but has resigned."
What I thought: "Whew. Got through that one OK. Is this
what's in store for me as the *Globe*'s society columnist? No
wonder Zena got Alzheimer's. Why doesn't rhoward, whoever
he is, stick to reporting from Ottawa? How many more people
are out there trying to trip me up?"

On Saturday, April 6, 1991, a front-page story on the Report on
Business section of the *Globe* concerned the top salaries of prominent Canadian businessmen. It had been written by Washington
correspondent John Saunders who, since some of the salaries were
in American dollars, had made sure, before sending the story in,
that all the amounts were converted to Canadian dollars. The copy
editor assigned to the story, without checking back with John,
made the mistaken assumption that all the dollar amounts were in
American dollars and converted the dollar figure given in the
opening paragraph back to Canadian figures. That meant, according to one of the silly and arbitrary copy editing rules, that all the
dollar amounts throughout the story had to be converted. When
the story appeared, they were all wrong.

　　John Saunders was incensed. He called the paper and demanded quite properly that they print a correcton notice. He spoke on
the phone to economics reporter Bruce Little, who agreed that
the *Globe* would make the retraction, but refused to make clear in
the retraction, as can be done in cases such as these, that the error
had been an editing error (otherwise, it looks as if the reporter
himself has made the error). Saunders appealed to Thorsell, who

stood up for Little. Saunders quit on the spot, though returned to the *Globe* three days later and still works there as an ROB reporter. Despite the experience, he, like Stevie, is a supporter of copy editors: "They save my bacon all the time."

Like the rest of us, copy editors are not immune from the vagaries of political correctness. One story that circulated in various American newspapers several years ago concerned a certain diligent copy editor who had been instructed to substitute the term Afro-American in the place of "black," as the latter was considered racist. Failing to notice the context of what he was reading, he excised the word black and substituted Afro-American on a company balance sheet. As a result the monetary results of the company were said to be "in the Afro-American." The American press had a field day, one newspaper speculating what would have transpired if the company had been in the red. "No doubt the sentence would then have read that the company was 'in the native or aboriginal American'."

For more than 20 years after his death in 1961, cardboard boxes filled with humorist James Thurber's unpublished papers lay around ignored and neglected. While going through these boxes, a man named Michael Rosen, who was editing a collection of Thurber works, came across an unpublished article titled "The Theory and Practice of Criticizing the Criticism of the Editing of *New Yorker* Articles," written in May 1959. Excerpts from this article were published in a December 4, 1988 edition of the *Sunday New York Times*, titled "He Edits Best Who Edits Least All Things, Especially Mine." It should be required reading for anyone planning to become a journalist.

After describing his boss Harold Ross's penchant for adding commas and excising repetitions, Mr. Thurber writes:

> Shakespeare used "to be" twice in one line and "tomorrow" three times in one line. Where were the *New Yorker* editors then? Ross used to say that we need a staff psychiatrist for the behaviour of writers, but we need a staff psychologist for . . . the seasonal ups and downs of individual editorial perception and ability. . . .

I was not so dismayed as amused when I discovered that

the editors, in a jittery mood or during certain phases of the
moon, are down readers. That is, they read the last word of
each line from top to bottom, and thus once encountered
"Dixie cups." When an editor becomes a down reader, mad-
ness is just around the corner. I am sure that the magazine's
back files, if read down instead of left to right, would produce
"girl laid," "trousers open" and God knows what other shocking atrocities. I always begin at the left with the opening word
of a sentence and read toward the right, and I heartily recom-
mend this method.

But it wasn't just the copy desk and its editors' foibles I had to
worry about. Under the new cost-cutting regime at the paper in
the early nineties, space was becoming a scarce commodity. On
January 25, 1991, at about 9:15 p.m., just as my husband, my son
and I were finishing our dinner, the phone rang. I picked it up. "It's
Eleanor Reading from the *Globe and Mail*," the person on the
other end said. "I'm sorry to bother you at home so late, but I've
just been informed that your column on the effect of the Persian
Gulf war and the recession on several balls will be cut." I was not
particularly surprised. Unknown to Ms. Reading, my columns had
been cut quite drastically on an ongoing basis for quite a while.
She, in fact, was the only copy editor for months who had both-
ered to inform me about the cuts. "How much will be cut?" I
asked. "Well, it's pretty bad," she answered. "We stopped it halfway
through the Canadian Stage Company Ball." Even a seasoned veteran of *Globe* copy desk cuts such as I was taken aback. It meant
that three-and-a-half paragraphs out of six would be lopped off
my column. Unfairly, I took my anger out a bit on the messenger,
who was just obeying instructions. "You know, Eleanor," I said
crossly, "I can hardly believe this. When John Cruikshank and I discussed my writing one column a week instead of three, he told me
that the column would be longer and I would be guaranteed
space. This is my third column under that regime, all of them
well-researched and noncontroversial, and every one has been cut
drastically."

"You were guaranteed space?" she asked. "That's the first I've
heard of it. I'll leave an electronic message for John Cruikshank

reminding him." My first inclination was to say, "Don't bother," but, feeling I'd already said enough, I bit my tongue, thanked her and hung up. (Nor did I reveal to her that I had also been promised by Cruikshank to be paid extra for my once-a-week column. The extra never did materialize on my paycheque.)

Unable to sleep that night (sleepless nights were becoming standard around our household with the new regime at the *Globe* firmly in place), I got up at 3:00 a.m. to take a peek at the newspaper on the doorstep to see the damage. Sure enough, the last paragraphs, which included descriptions of two major upcoming balls, had been excised.

Just the week before, for my first column under the promised "guaranteed space," the subject had been the Writers' Development Trust. Much to my chagrin and to the dismay of the organization itself, two major sponsors of the Great Literary Dinner and an upcoming event, the reason for writing the column in the first place, had been cut. I began to wonder what would happen to future columns. I didn't have long to wait.

Thursday, January 31, 1991, the telephone rang. "Hello, Rosemary. It's Edward Scissorhands from *The Globe and Mail* calling. I have a question about the column you sent down for this Saturday. You refer to Ms. Ferns as first a lawyer and then later as a Crown attorney. Which is she?" "She's both." "Uh, well, don't worry, I'll fix it up for you. Thanks very much, goodbye." And fix it up he did. The word lawyer was deleted from the column. I never did get a chance to explain to Mr. Scissorhands that one must graduate from law school in order to become a Crown attorney; I'm not sure he cared. Three paragraphs ended up being chopped from that column, including, again, the reason for the column being written, the announcement of an upcoming public meeting of the Ontario Secondary School Principals' Task Force on Violence.

Fortunately, in many cases, the cuts were not severe enough to detract from the impact of the column. The following piece on a successful young Toronto lawyer giving up his career to sing in a choir in England was discussed by Clyde Gilmour on his popular "Gilmour's Albums" on CBC Radio. I have reinserted the final two paragraphs excised by the *Globe*.

Lawyer Quits Rat Race to Sing in U.K. Choir

September 11, 1990
On Saturday, September 1, a small gathering took place at the Oriole Parkway residence of Ted Rowan-Legg, in-house counsel for the Royal Bank, as choirmembers of Grace Church-on-the-Hill bade farewell to fellow chorister Christian Van Dyck, who is leaving Toronto to live in England.

At the age of 30, Chris Van Dyck has decided to sell his house in Toronto's west end, get rid of his car, a 1989 Toyota Tercel, and abandon a lucrative legal career (present salary in his third year of practice—$70,000 to $80,000). He has chucked it all to go to live in a pastoral setting in a picturesque town on the edge of the Cotswolds to sing as a countertenor in the choir of the magnificent Worcester cathedral built in the tenth century.

"I enjoyed the practice of law," he explained, "but found the work highly strenuous and stressful. There's a lot of frustration in practising as a commercial litigator. Much of what I was doing was not terribly constructive in nature. A lot entailed deflecting issues and obfuscation." With an increasingly lengthy work week (60 to 70 hours), he was never home, and tension built up between him and his wife.

"Having said that," he added, "there are certain elements I'll miss. I enjoyed the drafting and negotiating." "And the money?" I asked. "The money, too," he said. "But money is a trap. It's going to be a difficult adjustment to make," he added. "We will be living basically at the subsistence level. But one of the great things is that we are going to get rid of our debts. In Canada, our consumption level was rising disproportionately with our income."

Their expenses in England will be low. They will live virtually rent-free in a flat in a lovely ivy-covered thirteenth-century manse on the church grounds overlooking the Severn River. He will travel free with the choir, which is touring Germany this coming spring and the Netherlands in the fall. His wife Donna, who is expecting their first child, is as enthusiastic about the move as her husband. She anticipates a closer, warmer family life with both parents involved in their child's upbringing.

Mr. Van Dyck's daily routine will be somewhat different than the one he had as a lawyer. On weekdays his working day will consist of a rehearsal in the late morning and a choral evensong at 7:00 p.m. (There is also a rehearsal at 8:00 a.m. on Saturdays and three services on Sundays.) He has engaged well-known countertenor James Bowman as a teacher and will travel into London once a week for a lesson. He will walk across a grassy common to the cathedral from his flat in the manse to go to work and will be home for lunch every day. A far cry from the daily commute on the crowded Gardiner Expressway arriving home some nights as late as 2:00 a.m. to fall into bed exhausted, only to repeat the same routine the next day.

"My friends tease me," he said, "about entering my mid-life crisis ten years early, but time is running out. A counter-tenor's voice should be at its peak at about my age, so now is the time to take the plunge. Besides, if I wait any longer, my wife and I may get locked into this fast-paced, expensive life-style."

Mr. Van Dyck grew up in Buffalo, New York, where he and his twin brother, Tim, began singing at the age of seven under the tutelage of their father, an organist and choirmaster. After high school he attended Cornell University for two years, ran out of money and spent a year in Nova Scotia, where his parents had moved, cutting fish. He then went to the University of Toronto to finish his degree in English and history, and Dalhousie Law School, before being hired by a large Toronto law firm where he articled and has practised for three-and-a-half years.

Tim Van Dyck flew up from the United States to attend the party. He, like his brother, is a litigation lawyer—in Boston, where the pace is even more frenetic than in Toronto. He logged 2,300 billable hours last year. And he doesn't have time to sing anymore.

On January 25, 1992, I used my lament concerning copy editors at the beginning of this chapter as the basis for a speech at the Granite Club. Surveying the crowd of several hundred beforehand, I was a bit nervous, but the guests seemed to get a kick out of my story, doubtless appreciating it more than its intended audience.

Exactly one year later, the *Globe* terminated my column, probably for a variety of reasons. Space was short at the paper and a society column was considered a frill; the recession had arrived and parties and social gatherings were not appropriate fodder at this time for a serious national paper; and after five years of writing on the same subject, I had probably gone stale.

So, instead of slogging away at my weekly column, I sat down to write a book called *The Glitter Girls*. Believe it or not, writing a book without newspaper deadlines and constant evenings out on the town was greatly therapeutic.

Best of all, much of the book was written on an old Radio Shack TRS-80 word processor that the *Globe* gave me when I started my column. Yet not one *Globe* copy editor was able to get his or her hands on my musings before they were published.

Chapter Seven

Exit from The Globe and Mail

As I soon learned out of necessity, a social event can mean just about anything, and I did my best to broaden my column to incorporate some of the more interesting gatherings. There's nothing quite as deadly as attending gala after glitzy gala. To the credit of the *Globe and Mail*, my supervisors never curtailed my activities. They did cancel some of my columns, but that was not because of the event I was covering, but because they didn't like the way I covered it.

After I had been at the *Globe* for just a few months, I sent down a column on a nursery school auction and a baby shower. I realized that, since the shower was held for my sister, there was a chance that the *Globe* might not run it, but I had also been informed by Geoff Stevens that conflicts of interest like that were acceptable, as long as they were declared, so I declared it. In any case, I thought, the paper could just run the nursery school piece if they didn't want me writing about a member of my family. Both events had a similar theme about women and children. I had worked hard on the column and breathed a sigh of relief when I sent it down.

But my copy editor at the time, Sam Carriere, saw the reference to my sister and took it to Gwen Smith, Geoff Stevens's assistant. She nixed the column and Sam phoned and told me. I called Gwen, who said I wasn't to write about my sister. OK, I said, I understand that, but what about the first item on the nursery school. "I don't like that, either," she said. "You're supposed to be writing about parties, not children. Send down something else."

At that time, just into the third month of my job, I was barely keeping up to my three columns a week, and I didn't have anything else to send down. To tell the truth, I was having trouble covering sometimes up to six events a week (two per column) and attending them all, as well as looking after my family, and trying to manage weekend travel and several households. A slow learner, I had yet to figure out shortcuts. My mail had gotten completely out of hand, and I was finding it difficult just reading all the invitations, never mind trying to choose which ones to respond to. I couldn't believe that all the work I had done on that column was for nothing.

Deep sobs erupted from my end of the line. "B-b-but I don't have a-a-anything else," I blubbered to Gwen, shocking even myself by my uncharacteristic emotional behaviour. "Well, don't cry, for heaven's sake," she replied, sounding utterly exasperated. I think she was as embarrassed as I was by the outburst. So there was no column that day. I never did find out what Gwen Smith had against the nursery school piece, except that she had no children, and maybe that made a difference. This is how the offending story went:

Oriole Nursery School is a small nursery school that was started immediately following World War II by parents wanting to take an active role in their preschoolers' education. As one of Canada's first cooperative, nonprofit nursery schools, it was quite ahead of its time. It has the same enrolment—56 children—as it did in 1948, and their ages range from 2-1/2 to 5 years.

Recently, the school held its fortieth birthday party and annual fund-raiser. The first one was held in 1948 at a parent's house, and it raised enough money for two new tricycles and a sandbox. In the mid-fifties, those attending paid admission to see a film on the Royal Family, but the projector broke down part way through the evening. This year's fund-raiser was an auction held to raise money for some playground equipment.

Almost every parent donated something to be auctioned off. Michael Miller, a master at Upper Canada College, offered six hours of tutoring. Michael Davies, a vice-president of Dominion Securities, offered his New York apartment for the weekend. Dr. Susan Schulman auctioned off a hypnosis seminar, which was purchased by Paddy-Ann Burns, a former parent.

The auctioneers were CITY-TV anchorman Gord Martineau and parent Valerie Pringle, host of CBC's "Midday." The school raised $6,800.

Past presidents of the nursery school board include former U. of T. president John Evans; AGO volunteer Susan Stone; and Lee Magwood, wife of SkyDome president Charles.

Other parents, past and present, include former Baton Broadcasting chairman John Bassett and his wife, Isabel, Arctic explorer Joe MacInnis and his wife, Debbie, and Bata chairman Thomas Bata and his wife, Sonja.

This year's president is Mary Beaton Nixon, whose son, Warner Bennett, attends. He is the son of architect William Bennett and the youngest of six children in the combined Bennett-Nixon household.

Baby showers aren't exactly in vogue these days, what with all the push for equality of the sexes and getting women out of the home and into the workplace. However, women are still having babies and their friends are still holding showers, as evidenced by a recent one for my sister, Minette Ross, at the Rosedale home of Marjorie Wallens, manager of public affairs for the TTC.

Most of those assembled were both mothers and working women, among them Angela Ferrante, assistant general manager at *Maclean's* magazine; writer Loral Dean; real estate agent Timmy Vezina; Ministry of Labour consultant Annella Parker Martin; and professional fund-raiser Beverley Howell.

After the traditional present-opening took place, revealing the expected baby blanket, quilted pram bag, baby towels from Holt Renfrew and a jumper from Mimosa, the mother-to-be was presented with two small containers, one of sugar and one of oil.

The oil was to wish her an easy delivery; the sugar a good-natured child. The presentation was made by Penny Williams, who has just resigned as editor of *Your Money* magazine. Burdened with neither a child nor a job, she departed after the shower to go helicopter skiing in the Rockies.

That evening I worried that I had made an enemy of someone above me at the *Globe*, so I asked Edgar what he thought I should do. "Why don't you call and ask Gwen out to lunch?" he suggested. So I did. The next day I got a call from Geoff Stevens. "Uh, Rosemary, Gwen has asked me to come along on your lunch together, so I'll see you tomorrow at noon." I still don't know to this day why Geoff was invited along (perhaps my sobs had led Gwen to believe she was dealing with a deranged woman), but anyway, the three of us had a pleasant-enough lunch together.

Near the end, Geoff turned to me and said, "Rosemary, we're really happy with your work here and I'd like to see you get a raise." I looked over at Gwen, who was glowering, as surprised as I was at this unexpected turn of events. "That's wonderful, Geoff, thank you very much," I gushed. "Yes," he said, "henceforth, your paycheque will go up an additional $25 a week." This time I didn't look at Gwen in case she was laughing at me. "Touché," I thought.

I have never forgotten how deftly Geoff Stevens handled two warring women on his staff at that lunch. He gave me a raise in front of Gwen, but it was nominal enough that I couldn't get too much of a swelled head. I think it was a clever way to defuse a potentially explosive situation.

But the relationship between Gwen and me was never a warm one. Gwen next raised her voice to me over my spelling: "Can't you even spell Sawatsky's name right?" I consider myself a decent speller, but that really hit a nerve because at the time (several years before his book on Mulroney), I hadn't even heard of John Sawatsky, so I couldn't even remember how I had spelled his name in the first place. Anyway, I thought to myself, what are copy editors for, if not to correct spelling?

I had various run-ins with Gwen Smith while she was at the *Globe*, but as long as the Webster-Stevens team was in place, I felt fairly secure. For those two years, I was treated fairly, and I felt that my column was, if not high on the newspaper's list of priorities, at least accorded some respect.

All that changed, once Stevens and Webster were shown the door. Although I was invariably treated with courtesy by William Thorsell, who actually took the time to write several encouraging notes on my columns (and who generously gave me a book of his on Paris after my Parisian articles), and, indeed, by Roy Megarry, who was unfailingly pleasant and helpful on the few occasions I ran into him, my columns were hacked to death after I sent them down to the *Globe*. The worst offenders were two male copy editors who, for some reason, took it upon themselves to rewrite or cut many of my columns, even ones that were completely inoffensive, such as a tame piece I wrote on the Canadian Federation of Friends of Museums, which they refused to run. I still have no idea why.

I didn't ever call the *Globe* to complain. With all the firings occurring with the changing of the guard, I didn't want to be considered a troublemaker, and I suppose I felt lucky to have a job at all.

As for the succession of new managing editors, I enjoyed working under Chris Waddell, a consummate professional, although it was clear he had no power. But, after he left, Tim Pritchard became my boss. One conversation I had with him went something like this:

Me: Tim, why wasn't my column "How (Not) to Marry Rich" run in the *Globe*?

Tim: I canned it.

Me: Why?

Tim: It's not an appropriate subject for your column.

Me: What do you mean?

Tim: Rosemary, what is the name of your column?

Me: "Society."

Tim: Well.

Me: Well, what?

Tim: Do I have to spell it out for you? That column had nothing to do with society.

Me: It had everything to do with society. For many society people, or at least wannabe society people, how to marry rich is a burning issue. In addition, Roxanne Pulitzer was one of the panellists.

Tim: Who is she?

Me: She was just involved in one of the most high-profile divorce cases in Palm Beach society.

Tim: Well, I don't know anything about that.

Me: Exactly.

Tim: Well, I'm sorry about this, Rosemary. I don't know what to say.

Sucky Me: Oh, it's okay.

The offending piece read as follows:

How (Not) to Marry Rich

Taping a television show isn't the easiest job in the world. It's bad enough when only 32 out of an expected 300 guests show up on a stormy night. It's even worse when your most celebrated guest happens to be stuck en route in the Philadelphia airport. But what if your panellists start to go at one another tooth and nail, disregarding the formatted script? But that's show biz. (That's also, I presume, why shows such as these are pretaped.)

The setting for the above-mentioned scenario was a taping of CTV's "Shirley" show on Monday night this week. The topic was How to Marry Rich, and I thought it might provide a few insights for those readers of this column who have not already done so. Well, it has, but not quite in the way I expected. . . .

To begin with, credit should be given where it is due. Shirley has a difficult task facing her every night, interviewing all sorts of people from all walks of life. She never flinches as the topics she covers range from interviews with victims of sexual abuse to unhappy spouses. Future topics suggested by the live audience, many of whom are regulars, ranged from nuclear holocausts to security guards.

Framed by purple walls and slanted white pillars illuminated with pink neon lights, Shirley began by questioning the most flamboyant of the six panellists, Gini Polo Sayles. (Gini is pronounced Jeannie; I never did find out what the Polo stood for—her second favourite sport, perhaps? But Sayles was the name of the rich oil tycoon she married, who smiled un-waveringly at her from the front row.)

Mrs. Sayles, who says she has studied the habits of such millionaires as Aristotle Onassis and J. Paul Getty, conducts seminars, conferences and field trips on how to marry a rich man. And for all those out there dying to know how it's done, she has some advice. Initially, she says, a girl has to get noticed by wearing body-conscious, sophisticated clothing. (She her-self came attired in a gold-sequined jacket, black see-through blouse, black striped nylons and gold-painted spike heels.) The next step is to move into the best part of town, "even if all you can afford is a teensy attic," and get to know your neighbours. It's all downhill from there.

"Now I know why I've been single for eight years," com-mented fellow panellist Roxanne Pulitzer. No slouch herself in the marrying rich department, Roxanne was married for seven years to Pulitzer fortune heir Herbert Pulitzer. Arriving late due to a delayed flight because of the storm, she rushed onto the set dressed down in a pair of blue jeans, white turtlenecked sweater and navy blue blazer. It wasn't only in her attire that Ms. Pulitzer differed from Mrs. Sayles. Her message to the audi-ence was you pay a high price when you marry rich. When her marriage broke up, she found herself out on the street and shunned by Palm Beach society. Her advice to the audience: "I came out of a seven-year marriage with nothing but my clothes and a $2,000-a-month allowance for two years from a man worth $25 million. Get a premarital contract if you can."

The other panellists were a smug young man from Texas who, since taking Ms. Sayles's course, says he refuses to settle for a woman worth less than $2 million; psychotherapist Sondra Gold, who runs her own matchmaking service; an overweight woman identified only as Catherine, who said she was tired of men running after her just for her money; and a Bay Street promoter who looked decidedly uncomfortable at finding himself on the panel. "It's a form of prostitution, real-ly," he said of Ms. Sayles's tactics. The audience, in response to the cue card, applauded with gusto.

Enlightened prattle, all of it. It will be fascinating to see what the show does with a hot topic like security guards.

Looking at the incident from Tim's point of view, I think that he did have some justification for criticizing the column. I had made fun in rather a scornful manner of people who appear on talk shows. And the *Globe*, under the new regime, was steering away from any controversy.

Had Tim told me to write with less sarcasm, I could easily have accommodated him. But he didn't seem to know how to voice a proper objection, so he scrapped the whole thing. This high-handedness is one of the reasons why the *Globe* is not the paper it used to be, and why many good people at the paper have left.

At this point I was becoming embarrassed about my columns, anyway. When I did write with some bite, it was taken out so that what was left was often just a list of names. I knew I either had to adjust or leave the paper. It was too hard to do all that work for nothing.

But as the weeks went by, I began to become more comfortable with the new regime. In a way, it turned out to be a good thing for me personally, if not for my reputation as a writer. Since I was sick and tired of going to all those parties, and the *Globe* was excising my little juicy tidbits, anyway, I just stopped going. It was easy to get over the phone what had gone on at a party without attending, especially since I was now expected to give a straight-out, nongossipy account. I was truly getting tired of the social scene, and this way I could do my job without actually being there.

I didn't want to do three columns a week anymore, either, but when I consulted my husband about cutting down, he said I would be crazy to be the instrument of my own destruction. As it turned out I didn't have to be. The *Globe* on its own initiative cut me down.

On October 26, 1990, I decided to give Tim Pritchard's successor, John Cruikshank, a rapidly rising star in the Webster-Stevensless *Globe*, a call. I made the call ostensibly to ask about the GST, but I really wanted to know the status of my column, since I had heard through the grapevine there had been more firings at the *Globe*. Edgar and I were planning a trip to Bermuda, and then I wanted to get ready for Christmas; if the *Globe* was going to let me go, I would just as soon find out now so I could relax over the Christmas holidays. The conversation went like this:

Cruikshank: John Cruikshank speaking.

Me: Hello, John. It's Rosemary Sexton. Have you got a minute?

Cruikshank: Not really, Rosemary. I'm really busy today. The editor for Focus is off and I have to edit that section.

Me: Well, I'll make it short. I'm just calling to ask about the GST. Starting January, since I'm a freelancer, I'll have to pay the tax. What is the *Globe*'s position on this? Will you be paying the tax for the freelancers?

Cruikshank: Well, I'll have to look into that, but I doubt it. We haven't dealt with that problem yet, but I doubt you'll get any satisfaction from us. I'll let you know. By the way, how do you feel about writing fewer columns?

Me: You mean two a week instead of three? I suppose if it meant that I got the allotted space every time for the two columns, it would be all right.

Cruikshank: I know what you mean. Your column doesn't have its normal impact when it's getting cut all the time. No, I mean one column a week, but maybe we could ensure that you got a certain amount of space. We're having trouble right now, you know. When you were first hired, our advertising was at an all-time high. Now it's the lowest it's ever been. It's not just our newspaper, it's all the papers.

Me: I realize that it's tough times for everyone and that the lack of space isn't your fault.

Cruikshank (proudly?): I fired six columnists last week, you know.

Me: While we're on the subject of less work, Edgar has a case in Bermuda next week. May I get a week off?

Cruikshank: I don't see a problem with that.

Me: And we'll talk about my column when I get back?

Cruikshank: OK. Talk to you then.

I had Christmas with my family, but had heard nothing from John about my reduced workload. I was getting worried. Usually I spent some part of my holiday trying to figure out my upcoming columns for the next couple of weeks. If I was cut down to one, it would be easy, but Cruikshank still hadn't called. Finally, I called him on the pretence of asking about my March holiday. It worked. "Remember the plan I mentioned to you," he said, "about cutting your three columns to one? We're going to start it now." So for the next two years, I wrote one column a week.

From that time on, after an initial settling-in period for my once-weekly column, I was treated well by everyone down at the *Globe*. I was rarely questioned by copy editors or edited at all except for length when there was a lack of space. I was asked to write for the front page of the Focus section, which I did under Sarah Murdoch, an extremely capable editor (now associate editor). And when Michael Valpy became managing editor (a post he quit after several years to go back to his column), the *Globe* ran three of my columns as front-page stories—one on falling prices in Rosedale real estate, one on the firing of Cartier president John Lauer and one on Princess Diana. I also wrote a feature on Conrad and Joanna Black's separation, which prompted an angry call from the inestimable Mr. Black to editor Thorsell.

Things seem to have settled down at 444 Front Street West, and though it is generally agreed that it is not the paper it used to be, mostly due to the extreme cost-cutting demanded by the Thomson regime, still for many Canadians the *Globe* is the newspaper of record.

And to give credit where credit is due, many newspapers these days seem to be under the gun. People are turning more than ever before to the electronic media for their daily news fix. In the past twenty years, newspaper readership is said to have declined greatly.

So maybe the papers have to use these stringent means just to stay in business. But it's a shame. The Thomson organization may be rubbing its hands with glee at the bottom line, but perhaps it should be taking a better look at the product it is creating. Ultimately, an inferior newspaper turns away advertisers and turns off readers.

"Although I will quit my column when *The Glitter Girls* comes out," I wrote in my diary in November 1992, "I will be sorry not to be able to say any longer that I write for the *Globe and Mail.*"

Well, the *Globe* beat me to it. In December, John Cruikshank called to say they were terminating the column, though he did present me with an interesting offer. The paper would continue to pay my salary at the same rate if I would contribute to a new political gossip column they were setting up, but I declined. The new column, titled "Tattler," had a fairly undistinguished run of six months.

Part Three

Life After
The Globe and Mail

Chapter Eight

Diary of an Author

Once my column at *The Globe and Mail* was terminated, I felt free to pursue a tack that during my five years at the *Globe* I had been prohibited from doing. I wanted to try to steer the proceeds of a future Brazilian Ball in the direction of Grenville Christian College, a small private school on the shores of the St. Lawrence River that I had sent my children to. A strict, but caring, back-to-basics Christian school, it had provided an atmosphere where my daughter and son had flourished, and I wished to thank the school in some way. I wanted this to be my swan song before retiring from fund-raising completely, but things didn't exactly turn out that way.

This diary begins after preliminary conversations and a tea and luncheon had already taken place between me, Brazilian Ball founder Anna Maria de Souza, Grenville headmaster Reverend Charles Farnsworth and school bursar Dan Ortolani, as a result of which Anna Maria had agreed to designate the proceeds of the next year's ball to Grenville and another co-beneficiary.

January 20, 1993
I left a message for Trevor Eyton (senator and chairman of Brascan), and he returned my call on an airplane telephone on the way to Mexico. It was a bit staticky so, after we chatted for a while, I got to the point. Could his wife, Jane, cochair the Brazilian Ball

to raise proceeds for Grenville Christian College? A highly successful fund-raiser for the school and one of its patrons, Trevor had already had a conversation with me, and he had seemed interested in the idea. Again he expressed interest.

I then asked if Jane would be willing to cochair the ball with Gay Evans, the wife of former U. of T. president Dr. John Evans. Gay is on the board of the Queen Elizabeth Hospital, and Anna Maria de Souza had told me she would be cochairing the ball. Trevor seemed enthusiastic about the idea. Gay's father, Grant Glassco, was Trevor's predecessor at Brascan, and John Evans, who Trevor said was his hero when he was a university student, preceded him as captain of the football team. Trevor also mentioned to me that John Evans knew Al Haig, the founder of Grenville, very well, since they had played football together. By the end of the call, I felt that he had given his promise. "It's a go, Rosemary," he said. I was very happy, since to have Trevor's clout behind the ball pretty well ensured its success.

I called Anna Maria to tell her. She seemed very pleased about this development, and asked if I would give Gay Evans a call to inform her. The call wasn't quite what I expected. A surprised Gay Evans said not only hadn't she known she was being considered for cochair, but that she didn't know that Grenville would be sharing the proceeds with her charity. But she was very pleasant and said she'd get back to me.

As usual, Anna Maria, a typical glitter girl, is telling different people different things. I got the feeling that, before I spoke to her, Gay Evans had been promised the ball all to herself and to her own charity, and that she had no idea that there would be a sharing of the proceeds.

Coincidentally, Kimberley Noble, a well-respected reporter for *The Globe and Mail*'s Report on Business, also called today to ask if I knew of anyone at the law firm of Tory Tory who had worked with Trevor Eyton in the 1970s. I left a message on her machine that it was doubtful that anyone at Tory's would be willing to talk since the Hees–Edper Group, which controls Brascan, still uses that law firm exclusively.

The two calls on the same day made me aware of the fact that now I'm no longer a columnist, I really have crossed over the line.

You can *either* work as a columnist and be out digging for stories on people, *or* be out making deals with those same people that the press write about. You can't play both sides of the fence. I can't be helping a reporter dig up dirt on Trevor at the same time as I need his help.

I like being back, for a while at least, on the dealmaking side. Giving up my observer status is a big relief.

January 22, 1993
Had lunch with *Globe* ROB columnist Bud Jorgenson. I picked him up at the *Globe*, and then, since we both wanted some exercise, we walked to Le Bistingo, where I had made reservations. Barbara McDougall and John Tory were there, and Barbara and I joked (since we had both recently been at Il Posto at the same time) about following each other around town. I asked John how his wife (who had been partially paralyzed with Guillain-Barré syndrome) was, and he said she was much better.

I guess I'm not the only one who's had trouble at the *Globe*. They tried to pull another one of Bud's columns, and again he stood up to them and won, though it may have been a Pyrrhic victory. After he noticed several want ads for an editor for the *Financial Times* in the paper, he made some calls and found out that they were fake ads that the *Financial Times* had to run because their editor is American. But the ads asked for qualifications that no one could fill so they could keep him. Bud, who feels that there's a principle here at stake, i.e., that Canadian publishers are hiring too many foreigners and not using their Canadian talent, wrote a column on the false ad. ROB editor Peggy Wente killed it. Bud argued with her and sent it down again. She killed it again.

Bud and two men from the newspaper guild went to Peggy to argue for the reinstatement of the column and got nowhere. They asked to speak to Thorsell and she said no, that Thorsell agreed with her. So they called up publisher Dave Clark, who said speak to the editor, which they interpreted as permission to go to Thorsell. They went to Thorsell, who gave the column the OK. But Bud still has to work on a daily basis with Wente, who now hates him, so he may not be there for long.

Now I am free of my column, I've been going out quite a bit for lunch with different people. It was fun for a week or two, but now I want to stop. Not only is it expensive, but it's a waste of time. I want to get back to my writing. But I've been invited to a luncheon with Mila Mulroney by Helen Vari, which I plan to attend this week, plus I have luncheon dates scheduled with Marilyn Lastman, Allan Fotheringham, Anne Delicaet, Jacquie Latimer, Ellen Roseman and John Lownsbrough that I should keep. But when the next two weeks are up that's it: it's back to work again. In some ways I find work easier than going to lunch, which palls after a while.

January 27, 1993
Attended the luncheon put on by Helen Vari at her Granite Place condominium for Mila Mulroney. Helen, who is in her sixties and a wealthy immigrant from Hungary, is one of Mila's best friends. Mila is in town for a Royal Ontario Museum gala tonight.

About 40 people were invited. Liz Tory was there wearing an Hermès blouse she had purchased at Hazelton Lanes. She came with Jennifer Carter, one of her daughter's friends, who manages the Hermès boutique.

Volunteers who have worked with Helen on one committee or another were there: Jill Farrow, who belongs to the Toronto Garden Club and whose husband is a doctor at the Toronto Hospital; Mary Nesbitt, who was Mary Molson; and lawyer Mary Louise Dickson, who used to spend summers in my hometown of Haileybury.

Also lawyer Anne Dubin, wife of the Ontario chief justice, in a grey plaid dress; and Nobel prize-winning U. of T. chemistry professor John Polanyi and his wife, Sue. While talking to John and *Sun* society writer Barbara Kingstone, I asked John if he knew Evelyn Huang (pronounced Wong). "Evelyn Waugh?" he asked. We all laughed. "Isn't he dead?" asked Barbara, who didn't seem quite sure. Barbara told me she will be moving to Hong Kong on March 1 because her husband Ed will be a visiting professor there.

Liz said she wanted to have a return luncheon for Helen at the York Club with Sue, Anne, me and some others, maybe on Helen's birthday, which is at the end of March.

Helen made a speech welcoming Mila and mourning the passing of Jeanne Sauvé, who, she said, had been to the apartment often and always admired the view of Toronto from its eighteenth floor. Mila was very gracious to everyone and amazingly good at small talk.

"Have you ever seen a stranger collection of people?" commented Liz Tory the next day. "There's nothing in it for Mila to go to things like that. I'm going to tell John." (Liz's son, John Tory, was Mulroney's campaign head.)

One of the reasons I always like to talk with Liz after a party is that she comes up with these incredibly funny and gossipy opinions which, as she well knows, I could never have used in my columns.

January 28, 1993

Gay Evans called. She is balking at being the cochair of the ball. "I've never heard of Grenville Christian College," she said. "Actually, Gay, I've never heard of the Queen Elizabeth Hospital, either," I told her. "Anyway," she went on, "no one has actually officially informed us that we are to be co-beneficiaries of the ball. We'd like a phone call from Anna Maria." When I told Anna Maria what Gay had said so that she could call her up, she instead became angry. "They haven't even got the ball yet, and they're making demands already."

She called me back later. "Rosemary, I've got a wonderful idea. Waterloo University has been bugging me for the ball. Why don't we team up Waterloo and Grenville? If you agree, you can have it for 1994." "That's great, Anna," I responded. It didn't matter to me who our co-beneficiary was, as long as we were one of them. And I knew that Trevor sat on the University of Waterloo board. But it seems surprising that she would discard the Queen Elizabeth Hospital just like that, with no discussion.

I called Trevor, who said it was fine with him to have Waterloo as a co-beneficiary, but he wasn't sure about Jane's commitments, with the ball now looming so close.

Globe sports editor Dave Langford phoned and asked that I not tell anyone that he and I went for lunch several weeks ago. The Alan Eagleson thing is going to blow up really big, he explained. I took it that he doesn't want to be seen consorting with the enemy. (Edgar is Alan Eagleson's lawyer.) I assured him I'd say nothing, though I didn't really understand his request. But then I'm not at the *Globe* anymore, so I probably have no idea what hoops he has to go through down there.

January 29, 1993.
The house is fairly quiet this week as the kids are all away. Robin's gone back to school after his mid-January break. He just called me with his exam marks—97 in math, 89 in Latin, 87 in biology and 86 in English. "Not bad!" I kidded him. We couldn't talk for long because he was late for a meeting of the yearbook staff of which he is assistant editor. Jen (my stepdaughter Jennifer) is in Vancouver visiting her boyfriend Andrew's father, and Steffi's in Bermuda, courtesy of my mother. (After they both graduated from Queen's University in 1989 with Honours B.A.'s, Edgar's daughter Jennifer and my daughter Stephanie lived in the coach house at the back of our house for five years.)

I had planned to go to a party for the Brazilian Ball commit-tee—just to keep in touch with them all if Grenville is to be a future beneficiary, but, at the last minute, I really didn't feel like it and went roller-blading instead. But a number of people called me later to fill me in.

The opulent affair was chaired by Cathie Bratty, wife of devel-oper Rudy, to thank the sponsors of the 1992 Brazilian Ball. It was held at the Bridle Path mansion of developer Shane Baghai, a builder from Iran. The grey stucco house with its long circular driveway was designed in the style of a French château and looks like something off a Hollywood movie set. It certainly knocked the socks off the invited CEOs who, according to their hostess, "were dropping their teeth and trying to look cool" at the specta-cle that greeted them. Some compared the 46,000-square-foot mansion to Versailles.

"I've never seen a house like that," marvelled Anna Maria de Souza the next day. "It makes the Campeau house look like a gate house." Those circulating marvelled at the high ceilings with their ornate mouldings painted in gold. The 200 guests went through a small hall into a bigger one, 40 feet square, with a circular staircase. In the centre of the hall was erected an island of coconut trees; brightly coloured serpentine decorations hung down from the bannisters. Guests then walked through the hall, where there was a receiving line, through various reception rooms including a massive ballroom, to the 6,000-square-foot indoor swimming pool area. Tables and a buffet were set up in the area around the pool. Two bands were playing, one in the hall and one in the swimming pool area. But the house is so large that a guest standing in the front hall could not hear the band in the swimming pool area.

What a relief it is neither to have to attend nor write up such events, though it would have been interesting to see the house, I guess. Just describing a house like that would bring dozens of wrathful letters down upon my head. But I liked writing those things up, because I wouldn't even have to figure out an angle. Just report straight on the overlavishness and ostentatiousness of the affair. Most readers with a sense of humour would just laugh at it all.

February 1, 1993
Got back from Brockville to find a message on my answering machine from Les Payette, executive editor for the *Toronto Sun*. I called him back and he asked if I would be interested in writing a column for the *Sun*.

I was very flattered by the request, and I wish I felt like column-writing again, because I would be proud to write for the *Sun*. It has some of the best columnists around, such as Peter Worthington, Douglas Fisher and Christie Blatchford, and it doesn't interfere with them to the extent the *Globe* does. I read four papers every day, the *Globe* and *Financial Post* in the morning, and the *Star* and the *Sun* in the evening. The *Globe's* still my favourite paper to read, but the *Sun* is my second favourite.

February 2, 1993
Had lunch with Fotheringham at his current favourite watering hole, Lakes. He's disturbed about Doug Creighton's firing from the *Sun* since he was one of Creighton's fair-haired boys. Maybe I'm next, he said. I told him not to worry. They'd be crazy to let him go. He said that Sondra Gotlieb, who was hired by Creighton, was fired by the *Sun* last week. He also said that after Creighton's firing, Cathie Bratty (her husband Rudy is one of the directors who voted Creighton out) went to the Creighton's house to see

Marilyn Creighton, but Marilyn refused to let her in. Adrian Macdonald was sitting at a nearby table and waved at us. She's a breath of fresh air—a nice friendly girl with seemingly no airs or pretensions about her.

February 4, 1993

Talked to another of my glitter girls today. She had attended Conrad Black and Barbara Amiel's Christmas lunch. "We know and like Conrad very much," she said, "but I'm reserving judgement on Barbara. She reminds me of a mutual friend of ours [Sondra Gotlieb]. They both come up to you and say, 'Please talk to me. Please don't leave me alone. I don't like anyone here in this room. Here is my number. Call me and we'll talk.' If you didn't know any better, you would think they were little fragile birds that had to be protected. But Barbara can't play on that vulnerability bit for too long. As time passes she gets less and less credible."

February 8, 1993

Last night Edgar and I flew in from Vancouver, where we'd gone for the weekend to celebrate Edgar's mother's ninetieth birthday. Vancouver was breathtaking; we're really lucky—it never rains when we visit. We used to stay at the Wedgewood, Eleni Skalbania's small hotel downtown, but there's no view. And we don't like the newer hotels like the Pan Pacific very much, because they're huge convention hotels.

So we booked at the Bayshore Westin in a corner suite with a two-sided view of the mountains and the harbour. Every morning, before ordering breakfast up to our room, we jogged over to Stanley Park and walked around the seawall. The temperature was a balmy 50 degrees. All I wore was a turtlenecked sweater of Robin's, a pair of stretch bicycle pants of Steffi's and my Birkenstocks, and I wasn't cold. And this was February! It's minus-20 degrees back in Toronto.

Over breakfast, which we had in our room, I was shocked to read in the morning paper of the death of *Globe* columnist Stephen Godfrey, who was only in his early forties. No cause of death was given in the obituary. (We discovered later it was suicide.)

Today at 2:30 p.m. was Stephen Godfrey's funeral at St. Simon the Apostle Church, practically just around the corner from my house. Two hours earlier Catherine Nugent and Cathie Bratty held a going-away luncheon for Barbara Kingstone at the Bradgate Arms. At first I thought I would go to both, and then I thought why should I? I knew that the funeral would be a mob scene, and I thought it would probably be uncomfortable for Barbara to have me at a party in her honour, since we were basically competitors, though friendly ones.

Instead, I sat down and wrote letters to Mary Godfrey, Stephen's mother, and to John Godfrey, his brother, both of whom I knew, though I had never met Stephen. And then I toddled off to the library, where I spent a glorious afternoon reading books about society to prepare for my speech to the Canadian Club.

Talk about luxury—having the time to spend browsing through books with no real deadline in sight. The first book I found on the library computer that interested me was in the rare book room of the Metro Library. There the staff took my coat and bag and made me fill out two forms. They even took away my pen and replaced it with a pencil so I couldn't damage the book in any way. The book was titled *High Society—Advice as to Social Campaigning and Hints on the Management of Dowagers, Dinners, Debutantes, Dances and the Thousand and One Diversions of Persons of Quality*. It consisted of a number of sketches by a woman cartoonist known as Fish (I wonder if she's the same A. H. Fish who illustrated my favourite Stephen Leacock paperbacks), accompanied by witty essays written by Dorothy Parker, George Chappell and Frank Crowninshield. It was funny and clever and documented such politically incorrect subjects as "The Seven Deadly Temperaments as frequently met with in the Ladies" (they included feline, nagging, maternal, romantic, practical, artistic) and "Getting on in Smart Society (If at first you don't succeed, dine 'em and dine 'em again)."

Dropped into Summerhill Market on my way home to pick up some groceries. Ran into Krystyne Griffin, who had been at the Godfrey funeral. "It was very moving," she said, "but there were so many people there that we had to line up in the cold for about fifteen minutes. Even Hal Jackman and Bob Rae had to wait outside for a while before they could get into the church."

Tomorrow and the next day I have lunches scheduled with Catherine Nugent and *Globe* business columnist Ellen Roseman; immediately afterward I'm going to the library for the afternoon.

February 9, 1993

Lunch with Catherine and her husband, David, was mostly fun, but a bit of an ordeal since they tend to bicker.

We had lunch up on the second floor of the Four Seasons. They both ate quite a bit and I ate almost nothing, mostly because Catherine is always asking me out to lunch and she always insists on paying. So all I can do, since I'm rarely very hungry at noon, anyway, is to keep my consumption down to a bare minimum. I do say no to about three out of four of her invitations—and to those of the other glitter girls—but it is important, when you're a writer, to keep in touch with the people in the know, which Catherine certainly is, at least about the glitter girl group.

I had a small salad and an Upper Canada dark ale, period. As for Catherine, well. While she was nibbling at the bread basket, there arrived a special pre-hors d'oeuvres plate of a pita-type bread spread with thick tomato sauce and olives, which she devoured. In the meantime, a large vodka and Coke arrived, which was downed fairly quickly. She then ordered a mushroom asparagus plate made up especially for her (it wasn't on the menu), and then a whopping dish of chicken and vegetables and noodles, along with a large side order of what appeared to be that white paste we used in art class in public school. "What's that, Catherine?" I asked. "Mashed potatoes," she said. By this time another vodka and Coke had arrived plus a bottle of red wine.

February 15, 1993

I almost ended up going to the Brazilian Ball after all, even though Edgar and I had breathed a sigh of relief that we didn't have to go this year now that I am columnless. He was in court for the Irvings in New Brunswick the day of the ball, and we were to meet in Brockville that evening. But his case took much longer than expected, so he missed his plane. We had already said no thanks months in advance to our friends Anne and Bob Lindsay when they asked if we could sit at their table, but Friday afternoon, after

I found out that Edgar was going to be late, I happened to be talking to Cathie Bratty. She and Rudy were sitting with David and Catherine Nugent and Shane and Marnie Baghai. The Baghais had cancelled as their daughter was ill, and Cathie, hearing Edgar was late, said, "Why don't you come along and sit at our table?" I was tempted because I'd be alone that night, and because it seemed that everyone I knew was going—my daughter Stephanie was covering it for Global Television; my stepdaughter Jennifer was there doing public relations on behalf of Heather Reid and Associates; all the women volunteers I'd worked with at the Wellesley Hospital were going (Wellesley is the beneficiary this year); Father Charles Farnsworth and Dan Ortolani from Grenville Christian College; not to mention all the glitter girls featured in my upcoming book, including Anna Maria de Souza, Carole Grafstein, Nancy Paul and Anne Delicaet.

But Edgar ended up catching a later flight to Toronto and he didn't want to go out; nor did I, after all, once I knew he was coming home. So we stayed in and ordered Chinese food.

We took the train to Brockville the next morning and had our usual quiet weekend. The snowbanks in Brockville are about ten feet high. Apparently the 32-centimetre snowfall we got on Friday was the largest since 1972. It was beautiful outside, and on Sunday morning we got up early and went cross-country skiing before breakfast. The snow was too deep to go along the river or on the golf course. So we followed Fernbank Road, a very pretty road along the river dotted with lovely old cottages located several miles to the west of Brockville. Then we came home and ate breakfast and read the papers. Robin visited in the afternoon, bringing me Valentine's Day cupcakes—pink and white—which he had purchased in an auction at the school. I really miss him when I don't see him from Monday to Friday. It's something that I look forward to all week. I'm glad that Steffi's in Toronto.

Later, February 15, 1993
We finally got into Toronto at 2:00 p.m. after getting up at six to catch the seven o'clock train. A freight train derailed ahead of us in Cobourg, so our train, to get by, had to be moved to another

track. But it was a CP, as opposed to a CN, track, and we had to wait for two men to come from Smiths Falls to show them how it was done. A three-and-a-half hour delay! Luckily, both Edgar and I had brought lots to read. I read all of *The Bassett Report* written by Isabel Bassett in the seventies on the role of women in modern society, and a tongue-in-cheek book called *Class* by Jilly Cooper, documenting the differences between Harry Stow-Crat and his peers, Mr. and Mrs. Nouveau Richards and Mr. and Mrs. Definitely Disgusting. The book was frightfully snobbish, as only the Brits can be, and quite clever.

Suanne Kelman, the copy editor down at the *Globe* who is compiling the "Tattler" column, has been phoning me to ask for help. When I took over Zena's column, the last thing I would have done is to call her for assistance. I get no sense of obligation with Suanne; in other words, she isn't someone who would ever appreciate what I'm doing for her or repay me in any way.

It's important in this business, and indeed in any business, to recognize who plays fair and who just takes. The trouble is, I'm one of those females who always try to be helpful even when they shouldn't be. I've already fed her two items. I've also identified people for her and given her phone numbers. This time she wanted some help on the Brazilian Ball. "I wasn't there, Suanne, but if I hear anything, I'll get back to you," I said, with no intention of doing so.

On the other hand, I'd be happy to give tips or help out in any way the Geoff Stevenses, Allan Fotheringhams, Stevie Camerons, Michael Bates and Bud Jorgensons of this world.

March 1993

Just got back from a relaxing ten days with Edgar on the island of Montserrat. To get there, you fly to Antigua and then take a small plane.

Back in the seventies some rock bands came to the island, set up recording studios and built large, luxurious villas to live in. Due to several destructive hurricanes, the rock stars left, but the villas remain and many are rented out to tourists.

Ours was perched on the side of a mountaintop with a spectacular view of the beaches and ocean below and the mountainous island of Nevis way off in the distance. It was massive with big pillars and indoor-outdoor courtyards and its own swimming pool. Quite the most beautiful residence we have ever stayed in.

But there are drawbacks to the island. First of all, there's nowhere to go and nothing to do. Edgar and I are hermits and we love to read and swim and walk, so we thought we would enjoy the isolation. But this was too much. When we went on walks, for example, we often ran into cows and bulls wandering freely on the island, and, unsure as to whether they would attack or not (probably not, but you never know), we would have to head back to our villa sooner than we wanted.

There were only two hotels on the island and one good restaurant that we saw. Plymouth, the capital of Montserrat, is a typical Caribbean town, not terribly clean, though we felt safe. Much of the food in the outdoor market and grocery stores looked and smelled bad, so we were pretty restricted in what we could eat. We ended up buying a lot of frozen chicken.

We also had a daily maid who woke us up every morning when she arrived at eight and didn't go home until the late afternoon. I'd really have rather cleaned and cooked myself and had the privacy. Agnes, the maid, was a bit of a tyrant, and tried to boss us around and to make us eat breakfast at nine. On holidays, I like to exercise and swim and then eat breakfast at about ten-thirty. She also wanted to talk all the time, and Edgar and I aren't great chatterers. We told her she could stay home and we'd pay her, anyway (it was included in our villa price), but she got insulted, so I apologized and we just put up with her.

Finally, the beaches on Montserrat are black sand, which is really sort of like mud. They're not great to walk along.

Funnily enough it was I, even more a hermit than Edgar, who didn't want to return another year. Edgar said he would be happy to go back. He loved our villa.

April 1993
The *Star* called me to ask if I had heard the news that Joanna Black is getting married to her priest friend. (After Conrad and Joanna separated, she started dating the Reverend Brian MacDonald, director of alumni and public relations at St. Francis Xavier

University, whom she then married.) I had not. They asked me for his name, and I told them to look at a back issue of *Frank*, which had the name in it. It's a little ironic that a mainstream newspaper has to go to *Frank* to find out things.

Another piece of news is that Stephen Godfrey's widow is pregnant with twins that are due in October, which means that she must have gotten pregnant in February just before Stephen died.

Despite his recent difficulties, Alan Eagleson had quite a large celebration for his sixtieth birthday down at his offices on Maitland Street. Nancy had left for England the day before, but Al, Jr., and Jill were there. Saw Johnny Esaw and chatted to Tom Wells, who's chairing the campaign to raise funds for the North York Performing Arts Theatre. Talked also to lawyer Walter Bowen and foundation head Don Rickerd and his wife, Julie, who said that Doug Creighton's speech at the National Magazine Awards dinner, decrying his firing, was not particularly well-received.

Catherine called me to say that a tea was held at Susan Davidson's house, cohosted by Carole Grafstein and Daniela Bruns, for the late Pat Appleton's daughter who's getting married. Michael was supposed to drop in but sent along his girlfriend, Marilyn, instead. So far Catherine hasn't been invited to the wedding, and she doesn't know why, but she suspects it may have something to do with Carole.

Catherine also asked if I'd ever heard of a woman named X. Apparently she's supposed to have carried on a fourteen-year affair with the husband of a glitter girl who's a good friend of Catherine's. I was surprised that Catherine would be telling me this, knowing about my upcoming book.

You know, Catherine, I told her, I could never put affairs in my book because it's unfair. First of all, if a marriage lasts long enough, at some point someone may stray, yet it may still be a good marriage. Secondly, it is unfair to the glitter girls if I talk about affairs they have had and leave out their husbands' affairs which I might know nothing about.

Krystyne Griffin told Catherine that Barbara Amiel has been complaining to her about all the travelling she has to do with Conrad as he goes around trying to meet up with important people. I'm exhausted, she told Krystyne. She's finding it hard to keep up with her writing with all the socializing she's expected to do. I never thought I would feel sorry for Barbara Amiel, but I certainly identify with her on that point.

June 2, 1993
Spent all day in a warehouse building at the corner of Coxwell and Dundas getting my photo shot for *Chatelaine* to accompany a forthcoming article on me and my book. Photographer Jim Allen had already come to my house to discuss the concept, which he said was to wrap me in newsprint. I said, "Sounds OK by me." Then, knowing what photographers are like with their "concepts," I elaborated. "I don't mind you having me look funny or sexy, I just don't want to be a laughingstock." He assured me that would not be the case.

Well, when I got to his studio, his assistants told me they wanted to do my hair fifties-style—back-combed with a flip. To add insult to injury, they weren't encasing me in newspapers at all. Instead, they had constructed a large, ungainly skirt out of *Globe and Mails* and had brought deeply cut, tight stretch tops to go on top. The stretch tops were bad enough, but I had a little temper tantrum about the hairstyle. At first I said I wouldn't pose at all, but then, feeling sorry for them, I agreed to pose with what they wanted, as long as they promised to take additional pictures with my hair my usual natural way. I probably shouldn't have panicked so badly; they may have known what they were doing. Especially since Jim Allen is supposed to be an excellent photographer and the makeup person was Barbara Allen, who's also supposed to be very good.

A few days later, Rona Maynard, the editor on the piece, called and asked me how the photographic session went, and I told her I was a bit worried about it. So right away she rescheduled the picture-taking. It wasn't really what I had in mind; I hate posing so much for the camera that I was willing to stick with the previous ones, no matter how bad they were. But she seemed insistent and she was just trying to help me, so I agreed.

What a mistake! It was awful. I had to go shopping with an assistant and try on about 20 dresses and narrow those, none of which I particularly liked, down to three. We went to Holts, where they have all kinds of dresses hidden away in cupboards that aren't out on view for the public and got a pink off-the-shoulder long gown, and then to Fetoun in Hazelton Lanes for a slinky turquoise number that cost the earth—several thousand dollars—which made me look like an aging mermaid. (Fortunately the stores were lending these dresses as a courtesy to *Chatelaine*; I didn't have to pay for them.) And then we went back to Jim Allen's for the fitting and the makeup and then out in a limo to do the shots. Of course it started raining right away, and by the time I was posed against a stone wall in the U. of T. campus, I was shivering with cold, my makeup was running down my face, and my very thin, wispy blonde hair was flat as a pancake.

I guess it serves me right for complaining in the first place. I'm sure both *Chatelaine* and Jim Allen are sick of me by now and rightfully so.

June 4, 1993
At the beginning of June, I got a call from Gina Mallet who, angry at the cuts made in her story by the *Chatelaine* editors, told me she was taking her name off the story. She was quite incensed. "I'm just calling to let you know, Rosemary, that I refuse to give my name to this story. And I'm writing a letter to *Frank* magazine, and Stevie Cameron is backing me up."

I tried to sympathize with her, but I really had no idea what to say, because I don't know what she wrote. It felt a little strange to be comforting someone whose piece on me got cut because of what she said about me.

I spoke to Rona a few days later. "It's too bad this happened," she said, "but I'm hired to do a job and I have to do it. There was another incident with Gina several years ago. I suppose you know about that." "No, I don't," I said. But Rona didn't elaborate.

June 7, 1993
Baton Broadcasting president Doug Bassett called to say that everyone is talking about my book. He says that he'll send down television cameras for my party and also put me on the news and on the "Dini Petty Show." "I hope you treated Susan [his wife] well in your book," he said, not really joking. He also told me that

the staid old Toronto Club, of which he is the president, just voted 82 percent to admit women members to the club. Only seven members didn't vote for one reason or another.

June 21, 1993

Eileen Whitfield, a fact checker at *Toronto Life*, called to ask some questions on the Liz Tory chapter, which *Toronto Life* is excerpting in their August issue. When I earlier spoke to *Toronto Life* editor Stephen Trumper, we discussed the magazine buying the Evelyn Huang chapter, but then *Toronto Life* called Evelyn to ask her to pose for a picture and she refused. They should have done it through me. I think Evelyn might have said yes if I had asked her.

So now they're doing Liz and I said I would call her, and she agreed to pose.

I gave Eileen the names and numbers of people to call and check on what I had written. I also found my notes on the Liz Tory interview and two sections of this diary, which corroborated what I wrote, and put them in a brown envelope in my mailbox to be picked up by a courier from *Toronto Life*.

In the meantime, Eileen started on her calls. One of the people she called was Sally Armstrong, the editor of *Homemaker's* magazine. The paragraph in question was as follows:

"Thank God, my coupon-cutting days are over" was [Liz's] remark at the same luncheon to an affronted Sally Armstrong, editor of *Homemaker's* magazine and author of a recent biography on Mila. "Liz, what are you saying? This woman is just back from Somalia!" responded a fellow guest, coming to Sally's defence. Seeing she might have gone too far this time, Liz quickly recovered. "We're living in different times when a society woman such as Liz Tory has to apologize to a career woman like me," commented Sally afterward.

When contacted by Eileen, Sally first denied everything, but then as Eileen questioned her little by little, she agreed that everything had happened, as written, except for the last sentence. Sally then called Denise Schon, my publisher at Macmillan, to complain that I was not telling the truth. Denise called me, and I stood by my story and told her to give Sally my number.

"You are very unprofessional, Rosemary," Sally said when she called, "to have recorded a private conversation like the one we had. You weren't interviewing me for your book." "That's right, Sally," I responded. "I called you up to ask if you would excerpt my book when it was finished in your magazine, and you asked me who the glitter girls in my book were, and when I said Liz was one of them, you related the incident. You didn't say what you told me was off the record." "It was a private conversation," she insisted. "Sally, my book is full of conversations I had with people, just like the one I had with you," I replied. "Thank you, Rosemary," she said, and hung up the phone.

The next furious phone call I received about the Liz Tory piece came from public relations consultant Heather Reid. "Every time I look at Roy Thomson Hall, I think of what a contribution Liz has made to our community," I quoted Heather as saying. Unfortunately, when Eileen Whitfield read that quote to her, Liz didn't like it. And called Heather to tell her so. "Who are you," Liz asked Heather, "to be making comments about me?"

When Heather phoned me, she was distraught. "Rosemary, you've got to take that quote out," she said. "Liz is furious." "Why?" I asked. "You were flattering her." "She thinks I'm not an important-enough person to be making comments about her," said Heather. "That can't be it," I answered. "Liz is no dummy. She's like the rest of us. She'll take compliments where she can get them. There must be something that bothers her about that quote. Maybe she wasn't as instrumental in getting the Thomson donation to Roy Thomson Hall as you imply. Or maybe she didn't want her name linked with her husband's employer in that way." So I called Liz and asked her if she would rather that part of the quote come out and she said yes, so I took it out.

These ridiculous complaints remind me of the ones I received in the first few years of writing my column. Why do some people think they can bully writers into eating their words?

Re the Brazilian. Trevor has obtained Bank of Montreal chairman Matthew Barrett and his wife, Irene, to be honorary cochairs along with him and Jane. It's a real coup, and it practically ensures that the ball will be a success. Today Father Farnsworth sent me a copy of a fax that Trevor sent him, suggesting I be the ball chairman. I was quite surprised, but turned it down as I'm sick of the ball scene. So we all put our heads together—Jane, Trevor and I—to come up with a ball chairman. Jane and Trevor suggested Susan Freeman, the wife of Ault Foods chairman Graham Freeman, and Mary Cassaday, wife of CTV head John Cassaday. They presently cochair the large and successful Kids Help Phone gala.

On Wednesday of this week Trevor and Jane are taking me, Susan and Mary to the York Club to lunch to see if we can't nail them down.

September, 1993

The fallout from *The Glitter Girls* has been quite extensive. The excerpt on Liz Tory in *Toronto Life* magazine appeared on coffee tables in Muskoka and got tongues wagging. The first reaction was summarized in a nutshell by the ex-sister-in-law of my Aunt Barbara, who has a locker beside Liz's at the Rosedale Golf Club. "My, Rosemary Sexton seems awfully impressed with Liz Tory," she told my aunt. I also got a call from Carole Grafstein saying how much she liked the piece and from Catherine, as well, who was somewhat more wary. "I hope you haven't printed things I've said about the other glitter girls," she said, worried at some of the remarks Liz had made. (She needn't have worried; in all the glitter girls' chapters, I used their names anonymously when they were saying things they wouldn't particularly want repeated. I didn't want to ruin their friendships forever, even though none had asked to be off the record.) But in general, the chapter excerpted was at first regarded as flattering.

The next week the worm turned. All the scuttlebutt became that Rosemary Sexton had really knifed Liz in the back, but she had done so in such a way that it had deceived everyone at first into thinking that it was a flattering account. Liz, who probably hadn't minded the piece at first (indeed, she called *Toronto Life* to thank them for the picture accompanying it), was reduced to telling everyone that she couldn't discuss it because she hadn't read it. John, her husband, told all those who approached the Torys at dinner at the Rosedale Golf Club one night that they were not discussing the book. John Tory, Jr., told people that it was the kind of interview he had always warned his mother not to give.

The *Chatelaine* piece in the September issue, which reached the stands in August, added fuel to the fire, quoting snippets of dialogue in the book and revealing that Catherine owed a $10,000 grocery bill.

By then Macmillan decided that they would have to release the book before its publication date on September 25, and it hit the stands just as excerpts were printed in the *Globe and Mail* of the Catherine Nugent chapter and in the *Sunday Sun* of the Marilyn Lastman chapter.

The cash registers rang up. Lichtmans at Yonge and St. Clair sold out and ordered another 100 copies. The Book Cellar in Yorkville sold out its 50 copies and ordered another 40. Ann Johnston, assistant managing editor of *Maclean's* magazine, was in the Book Cellar when an inebriated woman walked in and demanded "to see that horrid book that has my friend Catherine so upset." North 49, a discount wholesale store that sells to independent bookstores, sold out and ordered another 100. When Naomi Engel bought her copy at the Village Bookstore in Forest Hill, she was told it was the ninety-sixth copy sold.

I realize I'm just a small fish in a very big publishing pond, but it's gratifying to have these things happen, for a while, anyway.

September 8, 1993
Today I received a call from Marilyn Lastman.

"Rosemary. It's Marilyn. I'm just calling to thank you."

"Oh, you saw the piece in the *Sun*, Marilyn. I haven't even seen it yet."

"I've read the book and it's great. You know my son Dale, the corporate lawyer, the one who hates publicity. He said to me after I'd returned from Palm Beach, 'Mom, I'm really proud of you. You've come back as a celebrity.' 'What do you mean?' I asked him. 'I went away as a celebrity.' Mel's always worried about me and the press, and he was pleased, too. We're both coming to your launch party. Can we get three books for a hundred bucks?"

"I'm really pleased you like the book," I said. "Everyone loves your chapter."

"Well, why not?" she said, laughing. "I never did anything bad to anybody except my husband. I never stole anyone's husband. Also, I'd like to come to hear your speech at the Canadian Club. When is it? Can I bring Mel, too? If he's in town, that is. If he's not, I might find a handsome young construction worker to bring as my date."

Quote from Catherine in *The Globe and Mail*, also today in Michael Valpy's column: "Ms. Nugent, in a brief interview, described the references to her as 'mean and nasty' and the cause of a 'great deal of personal embarrassment' and said that the book 'was a terrible thing to do to a bunch of people who have done a lot of good.'"

Same day: John Fraser called to tell me to hold up even if I get barraged with criticism. His wife, Elizabeth, said that the reason the book was good was that I wasn't coy but just stated what I knew. He told me about writing his best-seller *Telling Tales* and all the adverse reaction he got, and said I wasn't to worry about Catherine's reaction. In a few months she will read the piece over and love it.

But he failed to follow up on his previous request to run an excerpt of the book in *Saturday Night*. A few weeks ago Macmillan told me he had called them and asked for an excerpt and said he would be in touch, but nothing happened. I didn't want to embarrass him by bringing it up (obviously he had changed his mind), so I said nothing. But I hear through the grapevine that one of his editors, Anne Collins, overruled him on the excerpt, though I don't know why. It could be because Conrad Black owns *Saturday Night* and perhaps the thin-skinned Mr. Black doesn't like the chapter in the book on him and Barbara.

The *Financial Post* also called me to ask for an excerpt, but when I called Denise Schon at Macmillan about it she refused, saying there were too many excerpts out there already and no one would buy the book. I don't agree with her on this, but since I'm the novice in the publishing world, I didn't argue. I probably should have.

September 27, 1993
Well, the launching party's over, thank God. There was a mob scene at the McGill Club, and we sold more than 100 books in

two hours. Global ran a segment on it three times the next day. Macmillan vice-president Bob Dees made a speech, and I followed, thanking everyone who had helped with the book and everyone who came. Susan Kastner in the *Star* and Marilyn Linton in the *Sun* wrote up the party, as well as Rosie Levine of *NOW* magazine. I also sent a piece to "Noises Off" in the *Globe's* Arts and Entertainment Section:

To: Val Ross
From: Rosemary Sexton
I've written up my party last night in case you can use it in "Noises Off." If you can, make whatever changes you see fit. Please excuse the arrogance of talking about myself in the third person.

Just what exactly was former *Globe* society columnist Rosemary Sexton wearing when a throng of about 400 guests milled through the McGill Club, while the melodious voices of the Grenville Christian College choir soared to the rafters, last Thursday evening (September 23) to celebrate the launching of her recently released best-seller *The Glitter Girls*?

For those who wondered, it was a large hooped skirt made of *Globe and Mail* newspapers, into which windows were cut to insert the shocking pink, purple and canary yellow covers of the book. Peeking beneath the skirt, created for her by freelance stylist Jimmy Moorehouse, were black velvet platform shoes by Canadian designer John Fluevog. Instead of the Vivienne Westwood corset she had planned to squeeze into (retail $725), the recession-conscious author substituted a black body suit from a Queen Street West discount store (retail $12.99) which she adorned with black beaded neck and wrist chokers by Katherine May.

And who came? Among the media types, lawyers and friends were Global anchor John Dawe, who will be interviewing Sexton on Tuesday (September 28) on the "News at Noon"; social scribe Sondra Gotlieb; former hockey star Red Kelly and his wife, Andra; composer-musician Hagood Hardy and his wife, Martha; *Chatelaine* editor Mildred Istona; lobbyist

Susan Murray; the *Star's* Susan Kastner with Dr. Allan Ross; and Bud Jorgenson and Ellen Roseman from the *Globe and Mail.*

"Eat your heart out, Anna Porter!" called out *Sun* columnist Peter Worthington, surveying the crowd; he came with his wife Yvonne Crittenden, book editor for the *Toronto Sun.* The proud new grandparents of twins Robert and Kathleen, Senator John Godfrey and his wife Mary were there; writer Stevie Cameron also came.

Other notables circulating included Eaton's chairman Allan Beattie; three Supreme Court justices Ed Saunders, Dennis Lane and Jack Ground; writer Ann Shortell and lawyer Herb Solway; investment banker John Bankes; longtime glitter couple Nancy and Derek Philips; Dr. Ken Walker, a.k.a. Dr. Gifford-Jones, and his wife, Susan; Dominion Insurance president George Cooke and his mother, Florrie; Allen Eagleson, Jr., and his wife, Yasmin; foundation head Don Rickerd, his wife, Julie, and mother-in-law, Kati Rekai; Mila Mulroney confidante, Helen Vari; designer Pat McDonagh; impresario Gino Empry; writers Gina Mallet and John Lownsbrough; lawyer Jack Batten and author Marjorie Harris; and *NOW* magazine's Rosie Levine.

As well, Robert Bundy and his wife, Trudy; former *Sun* society columnist Barbara Kingstone; Odette Ambar; and cookbook author Anne Lindsay.

Overheard, Sarah Band confiding to a friend: "I don't know what I'm doing here, the book is trash." That opinion was no doubt shared by others: 15 out of 16 glitter girls portrayed in the book failed to show up. But Marilyn Lastman made up for their absence by single-handedly working the room with husband Mel, and with sons and daughters-in-law by her side.

Maclean's editor Bob Lewis and Ann Johnston, assistant managing editor, came and left quickly.

There were also a few gate-crashers, including one-time Tory candidate Nancy Jackman who, famished after a lively set of line dancing downstairs at the McGill Club at the same time as the party, stole a few grapes from the hors d'oeuvres tables prepared by caterer Chris Klugman.

In her speech, in which she paid tribute to Macmillan

vice-president Denise Schon and thanked the Grenville Christian College choir, Sexton quoted a limerick that launch guest and fellow journalist Allan Fotheringham had whispered in her ear after catching sight of her newspaper skirt:

> There once was a girl from Bengal
> Who wore a newspaper dress to a ball.
> The dress caught fire and burned her entire . . .
> Front page, sporting section and all.

The *Globe* printed most of my write-up, but knocked out a lot of the names due to space problems, or because, as in the case of Sarah Band, they didn't know who the person was.

My family was also present—Edgar; Steffi, who brought along the Global television cameras; Robin, who sang in the choir; my stepson Chris and his wife, Wendy. My stepdaughter, Jennifer, was sick, but her fiancé, Andrew Bevin, who is the executive assistant to John Godfrey, M.P., came.

The party seemed to be a success, but I'm still getting repercussions from the book. "Canada AM" called to cancel my appearance. The rumour is that Doug Bassett was angry at what I wrote about his wife, Susan.

Last week Trevor and Jane took me to lunch at the York Club to meet Susan Freeman and Mary Cassaday, the two women whom they have suggested as possible chairs for the ball. I think they would do a very good job and hope that it all works out.

October 4, 1993

I spoke at the Canadian Club on To Work or Not to Work: Volunteerism in the Nineties. Surprisingly, I wasn't that nervous and I think it went over quite well, though I was nervous enough not to deviate from my text at all. I was allowed four head table nominees by the club, and so I picked Edgar, Trevor Eyton, Imperial Oil chairman Bob Peterson, a friend and neighbour of ours, and Allan Fotheringham. We sold out the Imperial Room off the main lobby of the Royal York and had to move to the ballroom on the convention level. About 350 people came, which, I was told, was the club's largest crowd that year after Conrad Black. Lucien Bouchard got only 158 several weeks before. I hope

Macmillan's happy, since it was their idea. My publisher Denise Schon and editor Kirsten Hanson were in the audience.

October 6, 1993
I received a curious letter from Anna Maria de Souza today. It read as follows:

> October 4, 1993
> Dear Rosemary,
> Congratulations on the success of your book *The Glitter Girls*. Unfortunately, its contents have resulted in too much hurt and unnecessary damage to the feelings of some long-standing, hard-working Brazilian Ball committee members. As well, the book is a great disservice to the good name of the Brazilian Ball, which was accomplished as a result of many years of dedicated and unselfish hard work.
>
> I regret to advise you today that the advisory board of the ball has decided not to give its support to Glenview [*sic*] College at this time. Perhaps you didn't realize that your comments in the book would affect the Brazilian Ball.
>
> Wishing you luck on the selling of *The Glitter Girls*, which I have heard is doing so well.
>
> Fondly,
> Anna Maria

Needless to say, I walked around all morning in shock after getting that letter. I was devastated that Grenville Christian College was going to be penalized because of my book. I called Trevor right away, who seemed as surprised as I was. I'll try to speak to Anna Maria for you, Rosemary, he promised. And I got this letter from him several days later.

> October 6, 1993
> Dear Rosemary,
> Thank you for including me as one of your guests at the head table when you spoke on the topic To Work or Not to Work: Volunteerism in the Nineties at the Canadian Club luncheon on October 4. . . .

I have also just talked to you relative to the Brazilian Ball and Grenville Christian College. It occurs to me there is no rationale for any exclusion of Grenville Christian College on the grounds you have stated and I will call Anna Maria to make that point in a gentle way.

All the best,
Trevor

October 14, 1993
Well, my two-week press tour to small-town Ontario is over. I think it was quite successful, but I'm such a homebody at heart, and I hated being away from Edgar. The worst part was the evenings, when he wasn't around to talk to and to go to bed with. My only stipulations to Macmillan were no evening appearances, and none on Mondays and Fridays since we travel to Brockville on those days. My media schedule sheets from Macmillan went like this:

Tuesday, September 28
10:00 a.m. CHFI at 25 Adelaide East
10:45 a.m. Mix 99 at Yonge and St. Clair
11:00 a.m. CFRB
11:45 a.m. "News at Noon" on Global with John Dawe
1:30 p.m. Dini Petty
6:15 p.m. Leave Island Airport for Ottawa

Wednesday, September 29
8:45 a.m. Meet publicist Jennifer Tiller in the lobby of the Lord Elgin Hotel.
9:00 a.m. CKBY FM at 112 Kent Street. Interview with Randall Moore.
9:30 a.m. Q101. Interview with Linda Steele.
10:30 a.m. CHUO FM. Interview with Bob Gougeon.
12:00 (noon) CHRO TV. Live at 12:30 with Dan Mooney.
2:00 p.m. CHEZ Radio.
3:00 p.m. Meet Derek Raymaker of the *X PRESS* at World Exchange Plaza coffee bar.
4:30 p.m. CJOH TV. Taped interview with Leigh Chapple.

In between those interviews I called up fellow journalist Roy MacGregor to chat and dropped into *Frank*'s offices. Michael Bate was not there as he was installing a new *Frank* person, Douglas Thomson, in Toronto, but Glen MacGregor was and we talked for a while. He showed me the latest issue of *Frank*, which I hadn't yet seen. It contained an article called "Glitter Girls Shun Sexton," describing my launch party.

At six-thirty that evening I took a flight to London, Ontario. In London, I was booked at the Station Park, a nice hotel with a central downtown location. Unfortunately, there was no room service. So my dinner that night, after I got to the hotel at about eight and had a bath, consisted of a tomato juice from the mini-bar (there was no vermouth with which to make Manhattans), a package of roasted almonds for my first course and a package of chocolate-covered almonds for dessert. My London day consisted of an interview and photo at the *London Free Press* and two television and two radio interviews. And then I flew home.

The next week was about the same. I spoke at the Canadian Club on Monday, had an interview on "Morningside" with Peter Gzowski on Tuesday, headed up to North Bay where I did one television show, one radio show, a *North Bay Nugget* interview, and a two-hour book signing before heading back to Toronto. After that, I had more radio and television in Toronto and a few short trips to an authors' breakfast in Burlington, and went to Kitchener for the "Bob MacLean" show.

The second-last day of my tour I spoke at an author's breakfast at the Burlington Golf and Country Club. About 250 people were present, and I thought my speech was OK. That is, until Honest Ed Mirvish followed me. Without a note, he had the audience in stitches in minutes. But it was a pleasure to be upstaged by such an old pro. Afterward, when he and I and the third author, novelist John Lawrence Reynolds, were signing books (Ed's line practically went right out the door), Ed's wife, Anne, came over to talk and bought one of my books, which was really nice of her. I think she felt sorry for me because my lineup was so much smaller than her husband's.

The next morning I went up to CFTO at Channel Nine Court to be a guest of Lin Eleoff's on "Eye on Toronto." It was quite a contrast to my appearance the week before on CITY-TV when I was interviewed on the noon show by John Major. There I was preceded by the Waltons, young kids in a new-wave country and western band, who changed out of their clothes right in my dressing room, and a comic named Jason from Yuk Yuks. It was a circus down at the CITY-TV studios, with people wandering in off the streets, lissome young girls with roller blades twirling around, guests meandering down the long corridors, and large groups of schoolkids cheering and waving or hissing and booing if they didn't like a particular guest.

At CFTO, I was preceded by two men from Oktoberfest in St. Catharines, one who sang and the other who played the accordion as guests sang "Edelweiss."

An interesting thing happened at CFTO as a girl named Adele Ilott led Elizabeth Crinion, my publicist from Macmillan, and me down to the waiting room. We have a request for you before you go on the show, said Adele. During your time on air could you please omit any mention of Douglas Bassett and his wife Susan? She seemed embarrassed to ask me that, perhaps worried I'd object or throw a tantrum or something. I assured her that I would have no trouble doing what she asked, that they'd just been mentioned in passing in my book. While waiting to go on, Keith Morrison came in to say hi. "I was looking forward to interviewing you," he said. "Do you think Doug Bassett cancelled the interview?" I asked him. "Oh, no," he answered. "Doug wouldn't do that." But what else could he say? "I'll inquire, Rosemary, and see if I can't get you on again." "Thanks, Keith," I answered. But I heard nothing, of course.

Today was my first day at home after the tour. I thought I would get back to working on my next book, but I was so exhausted that all I did was go shopping for groceries, clean the house, do laundry and have a nap in the afternoon with Beaumont the cat.

Deking into Summerhill Market quite early—around 9:00 a.m—after driving Edgar to work, I ran into Bob McMullen, the store owner whom I had not seen since *The Glitter Girls* was published. He was the one who had casually told me about Catherine's unpaid $10,000 bill.

"Catherine's been spreading the word around town that the

story about her bill is false and Summerhill's going to print a retraction," I told him. "Is that true?"

"Well," said Bob, "she's working on my father about it. He's the one dealing with her, not me."

"I'm sorry if I've caused you any problems," I said.

Bob smiled. "You owe me big on this one, Rosemary," he said. "That one line I gave you for your book has caused a lot of controversy. But at least one good thing has come out of it."

"What's that?" I asked.

"Catherine's outstanding account here has never been lower," he replied. And we both laughed.

Bob also told me that the sales of my book in Summerhill have been going very well, something that one of the grocery delivery boys had already told me. Apparently, Bob's father, Frank, got sick and tired of people coming in the store and oohing and aahing over things in my books, but not buying them. So he put cellophane covers on all of them.

November 1993

There's been another nice fallout from the book, and I guess my *Globe* column has something to do with it, as well. *Maclean's*, which had *The Glitter Girls* on its best-seller list for three weeks, called up and asked me to write for them. I'm sure this and the *Sun's* offer are my last chances. No one's going to want me in a few months from now, when all this has died down.

Maclean's managing editor Ann Johnston took me out for lunch at Bistro 990, where we hashed things over. *Maclean's* would pay a lot more than the *Globe* ($1,000 a page), but it would be a full-time job, I think, and I don't ever want to go back to that. I thanked Ann very much but declined. She very kindly said, "Think it over some more and if you change your mind, let us know." I don't think I will ever change my mind, but I'm sorry at the same time, because it's a great opportunity. I'm all talked out and really have nothing I want to say to anyone right now. And, above all, I'm really tired of being in the public eye.

December 1993

Ran into *Maclean's* publisher Brian Segal, Hughie's brother, who reiterated the *Maclean's* offer. Ann had talked about writing about whatever interested me, but he focussed on the visual arts and culture. I told him how flattered I was to even be considered for *Maclean's*, but that I really don't feel up to it. Brian and I were both attending a dinner put on by Bank of Montreal chairman Matthew Barrett for the Writers' Development Trust. Peter Gzowski, Farley Mowat, Betty Jane Wylie, John Brady and I were the guest authors. About 100 attended, including publisher Avie Bennett, broadcaster Betty Kennedy, realtor Sis Bunting Weld, former Grafton Group chairman Bill Heaslip and his wife, Nona Macdonald.

A funny thing happened after the dinner. Trying to sneak out without being noticed, I grabbed what looked to be my mink coat, which I had inherited after Edgar's Aunt Ella died last year. She purchased it more than 20 years ago at Holt Renfrew and her name was sewn into the lining. The next morning the Bank of Montreal called asking if I had taken home my own coat. Yes, I said, never dreaming I'd made a mistake. I decided to check just in case, and then I noticed that Aunt Ella's name wasn't sewn into the lining. When I called the bank back they were greatly relieved, because Nona Macdonald had called complaining that someone had taken home her coat. So the bank sent a car to drop off my coat and to deliver Nona's to her.

I really can't be trusted with expensive accoutrements such as jewelry or minks. I lose everything. Edgar and I are both the same that way. To us, paying a lot of money for such luxuries is a waste. However, Edgar says I do like buying houses. But he does, too.

February 1994

Well, the glitter girl network is still intact. I got a call from the *Brockville Recorder and Times* picking up on an item in this month's edition of *Toronto Life*, which read as follows:

Jungle Drums

When the Glitter Wears Off

The Glitter Girls, Rosemary Sexton's behind-the-scenes exposé of Toronto's high society women, continues to send little ripples through the Rosedale set. Miffed by Sexton's frank characterizations, several glitter girls have pressured Anna Maria de Souza, grand organizer of one of the city's most successful fund-raising events, the annual Brazilian Ball, to change the designated 1995 beneficiary. That was to be Brockville's Grenville Christian College, where the children of Sexton and her husband Edgar have been enrolled. Sexton had been asked to chair the event but declined; Brascan's Trevor Eyton and wife, Jane, and Bank of Montreal's Matthew Barrett and wife, Irene, will serve as honorary cochairmen. Sexton declines to comment, but the Ball would likely have raised $750,000 to $1 million for the school. Sexton's book is now in its second printing.

The reporter from the *Brockville Recorder and Times*, Eva Janssen, asked several questions about the above story, and then wrote a piece titled "GCC Dragged into Tiff between Toronto Socialites."

As a result, perhaps, of the *Toronto Life* item, there was a small surge in sales over the next weekend. One woman called Summerhill Market to ask to purchase nine books. Summerhill Market didn't have nine books and called me to ask where to get them. After I had hung up from that phone call, I decided to call Anna Maria. I had not spoken to her since her letter stating she was withdrawing the proceeds from the ball to Grenville Christian College. Nor had I replied to the letter, but the Brockville reporter had asked if she could speak to her, so I thought I had better tell her what was going on.

Anna Maria was very friendly, said she did not want to speak to the reporter, but that, yes, it would be correct for me to tell her that Grenville was still a potential beneficiary of the ball. She had decided to give the ball to Mount Sinai, after all (several months earlier she had asked me to call Valerie Fine, who was on the board of Mount Sinai, to tell her that Grenville would be getting the ball in 1995, not Mount Sinai), but Grenville was a distinct possibility after that. She said that her friends seemed to be getting over the book and asked me how it was doing. "Summerhill Market just sold 12 copies today," I said. "Poor Catherine," Anna Maria said, laughing.

I then mentioned that CBC had wanted to do a program with their cameras following me to the Brazilian Ball later on that week, but I had declined, not wanting to stir up trouble. "Oh, you should come," she said. "Anna Maria, I couldn't do that," I replied. "Catherine, Nancy et al. would be furious." "Some of them aren't even going to the ball," she said, and I got the distinct feeling that she would like me to go. But I continued to demur. Not only did I not want to cause problems, I just didn't want to go to the ball, period, or have a television camera follow me around, and I'd already said no to CBC.

We ended the conversation amicably and I felt quite good about how it had gone, until the next morning. I ran into Summerhill Market to pick up a few groceries, only to be confronted by Bob McMullen. "You sure gave Catherine an earful," he said quite pleasantly, but I felt he was displeased. "What do you mean?" I asked. "Haven't you been talking to Catherine recently?" he asked. "I haven't talked to Catherine since her chapter was excerpted in the *Globe* back in August," I answered. "Well, she stormed in here yesterday demanding to know what we were doing selling 12 copies of *The Glitter Girls*, and it was just about an hour after I talked to you," he said. "Heavens, Bob," I said. "I have no idea how she would know that. It certainly wasn't from me. Did you tell anyone?" "No," he said. And then the truth dawned on me. "I told Anna Maria right after you talked to me yesterday. In fact, she and I laughed about it. She must have called Catherine right away to tell her."

That was bad enough news, the fact that Catherine was right back to bullying the Summerhill Market people. But what was even worse was a phone call I received later in the day from Dan Ortolani, GCC's development officer. "I was just talking with some people from Sunnybrook Hospital," he said, "because we're working on a charity auction together. And you know what they told me? That they're the recipients for the 1996 Brazilian Ball proceeds. Anna Maria, at the request of one of your glitter girls, has said she will give it to them after Mount Sinai, not us." "Who's the glitter girl?" I asked. "I don't remember the name," he answered. "But if you mention someone to me, it might ring a bell," he said. "Liz Tory?" I asked. "Yes, that's who it is," he said. "Well, Dan, that should teach us, especially me, a lesson," I said. "Never believe anything Anna Maria says."

July 1994

I have a new interest, thanks to my husband. Golf. I absolutely loathed golf when I tried to play last summer. One time when we went I walked off the course in a rage; another time I lay down on the fairway and fell asleep because I was so bored. So Edgar gave up inviting me along. But he looked so forlorn going off by himself that I resolved to give it a real honest effort. Lo and behold, I began to like it and now I'm hooked. Nothing makes me feel better than coming in off the golf course after playing a tough eighteen holes. It's psychologically cathartic, since all you think about is getting that little white ball in the hole. And it's a great workout, since we don't take a cart. I don't think that most people know how physically tough golf is. Walking up and down hills pulling a golf cart and swinging at balls in between is much more exercise than I ever realized.

August 15, 1994

July's my favourite month, because we're at the cottage and Edgar's on holidays, but I like August, too, because Robin's at home and we can just hang out together. I'd better savour this while I can, because he just turned 17 this summer and I imagine it's the last summer I'll have with him before he has a summer job.

Tonight, after feeding Robin and Steffi and sending them off to a movie, I made pork chops with mushroom sauce, which I popped into the oven, baked potatoes, fresh green beans and baked tomatoes, and a peach-blueberry cobbler. When Edgar got home at eight, we both had baths and then dressed in our favourite loungewear—he in jogging pants and a T-shirt and I in a black negligée for drinks and dinner. Fell into bed around eleven. "What do you do every night now you're not out on the town anymore?" *Frank* editor Michael Bate recently asked me. If he reads this, he'll know.

September 6, 1994

Yesterday Robin went back to boarding school, and for the first time in a long time I feel like getting back to my writing. So I wrote for about eight hours today. I have two books in mind now that *The Glitter Girls* is done, one on my five years at the *Globe*, tentatively titled *Confessions of a Society Columnist*, and a fictional work about a family.

I don't want to go back to writing every day, just when I feel like it. Anyway, Mondays and Fridays are pretty hopeless, because I'm usually travelling and I don't have a portable laptop to take with me on the train.

September 7, 1994

Last week Popsy Johnstone called to ask that I pose for a picture today with Allan Fotheringham, along with a dozen others of his favourite ladies who lunch. The photo session wasn't until five, so I got in quite a few hours of work before going up to Summerhill and Yonge to pose for the picture, which will be made into a sort of collage to decorate Fotheringham's town house on Shaftesbury Avenue.

After the picture-taking session, where we women posed one at a time on a park bench with Fotheringham's arms around us, imitating the pose of a stone statue on the bench, we gathered at his place for drinks and hors d'oeuvres.

The town house was quite lovely—high ceilings, polished floors and an airy, spacious feeling about it. And the company enjoyable. I especially liked talking to Isabel Bassett, a striking woman at 55, who told me that her husband, John, was quite ill with a relapse after a heart operation. She will be running provincially for the Tories.

Sondra Gotlieb was there in a black fedora. She didn't look very well—her face was very flushed and she seemed quite fragile—but she was in fine form, telling funny stories about her back and neck problems and her daily physiotherapy and how she and Alan had rented a house with a swimming pool for the summer, not far from their own, so she could swim, but then they ended up hardly using it.

Sarah Band showed off photos of her latest squeeze, architect Gordon Ridgeley.

Phyllis Bruce went to her coat to pull her card out of a pocket when I asked her if we could have lunch sometime. She is presently an editor at HarperCollins, having left Key Porter, and she was one of the first people to read *The Glitter Girls* and give me some encouragement.

Adrienne Clarkson was there, as authoritative and lovely-looking as always. I expressed my concern to her that John Lownsbrough's piece on her companion, novelist John Ralston Saul, had been pulled from *Saturday Night* by Conrad Black and his new editor Kenneth Whyte. She wasn't very happy about it.

Honor de Pencier and I discussed golf. She's played for years. Also chatted with Lyn Carpenter, former personal assistant to Doug Creighton, who is now back at the *Sun* working. Although I didn't realize it when I was talking to her, she's the woman whose daughter died of anorexia and in whose name the *Sun* has started a support group for victims of eating disorders.

Also author Sylvia Fraser, who is soft and sweet-looking and writes about incest.

Other women who posed included Pamela Wallin, Geills Turner and Sylvia Ostry.

September 13, 1994

Last night we went to the opening party for the Barnes exhibit. Put on by the investment firm of Gluskin and Sheff, who had contributed $1 million to bring the collection of paintings by Picasso, Degas, Monet, Matisse and others here to Toronto (the NDP government contributed another $3 million), it was probably the biggest bash seen by Torontonians since the height of the eighties. Fifteen hundred invitees were hand-delivered engraved invitations accompanied by a glossy coffee table book of paintings enveloped in a wooden case. Edgar and I had considered not going since it was a Monday night and we get up at 6:00 a.m. to catch the 7:00 a.m. train, but there were two factors that caused us to accept. First of all, Gluskin and Sheff has hired Hughie Segal to do PR and promotions for them and we wanted to support Hughie, a friend, in his new job. And secondly, inside the glossy book, the wholesale price of which the *Globe and Mail* in a front-page story yesterday said was $85, there was a personal note from Hugh to Edgar and me. So we couldn't return the book, which we had intended to do when we initially decided not to go. And since we were keeping this expensive book, we felt obliged to go to the party.

Not that we ended up regretting our decision, because the party really was quite something. Police and photographers lined the steps to the front doors as we got out of our limo and approached the AGO. Once inside the building we walked down several long corridors, where we were greeted by copious tables of wines and champagne, and beautiful young people passing out exotic nibblies. After eating and talking and walking down more corridors, we were relieved of our drinks and ushered into the several rooms containing the original masterpieces. In the half hour spent circulating through these rooms we stopped and talked to the host Gerry Sheff; department store heir Fred Eaton and his wife Nicky, home from England where he was British High Commissioner; Eric Jackman; TVOntario head Peter Herrndorf and his wife Eva Czigler, who produces "Midday" for CBC; friends from Charleston Lake, Hartley and Peggy Nichol; lawyer Herb Solway and writer Ann Shortell, who's working on another book; U. of T. president Rob Prichard and his wife Ann Wilson; and lawyer Cliff Lax. Others seen were Gerry Schwarz and Heather Reisman, the latter in a pearl grey ball gown; Galen and Hilary Weston, she in beaded black and gold calling imperiously to her spouse: "Dew come awn dahling, you ah haulding us up"; TD Bank chairman Dick Thomson and his wife Heather; Bob Rae with Arlene in curly ringlets and wearing a short trapeze-shaped turquoise concoction that didn't flatter her at all; former finance minister Michael Wilson; former PR person Bob Ramsay and his new wife Jean (I didn't recognize Bob, he was thin and fit; he and his wife were in training for the upcoming New York Marathon); London, Ontario businessman Peter Widdrington; communications czar Ted Rogers and his wife Loretta, both of whom are down-to-earth and gracious; and former immigration minister Ron Atkey with his daughter Erin. Conrad Black and Barbara Amiel arrived with Allan and Sondra Gotlieb and former U.S. ambassador Walter Annenberg, Barbara wearing a short black skirt and silver and black blouse, which turned out to be quite casual for the occasion.

Emerging from the rooms with the paintings, guests were ushered down escalators and then walked into a large gallery around which were numerous food stations serving succulent rack of lamb, couscous, scalloped potatoes, roast beef and, for dessert, flaming orange crepes suzette. You could have stayed there all night and gone home filled to the gills, but down a long hallway there was another cavernous room with soaring glass windows and a square table set up in the middle groaning with gravlax, raw tuna, which was seared on the spot, salads and a special dessert plate of many colours.

That wasn't all. For those guests who ventured outside along a candlelit walk there was more food, and tables to sit at.

I wore a low-cut, slinky red dress that I bought at the Bay downtown on Friday on the way to catch the train to Brockville. It took me only about half an hour to find it and I love it—and it only cost $185. I also went to Holts to get my hair blow-dried, and I had my makeup done by Dana Joon, the makeup girl at Global and a friend of Steffi's.

I guess, now that it's over, I can say that it's fun to go to a party once in a while, but I can only say that in hindsight. When I'm expending the time and effort to buy a dress, get my hair done, etc., it seems like a horrendous waste of time—and money. But once I get there I have a great time, and Edgar has a hard time pulling me away. I'm exactly like my father that way. He would be furious if my mother had made arrangements for them to go out to a party on any given night, even just for a dinner party with close friends. He loved to stay home and read. But once my mother got him there, wild horses couldn't drag him away.

September 1994

My husband's law firm Osler Hoskin & Harcourt, known internationally as Osler Renaud, is holding a reception for its Hong Kong office this month. We decided to combine business with pleasure and stop off in Hawaii for a week of golf on our way back. I kept a diary of the trip as follows.

September 30, 1994

11:30 a.m. Toronto time. Ensconced in our wide business-class seats, my husband and I are airbound on our Air Canada flight to Vancouver. Instead of Cathay Pacific's direct flight to Hong Kong, which leaves at midnight and takes 16 hours, we have opted for this shorter flight. It has a four-hour stopover in Vancouver, where we plan to get out and stretch our legs and perhaps take in a bit of the scenery. This flight has the additional advantage of leaving at a decent hour in the morning instead of midnight. If all goes smoothly, we will arrive in Hong Kong at 6:00 p.m. tomorrow (Saturday) night, having lost a day travelling westward over the dateline.

We're settled in quite nicely, having bought three paperbacks at the airport bookstore, a Jeffrey Archer for my husband, an Anne Rivers Siddons for me and James Michener's *Hawaii*, as well.

4:30 p.m. Toronto time; 1:30 p.m. Vancouver time. On our four-hour stopover we took a cab to Shaughnessy and spent two hours walking through the residential streets, instead of our first choice, Stanley Park, which has dark purple clouds hanging over it. Old, stately houses, many Tudor-style on top and wooden on the bottom, large encircling verandahs and porticoes and beautiful gardens. The hedges and trees dwarf those back home.

3:20 p.m. Vancouver time. Back on plane. Discover that, unlike Air Canada, Cathay Pacific still has both business class and first class, and business class, as a result, is less luxurious. There is less room between the rows of seats this time. However, the seats are still roomy and the service is excellent.

7:30 p.m. Vancouver time. We have just finished drinks and dinner and have taken one sleeping pill each. There are nine hours left on the flight and these seats are definitely not as comfortable as Air Canada's, so we feel we need some help getting to sleep. I just finished reading Curtis Strange's book on golf tips called *Win and Win Again*, which I got from the library and started last week, and am going on to *Hill Towns* by Anne Rivers Siddons—but I'm starting to feel very s-l-e-e-p-y.

October 1, 1994
8:30 p.m. Hong Kong time. After our 12-3/4-hour flight, during which we mostly slept (declining the meal offered when we approached the city), we arrived at the Hong Kong airport to discover *no luggage*! Since we only have the clothes on our backs (Edgar in a plaid shirt, khaki pants and Nikes, and I in a turtlenecked

pullover, light tweed slacks and black leather walking boots) and it is 29 degrees Celsius, we anticipate an uncomfortable week in Hong Kong.

We register a complaint with the baggage people, who fail to inform us we can be reimbursed up to $100 each on new clothes to tide us over until our own arrive (it takes a helpful onlooker to do that!), then take a taxi to the Grand Hyatt, where we are staying. Its beautiful marble and glass lobby and the spectacular harbour view from our room help assuage our disconsolateness over the missing clothes. We take baths, enfold ourselves in white fleecy robes hanging on the bathroom door and order up mushroom soup, smoked salmon on rye and vanilla milkshakes before falling into bed. I make calls to Vancouver, Tokyo (our flight's next stop) and Toronto, finally locating suitcases back home in Toronto. Air Canada man promises to get them to us by this time tomorrow night.

October 2, 1994
9:30 a.m. Hong Kong time. Wake up to glorious, hot, sunny day with turquoise water and Kowloon skyline shimmering outside our large window. Numerous ships in Victoria Harbour, which is a constant hive of activity, both night and day. Aged junks propelled by great patched sails contrast with the speedy jet foils and hydrofoils that run between Hong Kong and Macau; the lozenge-shaped green and white Star ferries chug by sleek pleasure vessels; bulk cargo carriers, tugs and container ships dot the horizon alongside rusty red and yellow dredgers filling in the harbour to create more space for building. We stop counting at 100.

Call airport to confirm luggage on its way. I borrow a man's T-shirt from the concierge, so I don't have to wear my warm turtleneck (Edgar wears the white T-shirt he had on under his plaid shirt), and we head out to spend our $200 entitlement. Despite reports to contrary, find some good bargains in shopping complex adjacent to the hotel—a sleeveless top and silk shorts for me and shorts and sunglasses for my husband. I also buy a bathing suit so we can make use of the outdoor pool behind our hotel.

We don our new clothes and, feeling rather pleased with ourselves as a result of our successful shopping expedition, set out to do some typically touristy things. Take the Star ferry across Hong Kong harbour to the Kowloon peninsula for H.K. $1.50 and then a tram ride up to the Peak, Hong Kong's highest point.

Hong Kong is a shopper's paradise, and, indeed, there isn't much else to do besides shop. There is no land to speak of that has not been built on, few outdoor sidewalks except those beside noisy, polluted roadways, so the best places to wander are within the air-conditioned shopping complexes, which stretch literally for miles, and the indoor walkways that link them and most of the other downtown buildings.

There are virtually no houses, only apartments for people to live in. Today the papers report that the child of a wealthy Hong Kong businessman was kidnapped from his private school. The family lives in a 1,200-square-foot apartment that cost $5 million.

It's no wonder that residents of Hong Kong are snapping up the large houses in Rosedale, Forest Hill and Vancouver. They must think they're a bargain compared to what they see in their own city.

An interesting phenomenon peculiar to Hong Kong that we witnessed today in the area surrounding the ferry terminal was that the streets were literally strewn with hundreds of nannies, mostly Filipino, who gather here on Sundays, their day off, to sit and talk and eat and nap with their friends.

Hong Kong's official languages are Chinese and English, but English-speaking tourists may run into a little difficulty while conversing with most Hong Kong residents. Their grasp of the English language is less complete than we rather arrogant anglophones sometimes expect. When I went shopping for the bathing suit, for example, no one knew what I was asking for. Most times, I was sent to the men's suit section. When I switched to swimsuit, the store clerks found my request absolutely incomprehensible. Ironically, I finally found a bathing suit rack at a Lane Cameron department store right beside the children's clothes department to which a clerk had sent me, thinking I had said baby's suit.

I also had a bit of trouble inquiring about my lost luggage when I called the Hong Kong International Airport. The conversation went something like this:

Me: Hello, I am calling to inquire about my luggage from Canada.

Airport: Sorry, plane not in yet. No luggage.

Me: But my luggage was lost yesterday and is supposed to be coming in today.

Airport: Sorry. No plane yet today. Goodbye.

And the baggage person hung up. Surprised at this treatment, I tried again.

Me: Hello. Please don't hang up. I want to know where my bags are.

Airport: You get bags off plane when you arrive.

Me (trying to stay calm): But I tried to get bags off plane when I arrived. They weren't there.

Airport: Why you not put bags on plane in first place?

Me (voice rising): But I did put bags on plane in first place! You people lost them!

Airport: Lost them? Where they go?

Me (yelling): What do you mean, where did they go! You people lost them! *You* tell *me* where they went!

Airport: Oh, I understand. Please accept my apology. I very, very sorry about your bags. Hope you find them. Goodbye.

And he hung up again.

Needless to say, we were very, very happy to see our bags when they finally did arrive at two the next morning.

October 3, 1994

7:30 a.m. When our luggage came, we got up and unpacked, and I put rollers in my hair in preparation for the breakfast this morning, a briefing for the partners in my husband's firm and their wives about this week's coming events. Several of the lawyers at the breakfast turned down the main course—smoked salmon and eggs benedict—anticipating their heavy schedule of constant meetings, no exercise and large luncheons and dinners. I sat beside former prime minister Brian Mulroney, who since leaving politics has joined the firm's Montreal office, where his close associate Yves Fortier, appointed UN ambassador by Mulroney, is the chairman. I ask him where Mila is, and he says, Getting her beauty sleep. We discuss Chrétien, Clinton, all sorts of political gossip. The inveterate soul of tact, I do not bring up Stevie Cameron's new book, *On the Take*, soon to be on the book stands.

That night Brian and Mila and Edgar and I dine at a Chinese restaurant in the hotel. Mila looks spectacular. Her hair is redder than I remember and longer, and she wears a stunning white pantsuit. She's tall and very slim. I feel a bit dowdy sitting beside her in my 47-year-old face and ten-year-old cream wool dress. But Edgar always likes the way I look, and Brian and Mila both are such personable dinner companions that I quickly lose my self-consciousness.

October 4, 1994

12:30 p.m. A women's luncheon at the American Club at the south side of the island. Mila takes me in a chauffeur-driven car. Today she's wearing under her suit jacket a T-shirt that exposes her midriff. She looks like a sexy young teenager. Spectacular views of Repulse Bay from three sides of the building, which is glass from top to bottom. There are about a dozen of us and we sit out on a verandah at a long table, the intense heat of the sun cooled by a strong breeze.

This morning before the luncheon I awoke with a horrible sore throat. Walked to a medical clinic on the next block where the doctor I saw prescribed antibiotics, painkillers and cough syrup that I was given on the spot. The entire visit took about 15 minutes, which says something about Hong Kong efficiency. So the breeze on the veranda doesn't bother me as much as it normally would, given that I'm loaded up with pills. I do feel a little fuzzy, though.

On the way back to the hotel, I regretfully decline Mila's offer to go shopping because I feel so sick. Arrive back at the hotel at around four (Mila and Yves Fortier go shopping) and climb groggily into bed. As a result, miss one of the highlights of the trip, a dinner on board the private yacht of a Hong Kong millionaire who owns several downtown buildings, including the hotel at which we are staying. At this point I'm too sick to care about cancelling out on the evening, but feel sorry for my husband who, when he can't rouse me out of bed, heads off to the dinner without me.

October 5, 1994
Tonight's the big night—the law firm is holding a glittering reception for several hundred Hong Kong businessmen. All I want to do is get well enough to at least make an appearance. I sleep all day, only getting up at 2:00 p.m. to order a large glass of orange juice and some oatmeal with fresh fruit and a mug of hot milk. The room service here is excellent, but for some reason the oatmeal arrives stone cold, straight from the refrigerator. I haven't eaten since yesterday at noon and I want to go back to sleep, so, despite my initial aversion, I dig in. It's utterly delicious. Smooth, creamy, filling and, best of all, cool to my parched throat. I eat the whole bowl, climb back into bed and fall sound asleep in minutes.

Crawl out of bed at 6:00 p.m. and go down to party which is in full swing. Feel OK, and manage, without effort, to carry out my expected social role and have some fun at the same time. Flu seems to be diminishing. Sleep, and some pills to let me sleep, was all I needed.

After the reception, a group of us, including the Mulroneys and Yves Fortier, boards two buses to the Happy Valley Race Track to eat dinner and bet on the horses. Outside of a government-controlled lottery, racing is the only form of legal gambling in Hong Kong, and it is extremely popular. Last season's bets totalled more than U.S. $8 billion. Most of us are novices at betting, but we rally to the cause, picking a horse we favour to win or show. When each race starts we run out from the Jockey Club enclosure where we are eating dinner to scream and wave our hands around like the rest of the crowd in the grandstand. The whole experience is similar to watching a baseball game from a SkyDome box. As darkness falls, we descend in elevators to our waiting tour buses outside, passing what seem to be hundreds of chauffeur-driven Mercedes speeding into the entranceway of the grandstand to pick up their owners.

October 6, 1994

Thank heavens—my flu is gone. Edgar and I awake at ten-thirty
to a leisurely room service breakfast—plate of fresh fruit; freshly
squeezed orange juice; tomato, cheese and mushroom omelette;
basket of assorted baked goods; and hot milk with honey. Take a
cab to the Exchange Terminal where we board a two-tiered bus
for a sightseeing tour to the south side of the island. We manage
to get front-row, upper-deck seats from which the views are glorious. Less impressed with the outdoor market at the village of
Stanley. Stacks of jeans, T-shirts, sweaters, silk dresses and jackets are
piled unceremoniously on stalls, taking all the illusion out of the
not-always-genuine designer labels.

Return to hotel in late afternoon for a refreshing swim in the
pool. Try to book dinner at Gaddi's, an expensive French restaurant across the harbour in Kowloon Peninsula, but it is closed for
renovations, so eat in one of the hotel restaurants instead.

The Hong Kong that existed in the sixties with the prolifera-
tion of seedy bars and nightclubs, the city on which the movie *The
World of Suzie Wong* was based, is all but extinct, dwarfed now by
business towers and shopping malls. There were only a couple of
bars and tired-looking strip joints on the back streets of Wan-Chai,
the former centre of action for sailors and out-of-towners. It made
the Yonge Street strip look exotic and thriving in comparison. In
modern-day Hong Kong, the feverish preoccupation for making
money seems to have taken precedence over everything—including sex. "A pervert," goes a traditional Hong Kong definition, "is
a man who prefers women to money."

October 8, 1994

Leave Hong Kong at 2:35 p.m. with a stopover in Tokyo between
seven-thirty and nine and arrive in Honolulu at eight-thirty in the
morning. Then take a short 20-minute commuter flight to the
island of Maui. It is still Saturday; since flying east we have gained
a day. We pick up our rental car and drive about half an hour from
the airport at Kahalui to our rented condo in Wailea on the south-
west coast of Hawaii.

October 9, 1994

We are staying at a condominium complex called Wailea Elua, recommended by our neighbour, Yvonne Peterson, which has extensive rolling grounds and beautiful views of the ocean. Just across the road are two lovely golf courses called the Wailea Blue and the Wailea Gold.

Hawaii has been greatly built up since we last visited it ten years ago, but for the most part, the developments are well-planned and luxurious. After being in Hong Kong's central district where one rarely sees a blade of grass among the jungle of high-rise buildings, Maui's open spaces and fresh floral-scented air are welcoming. The Hawaiians are also very sunny-natured, pleasant people, in contrast to the residents of Hong Kong who, though very polite and hard-working, are not naturally gregarious.

Our condo, because it is only one bedroom and has no air-conditioning, is a reasonable $145 a night. We are pleased with this price because the greens fees to get on the Wailea golf courses, even for guests (which we are considered to be since we are staying at the Wailea Elua), are $60 each per day. That adds another $120 to our daily rate since we plan to play eighteen holes a day.

It was a mistake, however, not to reserve an oceanfront, air-conditioned condo, but they were all booked when I called. By midweek, it is 91 degrees Fahrenheit outside, and by midday our condo is like an oven. It is also too hot to play golf except in the early morning or late afternoon. Which we do. We also swim a lot, in the ocean and in the pool inside our complex. Luckily, it cools off to the 70s at night and we have no trouble sleeping. October is really off-season for Hawaii travellers, which we knew before we came, but we had no choice when to book, since we were tacking this on to our prearranged Hong Kong trip.

Maui has an island feel, but there's lots of action as well for those who wish it. Its only drawback for those of us in eastern Canada is the length of time it takes to get there—about ten hours in total. But even that can be considered a plus. Busy with golfing and swimming and walking and just resting, I never did get a chance to spend uninterrupted hours reading James Michener's *Hawaii* until we were on our long flight back home.

November 8, 1994

Back in Toronto, I attended a Scrabble tournament on Monday to raise money for literacy. Several hundred people paid $150 each to play a game of Scrabble with a so-called celebrity. Each "celebrity" was placed at a table with three paying guests. People I either talked to or spotted in the crowd included Peter Worthington and Yvonne Crittenden, Paul Godfrey, Robert Fulford, Pierre Berton, Peter Kent, Ralph Benmergui, Michael Coren, Susan Eng, Bluma Appel and Knowlton Nash. After drinks in the lobby of the Harbour Castle Conference Centre and nibbling on finger food, we were asked to go to our assigned tables. When I reached my table, it was empty. I stood there looking foolish for a few minutes. By this time everyone was seated at their tables ready to begin their games. I walked out of the room into the lobby, strongly inclined to walk right out the door and go home. But I stopped myself—I'd made a commitment to attend, after all—went and found some staff, and explained that no one was at my table. They quickly assigned me another table, and the problem was averted. Playing Scrabble was quite a lot of fun, though my table had pretty low scores. When Jack Batten and I were walking back to our cars, he remarked that he'd enjoyed the evening, but it had been a lot like work. "Actually, Jack," I said, "I find events like that harder than work."

December 21, 1994

Last night Edgar and I held our annual Christmas party. Actually, I shouldn't call it an annual party, because we didn't hold it last year. But basically, it's a party composed of neighbours and friends and all the Haileyburians I can find. Edgar says I go up to people in the street to ask them to come, because the party ends up being so big. This year 200 came.

To save money, I was going to do it all myself, but as the guest list grew, I realized I would be dead if I didn't have help. So I called Daniel et Daniel Catering and ordered $800 worth of food and another $600 worth of rentals and staff. And went out and bought the liquor and mix myself. I promised Edgar I'd keep the cost of the party under $2,000, and I think I did.

But even just getting the liquor and mix was no picnic. The liquor store will deliver, but I thought I could find cheaper brands if I went myself, which turned out not to be the case, since they mostly all cost the same, except for the very expensive ones. So that was quite a bit of lugging around—out to my car and then into the house.

But that was nothing compared to my misadventure getting the mixes and juice. I decided to go to a No Frills store at Parliament and Carlton, since it is fairly close to where I live and because it would be cheap. It was cheap, all right, but it was also a dreadful place. I actually felt afraid in there, and I'm not a fearful person. The store was littered with garbage, and half-opened boxes and tins. The cart I had was old and rusty, and the wheels wouldn't turn. I felt I was the only white person within miles. Stupidly, since I was coming from a luncheon at Jump, I was wearing Aunt Ella's mink coat. The hostile stares I got were incredible. Sometimes people blocked my way and refused to move. Two boys who worked there, who were, in fact, white and to whom I turned to help me carry the stuff out to my car, both refused. When I tried to ask them questions about prices, they were sullen and hostile.

The good thing about the excursion was that I bought a case each of Coke, diet Coke, soda, tonic, Sprite, ginger ale and two large cans each of tomato juice, orange juice and cranberry juice, all for $37. After I'd paid for it all, it took me about 15 minutes and 10 trips to bring it all to the front of the store (carts weren't allowed beyond a certain point). There I felt safer because the street was nearby and I could just run outside if anyone threatened me. But I still had the problem of getting my purchases out to my car, which was parked about a block away.

An old man who had been sitting on a windowsill at the front of the store watching me came to my aid. Would you like some help with all that? he asked. And picked up my cases at one end, with me on the other, and headed out to my car. It took us four trips. I tried to pay him, but he refused to take any money. "I'm a pensioner," he said. "I don't need money." So I asked him for his name and address and I sent him a Christmas card thanking him.

I won't make the mistake of going into that store again, but the old man's kindness helped cancel out my bitter feelings about the whole incident. Before then, I hadn't realized you could walk into a Toronto grocery store in broad daylight and be intimidated like that. The contrast between that store and the places I usually shop is beyond belief. I know for sure I would not want to be a poor person living in Toronto in the nineties.

With all the people who came to the party, the decibel level was pretty high. My mother and her new husband Jerry Smith flew up from Bermuda. (My mother married Archibald N. (Jerry) Smith, a Bermudian, five years after my father died of Alzheimer's.) Besides family, friends, business associates of Edgar's, never mind dozens of people from my hometown of Haileybury, there were also a number of prominent Torontonians.

Trevor and Jane Eyton came. Jane is very straightforward and says what's on her mind. She's not devious or hypocritical like so many society wives. And Trevor is a great guy. I mean, he could have dropped me like a hot potato with all the shenanigans that Anna Maria and Catherine pulled. But he didn't.

Allan and Sondra Gotlieb were there. I like her intermittent party pieces for the *Globe*; they're witty and topical.

Also Peter Herrndorf and Eva Czigler—he was on the cover of *TV Guide* this week. They're a popular couple on the social circuit, and, with their personal warmth and charm, it's easy to see why.

Donald and Adrian Macdonald talked politics with Hagood and Martha Hardy. Adrian, who's very kind, took me out to lunch after *The Glitter Girls* was out and said she'd like to try to get Catherine and me back together, but I told her not to bother.

Hagood has just decided to run for the Liberals in the next provincial election against Bob Rae in his own riding. That should be quite a contest, because in 1987 Alan Tonks came within 333 votes of defeating Rae. Hagood's great-uncle (the brother of his grandfather) was Arthur Sturgis Hardy, the premier of Ontario from 1896 to 1899, whose son, a Liberal senator, owned our Brockville house for 60 years. It was given to him as a wedding present by his in-laws when he married into the Fulford family, who made a fortune selling Pale Pills for Pink People all over the world.

More politicians were there. John Godfrey and his wife, Trish, whom I thought was pretty. Marriage in his fifties seems to be good for John. He looks settled and happy, and he and Trish have adopted a baby boy, Ian.

Isabel Bassett dropped in. She'll be running for the Tories in the same riding as Liberal Dr. Carolyn Bennett, and people are saying it will be a tough battle for her. I hope I look like that in my mid fifties, but I know I won't. She has a certain kind of cool, Grace Kelly elegance about her; I think I'm more the Judy Holliday dumb-blonde type. Her husband, John, has not recovered well from his heart bypass operation. As well, she has John's son David, a manic-depressive, living at home. But she never complains.

Al Eagleson and Nancy were there, he seeming to be his usual ebullient self. He has a magnetic personality, not unlike Mulroney's: people either hate him or love him.

Julian and Anna Porter came. Julian's always been kind to me since I worked for him in his political campaign, and Edgar and Julian get along well.

Former *Globe* columnist Dr. Gifford-Jones came with wife Susan. I used to work with her at the Wellesley Hospital; she's one of its most highly respected volunteers—quiet, unassuming and hardworking. Someone should write a book on women like her.

Former and present *Chatelaine* editors Mildred Istona and Rona Maynard with her husband, Paul Jones, were there, as were writers John Lownsbrough and Gina Mallet.

And a couple of neighbours: among them Dr. Peter Welsh, founder of the Arthritic Hospital on Wellesley Street, and his wife, Lynley, former New Zealanders. At a party their daughter held recently, some youths burst in and stabbed six of the kids. Luckily, no one was badly hurt, but Toronto isn't the safe city it used to be.

Globe business columnist Ellen Roseman was there with her husband, Edward Trapunski. Edward traipsed around after my daughter Steffi, who worked for him in a documentary he produced. A longtime friend of mine, Ellen has managed to outlast us all at the *Globe*. Good for her.

Epilogue

June 19, 1995

It's hard to believe, but it was exactly seven and a half years ago today that I started working at the *Globe*. Many things have happened in my life since then. Edgar and I are 58 and 48 respectively; and my children Stephanie and Robin are 28 and 17. Robin, whose character and accomplishments I am very proud of, has a summer job in Lake Louise, Alberta, and will be entering U. of T.'s Trinity College in the fall. And Steffi, my people-pleasing daughter, has a television career, a Labrador retriever and a new boyfriend—Bill Sebenski, director of correspondent services for the TD Bank.

In the decade that was my forties, I have put a five-year career as a journalist under my belt, as well as one book published and one book written. As I approach my fifties, I have started to pull back and concentrate more on hobbies and leisure time. Already I notice a flagging of the energy and resilience of my youth, but this lessening of my physical faculties is more than made up for by an increasing emotional and spiritual contentment.

It's funny how things never turn out the way you expect. Marilyn Lastman was a last-minute inclusion in my previous book and she turned out to be one of my favourite glitter girls. Many of my readers, judging from the comments I received, felt the same way.

Since the book came out in 1993, Catherine Nugent walks by me without speaking, though I felt the chapter on her was the fairest and the most well written, as I knew her the best.

I haven't seen Liz Tory lately, but her friends report she is as frenetic and witty as ever, and busy working on the 1996 Brazilian Ball.

I ran into Carole and Jerry Grafstein at the Barnes Exhibition opening party. "Where have you been, Rosemary? You seem to have dropped out of sight" was Carole's remark when she saw me. I guess it depends on one's perspective. Since the demise of my column, I thought it was she and her friends who had dropped out of sight.

Cathie Bratty has started a new life as a restaurateur, opening a restaurant, with husband Rudy's financial backing, on Bloor Street near the Kingsway. When a friend Sandi Hutchison took me there for lunch in the spring of 1994, Cathie greeted me with a hug and came and sat at our table for a few minutes. "I'm out of the fund-raising game," she said. "I got tired of it." She, like Marilyn Lastman, never forgot it was a game. Their late friend Pat Appleton is nodding her assent up in heaven.

God or fate, or whatever one calls the guiding force behind the human race, works in mysterious ways. I had asked the Grenville Christian College choir to sing at *The Glitter Girls* launch, in order to introduce them to Toronto society, since at that point they were to be upcoming Brazilian Ball beneficiaries. The ball may not have come through for them, but another happy result was achieved as a result of their Toronto appearance. Two of my guests at that launch were *Maclean's* editor Bob Lewis and assistant managing editor Ann Johnston. As a result of their attendance, last month's issue of *Maclean's* magazine, with a cover story on private schools, did a feature on Grenville Christian College.

"If you concentrate on such things as honesty, integrity and ethics," the magazine quotes Reverend Charles Farnsworth, the college's headmaster, as saying, "the rest falls into place." I have put much effort into treating my husband, our children, our co-workers and friends, glitter girls and society types included, with the honesty, respect and integrity espoused by Father Farnsworth, both in my life and in my writing. If I have sometimes fallen short, it is not from lack of trying.

Index